UNIVERSITY OF
WOLVERHAMPTON

05/07

Policing gender, class and family

Women's History

General Editor
June Purvis
Professor of Sociology, University of Portsmouth

Published
Carol Dyhouse
No distinction of sex? Women in British universities, 1870–1939

Bridget Hill
Women, work and sexual politics in eighteenth-century England

Linda Mahood
Policing gender, class & family: Britain, 1850–1940

June Purvis (editor)
Women's history: Britain, 1850–1945

Forthcoming
Lynn Abrams and Elizabeth Harvey (editors)
Gender relations in German history

Shani D'Cruze
Sex, violence and working women in Victorian and Edwardian England

jay Dixon
The romantic fiction of Mills & Boon, 1909–95

Ralph Gibson
*Women, faith and liberation: female religious orders in
nineteenth-century France*

Wendy Webster
Women in the 1950s

Barbara Winslow
Sylvia Pankhurst: a political biography

Policing gender, class and family
Britain, 1850–1940

Linda Mahood

University of Guelph

UCL
PRESS

© Linda Mahood, 1995

First published in 1995 by UCL Press

UCL Press Limited
University College London
Gower Street
London WC1E 6BT

The name of University College London (UCL) is a registered trade mark used by UCL Press with the consent of the owner.

British Library Cataloguing in Publication Data
A catalogue record for this book is available from the British Library.

ISBN: 1-85728-188-8 HB

Typeset in Sabon.
Printed and bound by
Biddles Ltd, Guildford and King's Lynn, England.

Contents

To my father
 Douglas Rupert Mahood
To the memory of my grandmother
 Nancy Mahood (1904–89)

❧

Acknowledgements

In May 1992, following a request that I had placed in a local Scottish newspaper for information about reformatories and industrial schools, I received a letter from a "78 year old person", who chose to comment on the documentary about girls' homes that I had worked on with BBC Scotland some months earlier. The letter warned: "If you are going to write stories and make films, try and get your facts right first. Your film . . . was disgusting, all lies . . . [It] did not upset people who know the facts . . . Try and do something useful with your talent." My first piece of "hate mail" disturbed me for a number of fairly obvious reasons. What it confirmed, though, was that there continues to be a wide range of emotions and contested interpretations surrounding these particular institutions of the social. I would like to begin, therefore, by expressing my sincere gratitude to the women and men who graciously permitted me to interview them for this book.

The research was supported by a number of sources that enabled it to grow from a thesis into a book. The Social Sciences and Humanities Research Council of Canada Doctoral Fellowship, the Committee of the Vice-Chancellors and Principals of the Universities of the United Kingdom Overseas Research Scholarship and the University of Glasgow Postgraduate Scholarship supported it during its dissertation phase. In the summer of 1990 a grant from the University of Saskatchewan allowed me to do some additional interviews and to present some early results at the International Sociological Association World Congress in Madrid. Financial assistance from the Dean of the College of Arts and Science and the University of Lethbridge Research Fund enabled me to participate in the BBC

ACKNOWLEDGEMENTS

Scotland documentary, *Washing away the stain*, to extend my study of homes for girls and women called magdalene asylums into the twentieth century, and to examine some newly discovered documents. The material in Chapter 3 appears in an abridged form in my "Family ties: lady child-savers and girls of the street, 1850–1925".[1] Chapter 7 draws heavily on L. Mahood & B. Littlewood, "The 'vicious' girl and the 'street-corner' boy: sexuality and the gendered delinquent in the Scottish child-saving movement, 1850–1940".[2] My interpretation of the material has benefited significantly by collaboration with Barbara Littlewood on this and other projects.

Many people supported me during my period in Glasgow, where I arrived in 1985. At Glasgow University, John Eldridge, Paul Littlewood, Ruth Madigan, David Frisby, Bob Miles and Eleanor Gordon gave me early support, but, most especially, my deepest appreciation goes to Barbara Littlewood, whose example and encouragement opened up the possibility for me to pursue an academic career. I am also very grateful to Janet Nobel and Hugh Corrigan, who always made room and time for me while I was collecting data in London.

On the other side of the Atlantic there are also a number of people who I met while an undergraduate and later an instructor at the University of Saskatchewan (some have since scattered) who continue to help me in various ways: B. Singh Bolaria, Terry Wotherspoon, Bernard Schissel, Nancy Poon, Kathy Kendall, Kiran Bolaria (an excellent research assistant) and Vic Satzewich, who has read and commented on every draft. At Lethbridge University, I would like to thank Carol Tomomitsu for her secretarial assistance with this manuscript and various faculty and students, especially Dr Patricia Chuchryk, Dave Brown and Diane Clark, Robin Bright, Ann Moritz, Jeff Ross and Natasha Cabrera, who became good friends. This book would not exist without the patience and support of my entire family, especially Lucy (born during the literature review) and Jack (born during the conclusion). Olga Satzewich's devotion to her grandchildren continues to enable me to interchange domestic responsibilities and academic commitments without worry. But it is Vic's strength, commitment to scholarship and gentle prodding that enables me to do it at all.

Linda Mahood
University of Guelph, Canada

Chapter 1

&

The genesis of the social

My brothers always would say to me, "Don't tell anybody we came from a home." I'd say, "What's wrong . . . I'm not ashamed of being brought up in a home . . ." It was a very good thing.[1]

You didn't need to get up to a hell of a lot to get put in one of these places . . . whatever problem they had they solved it by puttin' you out of the road.[2]

There were thousands of kids . . . who should never have been in places like that, but rather than the government of the time spending money on proper activities they'd rather capture the kids and put them into a place where they could contain them.[3]

[The Lochburn Home was for girls] who were taken away from their own parents . . . They had special frocks they had to wear and one or two of them had their heads shaved . . . We knew that they were *bad girls*, but I didn't know what that meant![4]

The memories of women and men who were inmates of Scottish juvenile reformatories and industrial schools in the early twentieth century reveal a range of confusing and bitter experiences. Such accounts suggest that the historical investigation of "youth" allows us to examine children as both the subjects of culturally constructed definitions and the clients of institutional practices.

The late-nineteenth-century child-saving movement was part of a massive intervention into private life whose strategies, institutions and consequences are still being debated by historians and social scientists. Then, as now, children were frequently the targets of theories and practices aimed at the wider regulation of family life.[5] Certainly, since the late nineteenth century public interest in children has been the wedge used to prise open families.[6] The current public outrage over issues such as domestic violence and child abuse, juvenile crime, homelessness and well-publicized cases of the apparent "failure" of child protection agencies has its roots in the late-nineteenth- and early-twentieth-century child-welfare ideologies and institutional regimes.

This study of child-welfare institutions in Scotland in the late nineteenth and early twentieth centuries brings together research from a number of social science disciplines and feminist frameworks that are often separate within the academic division of labour: criminology and social control, education, women's studies, men's studies and the sociology of the family. This book raises unique historical and social theoretical questions concerning child-welfare policies and social institutions.

Studies of the historical construction of social order[7] have documented the emergence of new social institutions, such as the police, an organized judiciary, prisons, poorhouses, schools and asylums in Britain by the late nineteenth century. The social control function of these institutions is widely recognized in the literature. According to some, the creation of the modern penitentiary in the 1840s was the "apex of this system, serving as a model of the new discipline and forms of regulation meant to bring a social and moral transformation to labouring women and men".[8] Others argue that the compulsory education of children in the 1870s was the pinnacle of social control. "Supervised by its trusty teacher, surrounded by its playground wall, the school was to raise a new race of working people – respectful, cheerful, hardworking, loyal, pacific and religious."[9] In addition to formal state institutions such as the prison and the school the mid-nineteenth century also witnessed the establishment of numerous statutory and nonstatutory "pre-prison" institutions. The history of these institutions is not so widely known, although their legacy remains with us today, embodied in the juvenile detention centre, the "lock-up" and the "secure unit" for young offenders.

Victorian penitentiaries for children and adolescents went by a variety of names, notably, houses of refuge, reformatories, industrial schools, certified industrial training ships, industrial day schools for truants and magdalene asylums, which were shelters for women and girls. These "child-saving"[10] institutions traversed the disciplinary continuum. Some were soft-end minimum security institutions while others were cruel and resembled adult jails. The establishment of child-welfare institutions raises a number of general historical questions: why did they emerge when they did? who ran them? how were inmates recruited? what regime of rehabilitation did they use? An examination of the histories of these institutions will form the framework of this study.

Complementing these general historical questions regarding child-saving institutions are a series of sociological questions concerning how these institutions are to be conceptualized: were they prisons, were they schools, or were they something else? According to Michael Ignatieff, a new social history of the control institution has begun to be written. He argues that the "new social history of the total institution" can be distinguished from the "timid empiricism" of the "history of an institution" because the former is a history about the "living battles of the confined against their suffering, and about the new professional classes [who] tied their social assent to the new institutions". This new social history analyzes the institution not as an "administrative entity, but as a social system of domination and resistance, ordered by complex rituals of exchange and communication".[11]

The main empirical focus of this book is the child-saving movement in Scotland in the period roughly from the passing of the Youthful Offenders Act in 1854 to the passing of the Children and Young Persons (Scotland) Acts in 1932. The year 1932 marked the beginning of a new administrative era for the institutions, in that management passed from the Home Office to the Scottish Education Department and certified industrial schools and reformatories were renamed "approved schools".[12] The historical framework of this book locates the activities of the child-savers in the social, economic and political changes of the earlier part of the nineteenth century, and the inclusion of some data from the 1940s provides a context for transformations in child-welfare practices after the Second World War. Of course child-saving was not unique to Scotland. Parallel systems for dealing with young offenders developed in England, Ireland and Wales, but many significant initiatives began in Scotland in the early decades of the nineteenth century. In Scotland most of the initiatives were undertaken by philanthropic individuals, magistrates and prison officials at a local level, whereas in England, influential social reformers such as Mary Carpenter and Matthew Davenport Hill formed the Reformatory and Refuge Union in 1851 and lobbied at the national level. Scotland's main contribution to the treatment of delinquency was the development of day industrial feeding schools, or "ragged schools", which aimed at preventing children from becoming delinquent rather than reforming those who had already committed crimes. Scotland also pioneered the juvenile reformatory; some of the largest and oldest institutions were in that country. Historian E. A. G. Clark argues that the "Scotch system" of ragged and industrial schools was adopted in at least 15 English towns. In 1862 an industrial school inspector stated that "we cannot have a better model for our English Industrial Schools than those of Scotland".[13] In 1917 Mossbank Industrial School for Boys in Glasgow was described as "undoubtedly the most progressive in Great Britain". The Chief Inspector for Industrial Schools declared: "Its spirit I should like to see in the management of every school."[14] By the early twentieth century the 48 reformatories and industrial schools in Scotland were dealing with nearly 7,000 girls and boys.[15]

Policing the population

Michel Foucault argues that the key features of the great transformations in the crime and deviancy apparatuses of Western societies in the late eighteenth and early nineteenth centuries are: increasing state involvement; increasing efforts to categorize deviant populations and to isolate them in separate institutions ("thieves into prisons, lunatics into asylums, conscripts into barracks, workers into factories, children into schools"[16]); the emergence of a new professional body of experts, technicians and professionals to administer the new system of corrections; and the shift from publicly punishing the body to making the mind, the "psyche", or character of the individual the object of discipline. These changes do not suggest that society became more liberal, but rather that punishment took new forms. The goal of the new rational system of punishment was not to inflict pain but to reform and rehabilitate. The new forms of corporal discipline included large dosages of scripture, prison labour, and moral education, which replaced a cluster of physical punishments directed at the body used in the previous centuries. Under the new regime talk of satanic temptation was replaced by assessment of the individual's lack of moral judgement and self-control. The magistrate replaced the priest–executioner, judging something other than crime, namely, the individual's potential to reform. The final judgement and sentence were diffused among a whole technology of experts: doctors, psychiatrists, parole officers, educationalists and social workers, whose responsibility it was to rehabilitate the offender and administer the system.

Behind changes in the perception of crime and the treatment of offenders, which Foucault outlines in *Discipline and punish* (1979), was a wider more general change in the perception of social life which he develops in *The history of sexuality* (1980). Foucault argues that the most significant advance of the period was the development of the scientific study of populations, in which Malthusian economics and social Darwinism became central. State officials began to perceive that they were not dealing simply with subjects or "people", but with a "population" whose characteristic economic, political, health, moral and welfare problems necessitated statistical analysis and social action. This developed, in part, into the formation of "a whole grid of observations regarding sex". The sex lives of the citizenry became a matter of governmental concern. "Sex was not something simply to be judged", however; "it had to be managed, inserted into systems of utility, regulated for the greater good of all, made to function to an optimum . . . Sex became a police matter."[17]

Moral statisticians established links between "sexual perversion" and racial degeneration. This demanded new agents of social control and new disciplines of medical psychiatry, pedagogy, criminology, social work and a discourse on sexuality which focused on the "surveillance of dangerous or endangered children".[18] It is this theme of the "colonization of children's bodies" that Jacques Donzelot develops in *The policing of families* (1979), where he argues that from the eighteenth century to the end of the nineteenth century doctors put together a series of texts attacking folk medicine, lay healers, wet-nurses and home remedies. These were directed to a popular reading public concerning the rearing, education and medical care of bourgeois children. The chief result was an alliance between social medicine and bourgeois women. It centred on the spread of household medicine: knowledge and techniques designed to enable the bourgeois classes to rescue their children from the harmful contact with servants and to place them under their mother's observation.[19] The organic link between the doctor and the bourgeois mother had profound repercussions on family life. It not only marked a privileged alliance with the doctor and the other family members, but it also paved the way for the profession's establishment within the existing structures of church, hospital court, and school.[20]

State intervention in working-class families went through other channels. At the poorest extreme of the social body, what was denounced was the administration of institutions for orphans and deserted children. Statistics revealed that 90 per cent of the state's orphans died before having been "made useful to the state", which got no return for the cost incurred in their upkeep during childhood and adolescence. The importance of these children as a natural resource did not go unnoticed and public discussion of the problem demonstrated the advisability of saving them for eventual service in national institutions like the military and the Navy, "for which they would be perfectly suited owing to their lack of constricting family ties".[21] The strategies for the working class aimed at diminishing the social cost of their reproduction and assuring an optimum number of workers at minimum public expense; this would be achieved by what Donzelot critically calls philanthropy.[22] Philanthropy, in his view, was not an apolitical pastime of Victorian gentlefolk, but a deliberate act of authority that created a dependent relationship between rich and poor.[23] It was a political act intended to depoliticize poor communities, at the same time that it effected an increasing insinuation of non-familial agencies into the family nexus.[24] Philanthropic activities reflected a wider concern over the creation of future citizens, workers and sexualities, all to be self-disciplining and self-regulating.

Donzelot discusses the different strategies directed at middle- and working-class mothers, and the different destinies envisioned for their children: supervised freedom for bourgeois children and surveillance for working-class children and their care-givers. His use of concepts such as policing, regulation and discipline require some explanation. Policing, for example, refers not to a truncheon-wielding constable, but to the administration of public welfare.[25] Regulation refers to the moral regulation[26] and administration of individual bodies, desires and pleasures at the level of the social aggregate, or what Foucault calls bio-politics.[27] The concept of discipline is equally important. Disciplinary techniques "centre on the body as a machine, optimizing its capabilities and integrating it into systems of surveillance".[28] For families, this entailed the increasing intervention by outside agencies. In her study of Scottish truancy Fiona Paterson argues that the family "is a practical target, being the focus of a series of interventions aimed at securing an upbringing for the future adult population which will reinforce the existing social order".[29] Thus, under the impact of the juvenile court, social workers and psychiatrists, the institution of the family is encircled, suffocated and invaded.[30] Donzelot refers to the French case as "the policing of families" and Christopher Lasch calls the American case the "proletarianization of parenthood".[31]

The disciplinary society: the social

Any critical history of such institutions has to place itself in relation to what Foucault has called the emergence of the disciplinary society and must respond to his claim that increasing surveillance and regulation actually created its own domain. Donzelot calls this new domain "the social", and defines it as a space midway between the private world of home and family and the public sphere of work and commerce. The social is closely linked with administration, ideology and discipline of new social institutions. The principal result was the emergence of a new social sector, comprising institutions, qualified personnel, legal apparatuses and relational norms that sought to take control of childhood and to police (albeit differently) middle-class and working-class family relations. It signifies the intensification of social discipline of private life in the nineteenth century and the increasing intervention in family life by outside agencies.

Recent studies of early social welfare programmes and practices support Donzelot's view that the totality of these movements and practices reflected the emergence of a qualitatively different sphere of society. In *Anti-social policy* (1990) Peter Squires examines the link between the administration of social welfare policies and disciplinary modes of social control. He argues that the social sphere contains both institutions and ideologies. It is his thesis, however, that the social has a dark side. The paradox of the social lies in the very forces that give birth to this constellation of principles, practices and ideals. While it promises "welfare", each wave of reform produces increasingly punitive, coercive and oppressive policies. According to Squires social policy becomes anti-social policy: when the "repressive, exploitative, or sectarian features of the welfare state intensify and develop to a sufficient level, they risk overwhelming the state's claims to welfare altogether".[32]

Drawing on the work of socialist feminist scholars like Michèle Barrett, Mary McIntosh and Nancy Fraser, this book will critically evaluate the concept of the social. In *The anti-social family* (1982) Barrett and McIntosh take issue with Donzelot. In their view Donzelot locates the blame for the demise of the patriarchal family on the middle-class women whom he claims collaborated with the physicians, experts and technicians. The bourgeois wife was to be the instrument who would stamp out the spirit of independence in the working man. They also claim that *The policing of families* is a "thoroughly functionalist"[33] text, a criticism that can also be applied to *Anti-social policy*. Squires argues that the social is constantly in flux.[34] "Social divisions giving rise to ideological disaffection . . . is indicative of . . . [the] failure . . . of the society's mechanisms of integration and its normative commitments to democratic citizenship."[35] Although he recognizes that there were conflicts in the social he does not develop this observation other than to say that it was the site of professional rivalries.

It is just this type of functionalism that Nancy Fraser finds so disturbing in academic analysis of social welfare policy. She suggests that "such analysis often screens out 'dysfunctional' events like micro- and macro-political resistances and conflicts".[36] The conceptualization of the social that she develops in her book *Unruly practices* (1989), which interestingly comes from another intellectual tradition, is clearly most insightful. Like Donzelot, Squires and other writers, Fraser also recognizes that the emergence of the social is closely linked with the rise of professionalization of a new class of experts to administer it. She warns us, however, of the danger of functionalist arguments because they obscure the active side of social processes. In her work on the modern American social welfare system, Fraser sees the social as the site of discourses about people's needs, specifically about those needs that have broken out of the domestic and/or official economic spheres that earlier contained them as "private matters".[37] For Fraser the social is an arena of contestation and conflict, which is a much broader definition than that found in Donzelot's or Squire's work. It is a space where conflicts among rival interpretations of people's needs are played out. "In the social", then, "one would expect to find a plurality of competing ways of talking about needs."[38]

Other helpful accounts of nineteenth-century family formation that have influenced my understanding of the genesis of the social are found in the growing body of sociological and historical literature on the family that place more emphasis on "agency" as a variable in family survival strategies. Anna Davin, for one, is sceptical about any alleged alliance between women and social work agencies. She suggests that "the philanthropist" was often perceived as an intruder by working-class families. While poor mothers participated in "free milk" programmes in order to get fresh milk for their children, many rejected the moralizing propaganda and the judgements that were being made about their "incompetence".[39] Other examples are Sean Damer's account of poor families in the tenements of Glasgow and Jane Humphries's work on English families. Both authors have cast the proletarian family as an important historical agent. In the case of Scotland, Damer stresses that working-class "men and women acted creatively on their grossly unfavourable working and living conditions to construct a culture which is uniquely tough, resilient, warm and witty".[40] Humphries suggests that the proletarian family was a defensive institution that enabled working-class people to survive the rigour and brutality of capitalism.[41] Linda Gordon questions the very notion of the invasion of the family. She indicates that what is referred to as "the family" is actually an institution of male/father domination and privilege. The problem of intervention, invasion or policing is more complex than first thought. "The critique of social control, both left and right, frequently points to the violation of civil liberties as evidence of the dangers of intervention into family privacy."[42] But we must ask the question: whose privacy is being invaded? This point alerts us to the central contradiction of familial ideology. State intervention frequently breaks up

9

THE GENESIS OF THE SOCIAL

traditional patriarchal power, the rights of the father to discipline his dependants, and replaces it with a more general state control of the rights of dependants, in other words, the rights of women and children. This is what several feminist scholars call the shift from private patriarchy to public patriarchy. Thus, "one man's loss in privacy was often another's (frequently a woman's) gain in rights",[43] albeit someone else's definition of what those rights should be.

There is a growing body of literature concerning "genesis of the social"[44] but few empirical studies of its operation. One of the ambitions of this book is to construct an aetiology of the social, using the child-saving movement in general, and residential schools in particular, as a case study. Through an analysis of the empirical data, three theoretical issues are brought to light that will provide a fuller conceptualization of the social than currently exists in the literature.

First, it is argued that the social is a material space. Other examples of new institutions for controlling working-class populations include workhouses, mental asylums and inebriate homes. Philip Corrigan, Bruce Curtis and Robert Lanning contend that while "the school, the prison, the park, the playground, the settlement house, the asylum, and other institutions were conceived by the ruling class as having an 'educative tendency' for the population they were also forms of police".[45] In this study we will question the social "function" of the child-saving institutions and their roles in the moral regulation and sexual surveillance of working-class girls and boys.

Secondly, the social is also an ideological space. It is the arena, the terrain, and the site of a rubric of laws, regulations, rules, policies and institutions, or what Foucault calls technologies-of-power.[46] It embodies the ideological practices, the conflicting expert discourses and the logic of the institution. The causes of juvenile delinquency were explained in terms of a familial ideology that espoused the virtue of the autonomous nuclear family headed by a male breadwinner, supported by his nurturing wife and their economically dependent children. This ideology established the parameters whereby the "normal" and "abnormal" family culture could be distinguished and families (by definition poor families) that deviated from this normative ideal were judged as deviant, pathological and productive of juvenile delinquency.

Thirdly, one cannot talk about policing families without talking about the disciplining of gender and sexuality. The role of incarceration in the social reproduction of labour is well documented in feminist studies of the prison.[47] Throughout the nineteenth century women were subjected to new forms of policing that were specific to them, and numerous examples of what Stanley Cohen calls "diversionary institutions"[48] were set up with specific class and gender roles in mind. For example, my own study of shelters for "prostitutes" in Scotland suggests that carceral regimes deployed by these magdalene asylums were based on both class and gender ideology.[49] The moral regulation of young working-class women was the goal of the asylum, where the directors were not interested only in producing ideal proletarian subjects out of the undisciplined real subjects who presented themselves as inmates, or even proletarian subjects reconciled to their status; they were producing *female proletarians* who were to take up quite distinct positions in the class and gender order.

Research on children in penal institutions has only partially begun to establish links between the construction of gender and class subjectivity. Noline Williamson's study of reformatory and industrial school girls in New South Wales between 1867 and 1887 demonstrates that reform school training was aimed specifically at devising an educational programme suitable for lower-class girls.[50] Similarly, Kerry Wimshurst's study of reformatory school girls in South Australia between 1871 and 1892 argues that "[t]here was never the least suggestion . . . that reformatory girls should aspire to the emerging professions . . . their futures . . . were seen solely as working-class wives and mothers".[51] But neither has compared the circumstances of reformatory girls with their male counterparts in boys' reformatories.[52]

In the 1990s we have seen the rise of men's studies, as more male academics have begun to investigate the construction of their own gender experiences. Recent contributions in this field have begun to enhance our understanding of how the construction of gender roles shapes identities for men as well as women. But work such as Anthony Rotundo's "Romantic friendship: male intimacy and middle-class youth in the northern United States, 1800–1900"[53] or Harry Hendrick's recent book *Images of youth* (1990)[54] echoes what has long been found in feminist research. Rotundo basically follows Carroll Smith-Rosenberg's path-breaking study of middle-class women's friendship,[55] while Hendrick admits his attempt to duplicate Carol Dyhouse's *Girls growing up in late-Victorian and*

Edwardian England. The results, however, do not advance the debate.[56] Simply substituting a "male" for a "female" gender-analysis fails to forge any new links in our understanding of gender socialization. Thus, our understanding of the process of social reproduction in some areas of gender and class analysis remains partial. The concept of the social as it is used by Donzelot and Squires also fails to locate the disciplining of gender within social institutions. While these authors recognize that classes are historically and socially constructed in the sense that people do not simply possess the roles and duties expected of them because of their class position, they portray the working class as genderless. This means that while class is regarded as a social construct, gender is a pre-existing trait. Gaps in the literature raise questions about the interrelationship between class, sexuality and gender. Put simply, what was happening to working-class girls and boys? Did they suffer repression and control (mainly) because they were working-class and regarded by the child-savers as morally corrupt? Or did the girls suffer "excessive drudgery and repression – not only because they were poor or 'bad' but also because they were female"?[57]

Few studies successfully integrate class, gender, sexuality and "race" in the interpretation of data and the elaboration of theory. Notable exceptions are Linda Gordon's (1988) study of the history of family violence and its handling in Boston, Mariana Valverde's (1991)[58] work on the Canadian social purity movement and Celia Haig-Brown's (1989)[59] study of Indian residential schools, also in Canada. These feminist scholars are sensitive to the "racialized" dimension of the interventions they document, a dimension that was evident in a rather different form in the Scottish context. The child-savers regularly referred to urban children as street "arabs" and to their parents' "heathen" backgrounds, especially those from the Highlands, but there is little evidence of the systematic targeting or stigmatization of minority ethnic groups in relation to their family life or morality, in spite of the migration of the Irish (and Roman Catholic) to Scotland's cities in the period considered here. Rather, a "racialized" discourse appears to float free of any anchoring in people's perceived racial category, and the labels are used as indiscriminate signifiers indicating inferiority and otherness. In this case, "savages" were perceived to inhabit not only the far regions of the Empire and Continent, but more alarmingly, the streets and slums of urban Scotland. In this form, Scottish racism relates more to what Etienne Balibar has called class racism, arguing that the notion of class is "ethnicized".[60]

Finally, the social is to be conceptualized as the terrain of contestation where opposition, rebellion and resistance are produced.[61] The history of the social construction of childhood allows us to examine children both as subjects of cultural definition and as clients of institutional services. In the context of the Scottish child-saving movement it is useful to point out that subject has, in fact, two quite opposing meanings, and this ambiguity will be explored in the following chapters. At one level it can mean someone who is subject to something, under surveillance, control or government; in the legal sense, subject to law or subject to rule. More broadly, it can also mean the initiator or agent, rather than the passive object, of an action, activity or policy. In the case of poor children and their parents the striking feature revealed by this particular project of historical sociology is the complexity of the working-class reaction to bourgeois child-saving initiatives. We must proceed, then, by regarding poor children and their parents as both subjects of their lives and subjected to external authorities and sanctions. This conceptualization of the social as the locus of resistance will enable me to analyze the process whereby class and gender resistance can occur. We can see poor working-class families as both the subject of state intervention into private life and the subjects or agents of social action.

Archives: a history from below

The main sources of data for this book are primary sources: archival and oral. Archival sources consist of the annual reports of the Inspector of Industrial Schools and Reformatories, the independent series of publications by various Scottish philanthropic organizations and the annual reports of reformatories, industrial schools, industrial day schools, the industrial training ships, female rescue homes and miscellaneous interest groups, published between 1800 and 1940. The annual reports of many of these associations were regularly submitted to local councils and magistrates and their contents often appear in official records. Valuable statistical and factual information about residential and day schools also comes from four Parliamentary

Commissions on reformatory and industrial schools (1852, 1896–8, 1914–15 and 1925), all of which were attended by representatives of Scottish institutions. These documents provide an officially sanctioned account of the theory and practices of state agencies and the problems they encountered administering child welfare. Another source of data is provided by the private files of the Home Office and Scottish Education Office, which administered certified reformatory and industrial schools between 1850 and 1932. These records consist of minutes, private correspondence, inter-office memos, formal and informal complaints from parents, teachers, school administrators and school board members, and letters from former inmates and their relatives. They contain information that never appeared as part of official state discourse or in the annual reports and their contents were never intended for public consumption. They provide us with a fuller picture of social processes than the public utterances of state documents would give if analyzed in isolation.

A methodological problem with dependence on archival data alone is that it will produce only the "official version" of events. It is important to consider the purpose for which administrative records were collected, why information was published, who had access to it (if unpublished) and also who collected it. Using only official state papers, for example those of Royal Commissions, would cause obvious methodological problems because participation in Royal Commissions by members of the public is a selective process. The people who wish to pursue particular interests associated with the issues covered under the Commission's terms of reference are more likely to participate in them than people who do not. The submissions presented in evidence generally share the ideas, values and goals of those who chose to participate.[62] It is for these reasons, however, that they can also be considered more useful than private documents, because they constitute "knowledge" in terms of which issues were targeted for discussion as part of public discourse and debate.

No single account can be truly comprehensive, therefore I have drawn upon evidence from a variety of different perspectives. In terms of the "history from below", my use of information from interviews, largely with former inmates, will enable me to make some tentative suggestions about how working-class youth and their parents reacted to the process by which they were perceived and defined. Ignatieff has challenged sociologists of the total institution to look beyond the inner walls of the institution. He urges the historian to ask questions about the relationships between the world inside the institution and the wider outside forces that create, shape and in turn are changed by the institution.

> In themselves prisons, workhouses, asylums and reformatories are only of antiquarian interest. They only become significant historical subjects when they show us, in the extremity of their rituals of power . . . their effects on society through the mythic and symbolic weight of their walls on the world outside, through the ways in which people fantasize, dream and fear the archipelago of confinement.[63]

Between 1989 and 1992 three attempts were made to contact former staff and inmates by placing requests on the letters pages of the *Evening Times,* the *Daily Record* and the *Glaswegian.* An advertisement was also placed in the *Glasgow Herald.* These requests for "assistance with historical research" yielded a total of 41 letters from men and women between the ages of 58 and 90 from all over Scotland and parts of England and Australia. The respondents offered general information about reformatories, industrial schools and approved schools. From these, 18 respondents (eight women and ten men) were available to be interviewed. Three interviewees were members of superintendents' families: two had lived in these institutions with their parents, as was customary. One man (born in the 1920s) took over his father's position as superintendent after he died in the 1940s. He remained in that position until his own retirement in the 1980s. Three women and one man had attended industrial day schools and seven men and two women had attended residential schools. Two women who attended regular state schools were also selected to be interviewed. I asked them to recall the circumstances surrounding their placement in these institutions, which necessarily included an appearance in court. I asked them questions regarding institutional life: what did they believe the schools were trying to teach them? How did it affect their relationship with their parents and other siblings? What was their daily routine? How were they disciplined? What was the curriculum? My goal was to find out what it felt like to be sent to a certified school and whether there was a stigma, and if so whether for their parents or themselves.

In November 1992, BBC Scotland began researching a documentary on magdalene laundries in Ireland and Scotland, called *Washing away the stain.* I assisted with the background research and preparation of the script. The journalists who succeeded in locating some lost records and arranged interviews with former inmates of Lochburn magdalene asylum have generously provided me with access to their data. I regret that my only contact with a former industrial training ship boy was through the mail.

At the time of research some documents on the Scottish reformatories and industrial schools were classified as "restricted access" or had only recently been declassified, presumably to protect the privacy of the individuals involved. I applied to the Scottish Office for permission to examine certain "closed files" and was granted it under the provisions of the Official Secrets Act. As chance would have it, the contents of these files did not turn out to be the "Pandora's box" I had hoped, consequently this book contains no information acquired directly from any closed files. Nevertheless, in compliance with the Official Secrets Act and the wishes of several of the informants, the names of all inmates have been changed and information about individual schools or staff acquired from interviews will be referred to generically, for example: "a residential school" or "a former inmate".

In this book my conceptual framework of the aetiology of the social progresses from chapter to chapter. Chapter 2 examines the ideological realm of the social, in this case how the perceived causes of juvenile delinquency were used to establish the normative framework for the child-saving movement. It is suggested that familial ideologies were deployed by the child-savers in order to fuel the demand for new legislation and alternative penal institutions for the cure and control of young offenders and children at risk of falling into crime. Chapter 3 shifts attention away from the popular concern over the causes of juvenile delinquency by providing a historical overview of the child-saving movement between 1800 and 1932. The chapter examines the material realm of the social, in other words, how specific laws, policies and programmes were translated into modes of intervention for the classification, surveillance and disciplining of families. Chapter 4 demonstrates that the emergence of the social is closely linked to the rise of a professional class of "experts" who administer it. It is the site where rival interpretations and discourses about people's needs are produced. In the case of the child-saving movement, shared ideologies clashed with intraprofessional rivalries and gender politics, making it a terrain of contestation. Chapter 5 develops further the assertion that the power of the social rests upon its modes of intervention and disciplining techniques, in this case the disciplining of class and gender. Opening with an outline of the recruitment practices, discussions follow on the formal curriculum of education and industrial training offered to girls and boys, and how the preceding modes of intervention were supported by a system of military discipline. The chapter ends with a description of the licensing or parole system offered to inmates who were ready to be released. Chapter 6 returns to the ideological realm of the social; it examines how sexual subjectivities were constructed for girls and for boys through the education and training they received and how these were manifested in the hidden curriculum of the reformatory. The seventh and concluding chapter assesses the conceptual value of the social. It suggests that the emergence of reformatories and industrial schools created a distinct social domain, a new physical space and new knowledge and ideologies about the causes and treatment of juvenile delinquency. It was within this distinct social space that class, gender and sexual ideologies were deployed, negotiated and resisted.

Chapter 2

❧

The child in danger

> To them drunkenness is in no sense disreputable, and sexual immorality no cause for reproach . . . They form a distinct *tribe* in the land. Their boys grow up without any manly purity of thought or respect for the honour of women. Their girls are strangers to that maidenly reserve and modesty which are the chief glory and protection of true womanhood and they have no conception either of the holy relationship of marriage or the sacredness of motherhood.[1]

This description of a poor family in Edinburgh in 1911 is fairly typical of those found in the reports of child welfare agencies, school boards and charity records between the late nineteenth and early twentieth centuries. It illustrates a number of concerns regarding the exact nature of juvenile delinquency and its relationship to the family, pauperism, educational destitution and a social milieu of unplanned urban growth.[2] A closer examination of this rhetoric reveals the presence of certain key figures or spectres: the brutal father and the feckless mother, filthy, drunken work-shy beasts who neglect their miserable children if not actually schooling them in vice and crime. Their unmanly sons grew up without "respect for the honour of women" and their immodest daughters were strangers to purity and chastity. Although this population was constructed in a class and "racialized" context, in the sense that they were marked off as a qualitatively distinct social category that inhabited the urban slums, the identities of the children were also gendered and sexualized. Thus in the discourses of juvenile delinquency two additional figures can be found: the "street-corner" boy and the "vicious" girl.

For social reformers writing on a range of social problems, including poverty, disease, drunkenness, irreligion, illegitimacy, and especially crime, which they saw as plaguing Scottish cities and towns, the street children became a paradigm for urban decay. They were increasingly concerned about the number of children in the streets who appeared to do nothing to earn their living except beg, busk and steal.[3] They did not differentiate between children with jobs and families and the destitute homeless orphan. To the bourgeois observer they were all alike, "drifting about the highways and byways of vice".[4] They were identified, "racially" and otherwise, as "arabs", "urchins", "savages", and "outcasts" and "as heathen and uncivilized, alien to order and progress".[5] These children were at once in danger and dangerous, to be pitied for their neglect but feared for the crimes they were destined to commit.

These concerns were not as novel as was believed at the time. Historian Geoffrey Pearson has documented a series of moral panics linking youth to social problems from Elizabethan times, but claims that there was a preoccupation with rising crime rates and social unrest in the early nineteenth century. As a result of agitation by the newly formed statistical societies, the question of juvenile crime burst into public awareness in the 1840s with a force previously unknown, "spreading fear into the hearts and minds of the early Victorians of impending social collapse".[6]

The child-saving movement of the nineteenth century has its roots in the prison reform movement of the 1830s and its critique of the justice system, which failed either to reform or to deter young offenders. This chapter examines the prejudices and preconceptions underlying the demand for state legislation designed to control juvenile delinquency. Following Peter Squires's suggestion that ideologies are constructions of the social,[7] it will be suggested that familial ideologies were deployed by the child-savers in order to fuel the demand for new legislation and alternative penal institutions for the cure and control of young offenders and children at risk of falling into crime. While the factors causing delinquency were said to lie within the family there was also a cluster of alleged factors such as pauperism, alcohol abuse and juvenile labour. However, these too were traced back to the permissive parenting and neglect of the children of the dangerous classes.

A portrait of the delinquent

Two themes linked the reformist rhetoric constructing the portrait of a "juvenile delinquent" throughout the period considered: the vocational and the sexual impropriety of the street children. The child-savers observed that delinquent and criminal patterns were different for boys and for girls.[8] As the terms "street-corner" boy and "vicious" girl indicate, what is often referred to as the Victorian ideology of separate spheres, with its separate yet complementary roles for men and women, is evident in the theory of delinquency, which was based on a model of sexual differences.

The street-corner boy

The child-savers observed that boys engaged in a continuum of disreputable activities, as the following interview in 1870 between a reporter from the *Daily Mail* and Bob and Jim, "the purest breed of city Arab",[9] reveals:

> "My fust name's Jim . . . I sleeps, I drinks, and I stand on my nose. But my pal there does the flying wheel dodge" . . .[Jim] and Bob lodged together . . . Bob's mother was dead, and he "never had no father". Jim's parents had gone to the bad, and his recollections of them were faint. Bob had been once or twice to a Sabbath school and was partly educated. That is, he knew there was a God, and he had heard of Jesus. Jim was profoundly ignorant on the subject. He thought these words were only of use for swearing with, and meant nothing. Neither boy knew the alphabet, or wished to know it. Jim *thought* he lived in Scotland, and, on being asked where Scotland was, hazarded a guess that it was part of Glasgow. He got his living by begging and standing on his nose at the doors of singing saloons and theatres. Bob's calling was more dignified. He occasionally sold matches, and sometimes did the revolving wheel with his hands. Both stole a little when they could do so safely.[10]

By the early twentieth century the unskilled street trader was held up as the antithesis of the disciplined skilled worker. Although it may sound like a fairly harmless way for a young person to earn extra money, it received almost universal condemnation from the child-savers by the late nineteenth century. Statistical surveys revealed that street pedlars were often undersized, badly nourished and poorly developed when compared to their peers who continued in school or found apprenticeships. Reflecting their own beliefs and experience of childhood as a time of innocent pleasure, child-savers were united in the belief that children belonged under the protective arm of their families. For them, the "purity of the home was understood in terms of its difference to the immorality and danger of the street".[11] In 1909 J. R. Motion, a Glasgow parish inspector, concluded that street trading had an "absolutely demoralizing and degrading" effect on boys.

> I am satisfied that this street trading . . . is simply, in the major-ity of cases, an open highway to a life of crime. The boys are continually associating with known and reputed thieves, and other undesirable characters. They openly enter public houses for the purpose of begging, and they are familiar with all man-ner of vices in their worst forms . . . They soon after entering upon this life, get addicted to betting, and when funds admit of it, they attend race meetings . . . and they can always be seen, big and little amongst them, scanning the racing columns of the newspapers.[12]

Most serious, from the point of view of the child-savers and the standpoint of prospective employers, was the belief that street trad-ing ruined boys for steadier employment. At their national confer-ence in 1909 the Scottish Council for Women's Trades announced that street trading by boys under 16 years of age ought to be prohib-ited, because it left them "unfit for a life of regular wage earning".[13] In 1910 a Glasgow police constable attributed the criminality of young adults to their earlier employment as street traders, who having "not learned any trade . . . wait about railway stations, hotels and places of entertainment looking for odd jobs . . . and they easily degenerate into thieves".[14]

Street-corner boys were regularly seen at the shows, playing pitch-and-toss or gambling in closes and, later in the century, outside the picture houses. They were readily identifiable by a seeming lack of parental supervision and their own defiant and unruly behaviour. "One could see it at once in their old-young look . . . the general air of impudence and devil-may-carishness."[15] Such boys were known to engage in a range of "crimes" from pickpocketing, pilfering, vandalism and begging to loud boasting, swearing, smoking and truancy. By 1925 too frequent attendance at picture houses was added to the list of major causes of delinquency. It was feared that films "of the blood and thunder type" would tempt "lads to burgle and thieve", and, more seriously, films of the "suggestive type" might encourage "lads to indulge in immoral habits, either by themselves or with girls".[16]

The vicious girl

In the case of girls, the child-savers also focused on their occupational choices and what they perceived as sexual precocity. Girls forced to grow up in the overcrowded slums of the large cities were feared to be in danger of drifting into prostitution by association with "vice". In 1859 a Scottish physician wrote: "If the first words a daughter hears are those of cursing and blasphemy; the only example her childhood sees is that of obscenity and vice; such youth is an apt learner; and at the age of ten or twelve, she may be both a prostitute and a thief."[17] In 1864 the editor of Edinburgh's *North Britain* wrote, "It is a sad sight to see the little daughters of working men fighting with each other for the *honour* of running messages to the prostitute and offering, sometimes for a crust of bread or a half penny, to sweep the broken bottles and glasses from the front door of the brothel-shebeen!"[18] According to a female parish inspector in 1911:

If the girl lives in a squalid overcrowded slum dwelling . . . where the common decencies of life can scarcely be carried out . . . where the children have been allowed to remain out to all hours in dark, ill-lit closes and stairs, where the father of the family bets and drinks, not to mention the mother doing the same, then I say, the girl would hardly be human if she did not fall prey to temptation.[19]

Girls "at risk" were readily identifiable by their defiant and "unfeminine" behaviours: going to theatres, dancing, flirting with boys, keeping late hours and associating with older girls of questionable reputation. With regard to work, street selling was thought to lead directly to prostitution.[20] In 1871, for example, after a midnight stroll through the slums of Glasgow two reporters from the *Daily Mail* reported that they had come across four sailors and some girls in a brothel-shebeen, "not one of whom was over sixteen . . . One of the girls [was] . . . the keeper of this juvenile pandemonium. [W]e recognized her face as familiar to us, not very long ago, amongst the little news-vendors who plied their vocation on the corner of Exchange Place, in Buchanan Street."[21] In September 1886 a 14-year-old paper girl named Mary Ann Campbell applied for admission to the Edinburgh Magdalene Asylum, a local home for "fallen" women. She "expressed a strong desire to be kept in the Asylum, explaining . . . that her object for doing so was to save herself from the evils to which she was exposed while selling the evening newspapers". Confessing that she "had already fallen under them", the asylum directors agreed that, despite her father's objections, it was "their duty to retain" the young pedlar.[22] They concluded that "the employment of girls in the sale of newspapers and other articles in the street at night, was the cause of much evil".[23]

Following the First World War the child-savers declared that the slackening of parental control during wartime, resulting from the absence of parents on military service, had contributed to a rise in juvenile crime.[24] But most serious was the appearance of a new breed of streetwise girl: the flapper! "Beneath the powder and rouge and despite her laugh and ever ready smiles, the flapper is a very pathetic little figure", an Edinburgh social worker explained in 1918:

> The product of a generation that had largely lost its faith before the war, in many cases she is a thorough-going little pagan only rendered precocious by a system of education which had no time for character building and no place for ideals. Her school contemporaries are those boys who provide the problem of the juvenile criminal.[25]

This social worker's concern was shared by the author of a letter to the *Evening Dispatch*, which stated that "all girls with any self-respect would shun being classed as a flapper for the very name breathes vulgarity".[26] In the 1920s tattoo shops were added to the list of concerns. A female probation officer indicated that she did not "think it [was] quite so disastrous for the boys, but with girls it just stamps them as belonging to the street . . . no nice girls would work along side a tattooed girl".[27] She had observed a distinct sex difference between the delinquency patterns for girls and for boys. She maintained that where boys fell into crime through hanging about with men at the docks, when girls went "adrift" they went "straight for the streets".[28] She was careful to point out that:

they certainly don't hang about the streets like old prostitutes, but they run about picture houses and little restaurants and ice-cream shops and these kind of places and everyone clearly knows what they are doing, but they don't actually invite in so many words. They have not the formula that the old prostitutes use.[29]

In 1930 the National Vigilance Association sadly agreed with the view of "a distinguished naval officer" that "no seaport town in the British Empire . . . [had] so many playful girls, pitifully ignorant, as in Edinburgh". The National Vigilance Association saw the problem as emblematic of an "age when parental control, teaching of high ideals, morals, and religion seemed to have gone by the board".[30]

Familial ideology and the child-savers

Most recent historical and sociological studies of the family demonstrate that it is not a natural but a cultural or social institution. These historical insights emphasize how the family has been subject to regulation by outside forces, whether impersonal ones, like changes in production, or deliberate intervention by state agencies as in the case of child welfare. Following the work of Michel Foucault, Jacques Donzelot attempts a deconstruction of "the family". For Donzelot, the family is more an effect or consequence, or site of intersection, than a pre-existing institution with its own history. He makes the analytical distinction between "the family" as a kin-group and "familialism", an ideological concept.[31] Donzelot's insight is useful here because it offers a framework for examining how modes of intervention into family life created a type of family that was subjected to external authority and how familial ideology was exalted.

To the average Victorian the central cause of juvenile criminality was intemperate and neglectful parents who allowed their children to roam the streets. This concern with "deviant" family values was informed by an unstable mix of three popular Victorian philosophies: Calvinism, environmentalism and eugenics. Although these changed over the period in question, especially after the introduction of psychology into social work in the 1930s and 1940s, there was never any definitive break in the preceding paradigm. One can

25

certainly recognize elements of the Calvinist view that vice and crime were sins and features of people who were not destined to be saved, but early-nineteenth-century evangelical reformers believed that individuals, especially children, could be transformed. It was their goal to help each to make his or her way to the "throne of Grace".[32] But their programme was confined to the spiritual field, to preaching the gospel in the hope that the spirit and power would fill the world with converted women and men, thus, social problems would take care of themselves. By the mid-nineteenth century Scottish evangelicals recognized that their church missions and inspirational preaching had not disposed of social injustice. More aggressive strategies were needed.[33]

The child-savers acknowledged that young offenders were not totally responsible for their condition or their actions. "Adult paupers might be held responsible for their misfortunes . . . but when children were destitute it could not be their fault, since they were by nature dependent."[34] Thus, young offenders were seen as victims of bad families rather than born criminals: "more sinned against than sinning".[35] This marked a shift away from the evangelical tendency to see social problems in strictly Calvinist terms, as divine retribution against spiritual weakness. According to an Edinburgh child-saver, delinquent behaviour in children was evidence that they were "acting upon the only education they had received from vicious parents".[36] Mid-nineteenth-century theory adopted an environmentalist philosophy that located social problems in ignorance.[37]

> You may wring your hands and bewail the power of sin. But you will be wiser if you take the sinner's child and begin to create in his mind a rich circle of thought. The parent is impenetrable. No earthly power can save him. With the child it is different. His character is unformed. You can make of him what you will . . . He has inherited nothing but the evil environment which his parents and a bad social system have created in which we allow him to grow up. The whole stress, therefore, falls upon the environment, above all the social environment, into which from birth the child enters.[38]

In contemporary terms juvenile delinquency was located in the problems of home environment and anti-social conditioning. Richard Johnson argues that the nineteenth-century moral entrepreneur combined liberal theories with the observation out of bourgeois culture, of working class behaviour. They saw industrialization as being progressive but were concerned about its accompanying problems . . . Problems which were not seen as "natural" were not held to be connected with large-scale industrial capitalism. So they were discussed in terms of "invasion", "infestation" and "disease" and were viewed as problems of the principles and habits of the population.[39]

Metaphorically, juvenile delinquency was a "disease", affecting both girls and boys, albeit differently; caused by a contaminated home environment, and cured only by removal to a reformatory.

"As the twig is bent the tree will grow" was the oft-quoted maxim that summed up the situation for thousands of urban slum children. Victorian environmentalism also appeared in the idea that great social evils of the day – alcoholism, venereal disease and illegitimacy – could be cured by radical interventions, including housing reform, medical reform, female suffrage, and temperance. Many argued, for example, that alcohol abuse lay at the heart of the dysfunctional home environment. According to the director of an industrial school in Glasgow, the main cause of delinquent youth was "the drunkenness of the people".[40] The director of a Dundee residential school predicted that "as long as there are wine stores, there will be waifs' homes".[41] And the Reverend T. Guthrie, the author of *A plea for ragged schools* (1847) and founder of the Edinburgh Original Ragged School, stated that "If there was a white slave-market in Edinburgh they would sell their children for drink."[42]

The characteristics of the deteriorating and squalid urban neighbourhoods in which the children lived were transferred directly on to its inhabitants. Describing Edinburgh in the 1860s, one journalist wrote:

> The time was, and that not long ago, when brothels and the homes of the people were as distinctly apart and kept separate from each other as the Police Office and the Church . . . But a sad and withering change had come over us . . . The scarcity of accommodation for the labouring classes [is] prominently visible, the brothel-keeper and his harlots are in hundreds of cases the near neighbours, and, I regret to say, in some instances, even the associates of working people and their families . . . It is a sad thing that the working fathers and mothers of Edinburgh,

for want of proper house accommodation in our streets, are driven to seek homes for their families in our dark closes and wynds, where the atmosphere of prostitution is most deadly. It is a sad thought to think that the aristocracy of our closes are brothel-keepers and prostitutes, and that the rest of the crowded population are living in misery and degradation . . . The children of the working man are compelled to grow up familiar with the language, the manners, and the *morale* of the brothel; and it is next to impossible but that when they become of age they will adopt the same profession.[43]

Juvenile delinquents were distinguished from healthy, respectable and well-tutored girls and boys by means of concentration on attributes like dirt, wage earning, and forms of "knowledge". Knowledge of the adult world and familiarity with its pleasures found among slum children conflicted with middle-class standards and notions of childhood propriety.[44] As a journalist noted in the 1870s:

To [the young delinquent] oaths and curses are indeed "familiar as household words". Ere they have yet learned to lisp, their ears are familiar with everything which is evil and abominable; and before they have arrived at sufficient maturity to enter into the pleasures of vice they have become proficient in all its arts. They are taught from their infancy to beg, to cheat, and to steal, and if they do assume to earn an honest penny in the sale of matches and such other articles as constitute the stock-in-trade of mendicant merchants, it is but too often to cloak some more nefarious mode of obtaining money.[45]

By the late nineteenth and early twentieth centuries the influence of population genetics began to figure in the discourse, which was said to be more scientific than environmentalism. According to Frank Mort, at the "heart of the eugenicist strategy lay a sustained attack on nineteenth-century environmentalism . . . [which] was at best a mere palliative and at worst it actively sustained the unfit and degenerate elements of the population in their reckless over-breeding".[46] Eugenics contained the promise that the human race might be improved by the adoption of a positive genetic policy based on the principles of heredity and the "survival of the fittest", which entailed the prohibition of the reproduction of children by parents who were allegedly of inferior stock. In the 1870s Scottish child-savers began to talk in terms of a "race" or population of physical and mental defectives who had to be identified and segregated lest, through their unrestrained breeding, they swamped the superior part of the population. An example of this concern is found in this Glasgow newspaper article of 1870:

> we may as well expect to gather grapes from thorns or figs from thistles as to find good citizens grow up from among the children who are born and reared in such dens as the Laigh Firk Close, Princess Street and the Havannah. Already these localities have begun to produce a type of humanity peculiarly their own, both physically and morally . . . Every day that is allowed to pass without some well and powerfully organized and sustained effort to rescue the young children . . . from their dreadful surroundings is simply losing ground.[47]

As a social movement eugenics was influential in both the United Kingdom and North America, where it was associated with Darwinism, between 1890 and 1920. Early-twentieth-century commentaries focused on genetic and material factors, venereal disease, alcoholism and diet, which had produced a "race" of inferior human beings who threatened national progress. In 1914 Anne Mercer Watson, medical officer at Aberdeen Female School of Industry, reported that the girls

> as a rule [were] very poor material. We have a great many tubercular children. Syphilis is a disease that is by no means rare. We have these two diseases, and I have a very strong feeling if one were to examine the blood for these two diseases that 90% of the girls of the school would probably show some traces of one or the other.[48]

At a meeting of the Reformatory and Refuge Union in Edinburgh in 1924, "juvenile wrongdoing" was associated with "lack of mental endowment". The committee suggested that the first step was "to stem the source of the evil", which required that "something must be done to prevent those who are seriously defective in intellect from going out into the world and multiplying their kind".[49] A girls' reformatory superintendent in 1926 revealed, "there is a relationship between satisfactory physique and honesty".[50] Like her, many believed that the true sources of delinquency in Scotland were the Irish, the Highlanders, and the Lowland Scots. "Many have not lived in any very advanced state of civilization at home, and have had primitive ideas of cleanliness and comfort. When removed from the restraints of home, and lost in a Glasgow slum, they are apt to sink to very low depths indeed."[51] One Glaswegian pointed out that crime in Clydeside and the southwest of Scotland was caused by the " 'aliens' . . . who are producing a demoralizing effect on the standard of cleanliness [and] morality of our own people. An enormous proportion of low-type Irish are summoned before the various courts."[52] In the case of Edinburgh, another pointed to the existence of "a great company of men, women, and children who are morally and socially and intellectually a hundred years at least behind the higher civilization".[53]

Understanding the rhetoric that underlay the child-saving movement as it developed in the nineteenth century involves first appreciating how cultural and class differences were translated into the category of a pathology by the middle-class child-savers. Throughout the nineteenth century industrialization brought increasing wealth and prosperity to middle-class homes. Bolstered by strong kinship networks, the middle-class family emerged with a new self-confidence. This climate gave rise to a set of normative values and prescriptions that defined the normal, "healthy" productive family as the autonomous nuclear family unit, headed by a male breadwinner, supported by his nurturing wife and their financially dependent children. This form of familial ideology is known in the literature as the doctrine of separate spheres: the notion that the role of women should be exclusively within the domestic sphere,[54] which since the Victorian era has became the normative ideal for many middle- and working-class families.

Aspiring to inclusion in the governing stratum, adult members of the prosperous middle-class family were eager to insert themselves into the "public gaze" through a myriad of religious, philanthropic and scientific societies.[55] As will be seen in Chapter 4, it was largely to the activities of this class fraction of women and men that the emergence of juvenile delinquency as a distinct social problem and the rise of child-saving institutions can be traced. They became the key players, the lobbyists and agitators, who were the "experts" of the child-saving movement. In their work on the middle-class family Leonore Davidoff and Catherine Hall have argued that evangelicalism "fostered humanist compassion for the helpless and weak: women, children, animals, the insane, and the prisoner". Benevolent concern, however, was tempered with the drive to control these same groups.[56] This is supported by Olive Checkland's study of philanthropy in Victorian Scotland. Smout states that Scottish philanthropists never ceased to be orthodox Calvinists and Presbyterians; they were fervently religious, puritanical and anxious to see their ideals adopted by society as the accepted norms.[57]

The first generation of "experts" agitated for penal reform and therapeutic strategies in treating juvenile offenders.[58] In Scotland they acquired their audiences through the pulpit, the press and newly formed statistical societies of the 1850s and 1860s. Using their professional status as magistrates, ministers, industrialists or, in the case of women, the wives and daughters of these professionals, the picture they constructed was widely accepted because of their social status. Their activities were largely philanthropic and the first child-saving institutions were intended to be run as charities. The second generation of "experts", many of whom were called to testify at the Royal Commissions on Reformatory and Industrial Schools in 1897 and 1915 and the Secretary of State's Youthful Offenders (Scotland) Committee in 1925, lobbied for more interventionist legislation, such as the Criminal Law Amendment Act 1885 and the Children Act 1908, which are discussed in the next chapter. Like the first generation they also composed a loose network of public and private organizations, linked by overlapping membership in diverse local and national child welfare organizations, such as the Scottish Society for the Prevention of Cruelty to Children, the Charity Organization Society, the Reformatory and Refuge Union, and various youth clubs, such as the Boy Scouts, the Boys' Brigade and the Band of Hope. There was also a new feminist group of social workers, teachers and physicians with professional aspirations of their own.

The working-class family

In stark contrast to the families of the middle-class child-savers, the working-class family did not weather the industrial revolution nearly so well. In the households of the labouring classes where the main breadwinner was a skilled tradesman who earned a regular wage, the family enjoyed some degree of material comfort, the women might not work outside of their homes, and the children might be fairly well fed, dressed and sent to school.[59] In Victorian Scotland these families were regarded as fortunate. But there was a great range in the standard of living among the urban proletariat. Generally, middle-class familial ideology bore little, if any, relation to the realities of life for the thousands of unskilled and casual workers or unemployed men and women who populated the poorest districts of Scotland's industrial towns and port cities. It was the visibility of the poor urban working class that led to considerable concern over social order.

Throughout the nineteenth and early twentieth centuries British journals and the popular press were marked by a proliferation of debates about the social problems of the growing cities. Disorder and popular protests, once relatively tolerated in rural areas, began to be seen as more threatening, even revolutionary within an increasingly urbanized Britain. The massive urban growth of the first decades of the century made already existing social problems appear more prominent than ever before. By the 1840s Glasgow was by far the largest city in Scotland and the second largest in the United Kingdom. At 275,000 in 1841, the population of Glasgow was 12 times larger than it had been in 1775, and between 1831 and 1841 it grew by more than one-third. Edinburgh, at 138,000, was only half Glasgow's size, and Aberdeen, Dundee and Paisley were each only half the size of Edinburgh.[60] Waves of immigration had dislocated traditional kin networks and left poor families to struggle with new problems: slum living, disease, overcrowding and unsteady wages, with no external support. This made it extremely difficult for poor rural and urban parents to combine long hours of employment with the care and nurture of their younger offspring, thus parental supervision for children over the age of 12 was unlikely.[61] Moreover, the working-class family was still very much an economic unit and its continued survival depended on the financial contribution of all members. At very young ages girls and boys were expected to work outside of their homes and the pennies they earned baby-sitting, running errands, street-selling or doing small jobs in local businesses and factories contributed to the family coffers. Working-class child-rearing practices such as these contradicted familial ideology and aroused indignation and pity among middle-class observers. The parents who depended on the earnings of their young children were regarded as having failed in their most fundamental duty.

Politics, pauperism and population

The initial impetus behind the juvenile prison reform movement was based on the justice system's previous history of failure to deter or convert young offenders and "also on a new awareness of the nature and extent of juvenile delinquency".[62] This new awareness was due largely to the publication of an increasing number of statistical exposés into the living conditions and habits of the urban poor. The rise of statistical societies by the middle of the nineteenth century and the intense preoccupation with a rubric of ostensibly social questions, including health, morality, idleness and crime (what Foucault calls bio-political interventions), have been linked by many historians to the emergence of a capitalist mode of production and its attendant class structure in Britain. Squires argues that the emergence of statistical and social sciences at this time testifies to the close connection between the development of capitalism and the emergence of a uniquely "social" form of discipline.[63]

Branches of one of the earliest statistical societies, the National Association for the Promotion of Social Sciences, were formed early in Scottish cities and the most prolific writers on the juvenile delinquency problem, both men and women, congregated annually to discuss the most pertinent issues. Papers on the juvenile crime question and the role of reformatories and industrial schools were read at the National Association for the Promotion of Social Sciences conferences that were held in Glasgow in 1860 and 1874, Edinburgh in 1863 and 1880, and Aberdeen in 1877.[64] In the 1900s Scottish branches of the Reformatory and Refuge Union and the National Vigilance Association were formed and dedicated themselves to dealing with publicizing the problem of juvenile crime. In the 1940s district Juvenile Organizations assumed the responsibility. It is in this context that this section will examine how one social problem – juvenile delinquency – was conceptualized in terms of politics, pauperism and population.

In the 1840s juvenile delinquency was linked to another form of impending social collapse: Chartism. Early Victorian perceptions of juvenile lawlessness associated it with the possibility of political insurrection among the lower orders. G. Pearson argues that this response to the early writings of Karl Marx and Friedrich Engels fuelled the wings of charity. The Victorian philanthropic movement "repeatedly justified itself in the conviction that, unless a system of moral instruction were provided for the poor, then crime was a prelude to social revolution".[65] In Scotland conservatives feared the overtly oppositional challenge mounted by working-class organizations. The threat of trade union activity and Chartist demonstrations during the 1830s and 1840s, for example, suggested to the bourgeoisie that "Armageddon might be just around the next bend".[66] A belief arose among segments of the bourgeoisie that the tide of insurrection could be overturned by voluntary initiatives and legislation. According to Russell Dobash, by the mid-nineteenth century new institutions emerged within the criminal justice system to survey, punish and reform the labouring classes. The creation of the modern penitentiary in the 1840s is an example of one institutional response, "serving as a model of the new disciplines and forms of regulation meant to bring a social and moral transformation to labouring women and men".[67] Beside the demand for prison reform was a growing lobby for state education. Johnson argues that the "synchronization between the demand for state education, and the growth of Chartism was exact. All the educationists were hostile to Chartism, Owenism and trade unions."[68] He argues that the working people were not seen as merely ignorant, but it was increasingly recognized that they had their own kinds of knowledge and this knowledge threatened the bourgeoisie. "Supplying what was absent" was no longer the goal of philanthropy, now "intervention must correct what was present already".[69] The creation of juvenile reformatories and industrial schools in the 1850s, which pre-dates the education acts by some 20 years, was one important measure whereby the children of the dangerous classes could be educated "to the ranks of conformity".[70]

Concern about the dangers of trade unionism at home was compounded by the debate around the question of "national efficiency": in essence, the fear that the military force of the Empire might be weakened by the sickly state of would-be soldiers and the mothers who produced them. This fuelled the debate about the most pressing needs of poor children. Philanthropists' writing on poverty, public health and housing linked these concerns with juvenile delinquency. The children of the poor were both the endangered and dangerous victims of their parents' ignorance and immorality. At the Select Committee appointed to enquire into criminal and destitute children in 1852, testimony after testimony revealed the shared belief that "it is from the mismanagement or low moral condition of the parents, rather than from poverty, that juvenile crime flows".[71] A distinction was made, however, between poverty as a problem of inadequate income, a difficulty against which "worthy" people struggled, and the wastage of money through drinking and gambling.[72] Writers on the poverty problem chose to define the problem in terms of the conditions of "pauperism", a condition of individuals, rather than poverty, a condition of capitalism inflicted on exploited workers.[73] By implication pauperism was seen as a consequence of an individual's chosen lifestyle: idleness, drunkenness, irreligion, imprudent marriage and sexual promiscuity. Like other Victorian social reform movements, the agitation around juvenile delinquency was an attempt to analyze a social problem in a dispassionate and even scientific way. Reformers chose to see juvenile delinquents as victims. "Any other way would have forced them to see the cause of juvenile delinquency in an exploitative economic structure."[74] This was a critique that would have demanded a much more radical transformation of the structure of society than the reformers were willing to assume.

Moral statisticians engineered unofficial enquiries into the living conditions of the nation's poor.[75] What they discovered violated their image of the "ideal" childhood. Thus, "moral interventionism arose from the contrast between the lived culture of the middle class and what was observed of working people".[76] In the case of children, early writings on juvenile delinquency reveal a great gulf between the realities of slum childhood and the middle-class experience of a protected childhood.[77] They hypothesized the existence of a moral or criminal career, where the neglected children of the poor would move from being themselves at risk to being a risk to others. It was admitted, however, that street girls and boys were seldom naturally or innately criminal, but just following the example set by their parents and older siblings. Not guilty then, but not innocent either; it was argued that permissive parenting would be the downfall of all these children.

Evidence drawn from the collections of moral statistics that proliferated in mid-century Scotland enabled the child-savers to turn familial ideology into a scientific strategy for diagnosis and intervention. The identification and classification of precipitating factors and of types of child were facilitated by this accumulation of data. In their efforts to determine the causes of juvenile delinquency, the child-savers focused on the conditions of family life among the very poor. At best, the poor family was seen as overcrowded, dirty and lacking in positive moral training. At worst it was notorious for the promiscuous mixing of the sexes and for schooling its children in vice and crime. Even though statistical surveys revealed that many of the conditions that prevailed in the backgrounds of delinquent children (poverty, family disruption and bad housing) could also be identified among noncriminal children, the environmentalists' influence on early criminal theory was strong enough to turn this observation into a necessary if not sufficient cause. Social problems were regarded as the outcome of individual weakness and vice, although certain social situations might exacerbate tendencies and frailties. Mary Carpenter, an English leader of the ragged school movement, made a distinction between what she called the "perishing" and the "dangerous" classes.[78] Children of the former class were those who had not committed any crime but were likely to do so, through destitution, ignorance and bad example. The child in danger would in time become the dangerous child.

Conclusion: ideology and the social

The definition of, and solution to, the problem of juvenile crime and delinquency emerged through the child-savers' investigations. The juvenile reformatory experiment first removed convicted children from the adult prison system; the influence of mass industrialization, urbanization and environmentalist philosophy then created another category of child, the child in danger. The focus of the discourse was the large group of orphan, semi-orphan and destitute children who, though not technically law-breakers, shared their characteristics, for example, working-class background, bad housing conditions and poverty. This was a category of children who, through no fault of their own, were seen as being in moral and physical danger of falling into criminal habits.

The child-savers professed a strong commitment to family life and they argued that it was wrong to break the family tie without a very good reason, but evidence suggests that grounds for intervention ranged from seemingly innocuous swearing to habitual laziness, drunkenness and violence. One residential school mistress admitted that not all parents who "swear or get drunk, or are violent in their temper were all together bad" but, according to her, history had proven that "few parents are guilty only of these faults; there is something more usually".[79] As environmentalism gave way to eugenics, the focus did not shift: the conditions of family life among the very poor which violated the middle-class familial ideal remained the locus of concern. The average Victorian did not question the social system but saw the problem in moralistic or pseudo-scientific and policy-oriented terms, attributing the problem to neglectful parenting. The reformation of the rising generation was the only means by which to maintain effective control over the population. The education of the young would prevent the working class from reproducing itself "in its present condition – vicious, criminal, heathen, drunken and dangerous".[80]

The strategic significance of diagnosis in terms of parental neglect is that it facilitated concrete action. For reformatory and industrial school supporters it mandated the right of the state to have children removed from their homes. As May argues, after 1850, the character of nineteenth-century family law suggested that where the parents abrogated their duties the state had the right to act *in loco parentis*. Parents who did not provide physical, mental and moral care "signed away their rights to their children".[81] The principle of *in loco parentis* provided the legal framework for subsequent child welfare legislation and the admission practices of reformatory and industrial schools were based largely on the courts' perceptions of family circumstances.

Chapter 3

❧

The dangerous child

> I was always plunking school . . . I used to like to jump on a
> lorry and go out in the country and walk around all day. Lat-
> terly, I had to go into the court . . . This day there was no
> reprieve . . . I had to get three months sentence in this indus-
> trial school . . . You were taken away from your mother . . . My
> mother was crying . . . If you come back again you got six
> months [then 9 months] . . . and then it was the Training Ship
> Mars . . . I didnea plunk school again . . . It cured me. I was the
> first at school every morning [after that] for fear of goin' back
> there again.[1]

Remembering the circumstances surrounding his own court appearance and placement in an industrial school for truancy in 1908, a
former inmate of a Glasgow industrial school reveals a knowledge of
the logic of the reformatory and industrial school system that was
shared among the urban poor by the end of the nineteenth century.
"They would take you quicker then, than they would do now"[2] is a
sentiment that was shared by many families, who lived on the look-
out for the parish inspectors and truant officers: the agents of institutions that called themselves "homes". By the early twentieth century
a network of juvenile reformatory and industrial schools had
emerged that contemporaries described as being analogous to a set
of sieves. It was hoped that the first sieve, the day industrial school,
would "retain by far the largest number; a smaller will pass to the
second sieve, or certified industrial schools; a still smaller on to the
reformatory, and few, if any, to the prison".[3] After 1907, probation
was added to the list, and it replaced the day industrial school as "the
first step".[4]

This chapter will shift attention away from the popular concern over the causes of juvenile delinquency and focus on the treatment of convicted children. Peter Squires argues that where the integrative function of social institutions like the church, the school or the police appear eroded and the least secure, the liberal-democratic regime becomes all the more punitive and disciplinary. Hence, around society's key "social divisions – the 'fault lines of the social' – a whole array of mechanisms and procedures . . . are deployed – with profound consequences for some sections of the population".[5] The purpose of this chapter is to examine the modes of social intervention and how contemporary discourses on juvenile delinquency were translated into legislation for the classification, surveillance and disciplining of poor families. First, it examines the prevention era, the first pioneering experiments in the treatment of juvenile delinquency; secondly, the reformatory era, the period spanning the introduction of the Youthful Offenders Act 1854, Dunlop's Act 1854, the Reformatory and Industrial Schools Act 1866 and the Education (Scotland) Act 1872. Finally, the protective era is examined – that is, the period from the passing of the Criminal Law Amendment Act 1885, the Probation of Offenders Act 1907, the Children Act 1908 and the Children and Young Persons (Scotland) Act 1932, which resulted in the transfer of reformatories and industrial schools in Scotland from the Home Office to the Scottish Education Department.[6]

The prevention era, 1800–54

The early history of the treatment of juvenile offenders is a "history of coarseness and brutality". As late as 1833 it was recorded that a nine-year-old Scottish boy was sentenced to be hanged for breaking a window and stealing 2 shillings' worth of paint. He was reprieved, "but the fact is indicative of the spirit of the age".[7] Prior to the second quarter of the nineteenth century little, if any, attention was paid to age or sex of the offender, and girls and boys were thrown into prison alongside adults for the most trivial charges. Critics of the prison system argued that prison did not rehabilitate or deter young offenders. In fact, subjecting poor children to short prison sentences actually did them a favour, because the bath, meals and clean clothes they received were luxuries. Others took a different view, claiming that the repeated prison sentences actually hardened the young offender. By the end of the eighteenth century it became the passionate conviction of early British prison reformers like John Howard and Elizabeth Fry that the imprisonment of children was too harsh and brutalizing, and philanthropists throughout Britain, following their lead, demanded the removal of children from adult forms of punishment.

In Scotland the first institutional attempts to rescue and reform young offenders occurred in Glasgow. Initiated by a divinity professor named Stevenson MacGill, the Glasgow Society for the Encouragement of Penitents was formed in 1801 to assist juvenile offenders, specifically "vagrant boys" and "magdalenes". The Society proposed the establishment of two charitable institutions. The first would be a type of "half-way house" for Bridewell boys to prevent them "from returning to their idle and pernicious courses".[8] The second was an asylum for teenage prostitutes, whom they referred to as magdalenes.

Drumming up support for a boys' reformatory proved to be difficult. A letter to the editor of the *Glasgow Courier* in 1805 reported that the Society for the Encouragement of Penitents "could not trace one benefited individual of either sex, except an unfortunate lame boy who could not run away from his apprenticeship when his comrades did".[9] By 1815, the Society too admitted its failure and abandoned its efforts on behalf of vagrant boys, confessing that notwithstanding "the attention, zeal, and prudence . . . their success has hitherto been small". They attributed their failure to two factors: the "interference of foolish and unprincipled" parents and the lack of statutory authority.[10] For success they concluded that they would need the legal authority to keep a boy's parents from interfering, and a state-supported institution for the "tuition and reformation of boys who have been convicted of crimes . . . supported by the authority of law".[11] After abandoning their work among boys, the Society for the Encouragement of Penitents turned its attention to its second project, and a magdalene asylum opened in Glasgow in 1815.

It was not until 1826 that a second attempt was made to establish a reformatory for boys. Inspired by MacGill's work a decade earlier, the governor of Glasgow City Bridewell, William Brebner, launched a public appeal for an institution for the punishment and reform of male juvenile prisoners. Regarded as the "founding father of the

Scottish prison system",[12] Brebner was the first to classify Scottish inmates by sex and age. He also recognized the importance of rehabilitating juvenile offenders and emphasized the necessity of teaching boys a trade. In a letter to the Lord Provost in 1826, he stated his objectives. He did not question the importance of incarceration, but argued that Bridewell did not go far enough in controlling crime or rehabilitating offenders. He believed that sentences of between two and six weeks handed out to third- and fourth-time offenders were too short to break up the "street gangs which plagued city streets".[13] In his opinion these short sentences were more likely to "inure, harden, and gradually train offenders to endure confinement, without feeling it as punishment".[14]

His work among boys had alerted him to the presence of two classes of young offenders: those he called "desperately wicked" and a second group that he described as the "offspring of ignorance, depravity, and neglect". The former group of hardened repeat offenders made up half of the Bridewell boys. This group regarded prison, with all its privations, as a "comfortable asylum". They were the class who, if fortunate enough to escape capital punishment or transportation, inevitably became "disabled and diseased and ended their days as 'depraved paupers' and burdens on the public purse".[15] It was the mixing of this class with first offenders in the prison that most disturbed Brebner. First offenders "get into contact with the idle and vicious and soon become their tools and associates".[16] The originality of his mode of intervention was that he thought it possible to intervene in the criminal career, thus preventing the potential delinquent moving from the "depraved and neglected" stage to the "desperately wicked" stage. A House of Refuge for boys that focused on the first-time offenders would provide a preventative service and be an intermediate step between the prison and the community. His unique approach entailed using custody in a positive manner, through the introduction of vocational training.

> Here the friendless outcast would be . . . trained up in habits of cleanliness, regularity, and order – subjected to vigilant inspection – and permitted to remain until industry, education and the force of good impressions, should in some degree have subdued the strength of criminal desire.[17]

The reformatory school

Institutionalized rescue work among boys did not actually begin until 1838, when Brebner and Captain Miller, the superintendent of the Glasgow Police Office, finally succeeded in securing pledges totalling £10,000 to go towards the construction of a House of Refuge. A board of directors was appointed and the doors of the Glasgow Boys' House of Refuge opened on 18 February 1838.[18] This was intended to be more than just a "half-way house" for some 300 juvenile offenders; it would serve a symbolic function as well. The building, with its "commanding eminence", spire, belfry and tower, would be a "monument to the philanthropy of the citizens of Glasgow".[19] It would set an example to be followed by the "other great cities of the Empire".[20]

Evidence from the Glasgow police records suggests that the House of Refuge rapidly became an integral part of the city's provision for boy delinquents and first offenders.[21] It was used by magistrates as an alternative to sending juveniles to prison. Within the first 11 months 164 boys were admitted into the House and the Superintendent of Police claimed personally to have recommended 110 cases. In fact, the House of Refuge proved to be so successful in reducing both crime and the cost of prosecuting juvenile offenders that in the same year the Lord Provost was exhorted to open a similar institution for girls. The magdalene asylum was regarded at the time as the obvious location for a home for criminal girls: "the object of that Institution being so nearly the same, there could be no objection to such an arrangement".[22] In October 1838 the Lord Provost requested that it be converted into a House of Refuge for girls. Putting female thieves in with prostitutes might appear curious, but it must be remembered that at the time very little difference was perceived between the two classes. The asylum's directors agreed to the merger on the condition that accommodation be reserved for 40 magdalene cases under 25 years of age. The remaining 120 places were turned over to convicted girls and adolescents who "consented" to go there after a preliminary two-week prison term expired. A few places were also allocated to destitute and orphan girls who were considered at risk of falling into crime or prostitution. The new institution, which began to admit inmates on 12 October 1840, was called the House of Refuge for Females.

Almost immediately it became clear that although charitable contributions could build an institution they could not sustain one. In Glasgow steps were taken to obtain an act of Parliament to raise a small assessment from the rates to support the refuges and in 1841 the first act of Parliament was obtained. The Act for Repressing Juvenile Delinquency in the City of Glasgow was unique to Glasgow. It placed the girls' and boys' reformatories under one board of commissioners, and provision was made for their support by a tax on ratepayers.[23] According to historian Andrew Ralston, Scotland pioneered reformatories. The Dean Bank Institution for the Reformation of Female Delinquents was opened in Edinburgh in 1832[24] and the Glasgow Boys' House of Refuge became the largest reformatory school in Britain. The only other institution in Britain at the time was the Juvenile Prison at Parkhurst (1838), "a brutal institution, which trained boy transportees before embarkment".[25] Glasgow reformatories were the only ones in Britain to have a special act of Parliament; nevertheless, the grant fell short of the amount needed to maintain the institution so the commissioners continued to rely on voluntary donations to meet its costs.

The industrial school

At the same time that reformatories were being established, the similar industrial school movement was getting underway in Scotland. Full-time education in Scotland did not become compulsory by law until 1872. Prior to this time, however, there is evidence of a democratic tradition of national education dating back to the seventeenth century; in 1696 a statute decreed that schools, under the control of the Kirk and financed by a property tax, be erected in every parish and burgh in the kingdom. This was influenced by the Calvinist view that children were born ignorant and godless and that education, structured by a regime of "godly training", would prepare the child "for the business of life and the purpose of eternity".[26]

Scottish parish education can be distinguished from the system of education in England, where all schools were either private profit-making concerns or dependent on charity. The Scottish system resulted in the highest literacy rate in the United Kingdom. However, the parish system was not the only education option available in Scotland. By 1818, of the 5,081 schools involved in elementary education only 942 belonged to the publicly financed sector; 2,479 were fee-paying schools, 212 were charity schools, and 1,448 were charity Sunday schools. Of the pupils attending these schools, only 54,000 (a little more than a fifth of those being educated and perhaps a tenth of those requiring education) were going to publicly financed schools; 112,000 were in private schools, 10,000 were in charity day schools and 75,000 were in Sunday schools.[27]

According to most historians, it is doubtful whether the "national system of education" survived the early decades of the nineteenth century, or if, in fact, it ever had existed. Nineteenth-century sceptics, such as the Reverend George Lewis, author of *Scotland: a half-educated nation both in quantity and quality of her education institutions* (1834), revealed that only one in 12 of the population attended day schools, and that in this Scotland was lagging behind Prussia, France and parts of the United States and was only marginally ahead of England.[28] The disruption of the Church of Scotland in 1843 fragmented the system further as the new Free Kirk began to set up its own schools, making three principal educational bodies: the old Kirk, the new Kirk and the Roman Catholic Church, plus profit-making private initiatives that catered for those who could afford higher fees. Nevertheless, there was still a shortage of schools.[29] The Argyle Commission of 1866, established to examine the lack of adequate provision of schools for Scottish children, concluded that of 500,000 children needing education, 200,000 received it under inefficient conditions, 200,000 were at schools of doubtful merit with no inspection and 90,000 were attending no school at all.[30] In Glasgow, for example, of 98,767 children between 3 and 15 years of age, only 48,391 were on school rolls.

According to T. C. Smout figures such as these make it difficult to escape the "conclusion that the boasted tradition of the Scottish system had either collapsed over large areas in recent years as the result of industrialization . . . or that it had in fact never worked at all".[31] Similarly, Thomas Ferguson argues that by the 1850s the "major social and religious changes which had been taking place in Scotland had necessarily played havoc with the traditional education system in the country".[32] He admitted that the parochial school had done a great deal for Scottish education, providing a link between primary and secondary education and universities, "but it was evident that the parochial system had served its day and that education must enter a new phase"[33] if the growing demands of the population were to be met. This was especially true in the cities, where the high juvenile crime rates alerted many to the urgent need to train poor children. For those who believed that education was a panacea for all social problems, the solution lay in the extension of voluntary aid to poor children through the ragged or industrial school movement.

One of Scotland's most important contributions to the nineteenth-century child-saving movement in Britain was the development of industrial schools for needy and destitute children. The pioneer of these institutions was William Watson (1796–1878), whose interest in the subject was aroused by his daily contact with young offenders in his capacity as Sheriff-Substitute of Aberdeenshire. "When I find", wrote Watson, "that there are two hundred and eighty children under fourteen years of age who have no means of subsisting but by begging and stealing, I think it is high time to attempt another new institution."[34] In 1841 he instructed the police constables to bring all vagrant children to the city's poorhouse, where a room had been set aside for the purpose of an industrial school. Food proved to be a sufficient incentive for the children to continue attending, but Watson recognized the need for wider powers and in 1845 he persuaded the magistrates to authorize the police to bring all vagrant children to Aberdeen's soup kitchen, where he established a larger school. Such authoritative backing helped the schools to expand and by 1851 there were four industrial schools, catering for a total of 300 children.[35]

Other Scottish towns were quick to follow Aberdeen's example. Another well-known pioneer of the movement was the Reverend Thomas Guthrie of Edinburgh (1803–73). Influenced by Watson's success, he used his powers of persuasion in writing A plea for ragged schools (1846) and thereby raised sufficient money to open the Edinburgh Original Ragged School in 1847. It was not long, however, before the school, which was strongly supported by the Free Church, was accused of proselytizing. A second, the United Industrial School, was opened and unlike Guthrie's it offered religious instruction to both Roman Catholic and Protestant children. Between 1841 and 1851 day industrial schools were opened in most Scottish towns large enough to experience problems with juvenile vagrancy and delinquency, including Aberdeen, Ayr, Dumfries, Dundee, Edinburgh, Glasgow, Greenock, Paisley, Perth, Stirling and Stranraer.[36]

Scottish historians generally accept that industrial schools grew out of the ragged school movement of the 1840s, whereas the reformatory movement grew out of the prison reform movement a decade earlier.[37] We should be careful not to draw too rigid a distinction between reformatories and industrial schools at this point, however, because "the distinction was not yet clear cut; the ideology of a dual system of industrial schools for preventing juvenile delinquency and reformatory schools for treating it was not yet developed".[38] What distinguished the first industrial schools from reformatories was that the founders intended them to be nonresidential. Watson argued that the parents should never be entirely relieved of their responsibilities. To institutionalize children in dormitories would cut them off from learning "all the practical lessons they can from the circumstances in life".[39]

Most reformatories and industrial schools admitted boys and girls whether they had prison records or not. Watson, for one, was not particularly concerned about separating children with criminal records from others, because they all belonged to the same class. In some cases, however, a common class background was the problem. By the 1850s the admission practices of the Glasgow Girls' House of Refuge were under attack because the wisdom of mixing petty thieves with prostitutes was questioned. Critics observed that on admission days the lobby of the Girls' House of Refuge "was thronged with homeless creatures, from childhood upwards, filthy, wretched, and often diseased". The house was continuously overcrowded and due to lack of space "the indiscriminate intermingling of all ages of girls and young women in varying degrees of delinquency was unavoidable".[40] Renovation in 1850 led to some improvements but, nevertheless, young women and girls suspected of prostitution were placed in the magdalene division rather than the House of Refuge, even where they were charged with theft. This upset the directors of the magdalene division, who resisted association with the criminal element. Each side feared that it would be contaminated by the other side, so in 1860 the magdalene division moved to a new location on neighbouring grounds and became the Glasgow Magdalene Institution; the House of Refuge became certified as Maryhill Industrial School for Girls.

The reformatory era, 1854–85

Although the reformatory and industrial school system was built on the voluntary principle of social welfare dominant at the time, by the 1850s the system had grown to a size and scope warranting state administration. As Table 3.1 indicates the child-savers campaigned hard for legislation for the regulation of reformatories and industrial schools. In order to fuel their lobby, child-saving propaganda frequently played on class fears. The image of swarming bands of youth preying on society and corroding the social order coincided with the abolition of the transportation of convicts to British colonies in the early 1850s and the rise of trade unionism. The response of a threatened middle class was essentially defensive; social chaos was to be contained by reasserting domestic values of home and family life. This section suggests that children acquired a new status in the eyes of the law between 1854 and 1885, via the enactment of new laws and the expansion, in size and scope, of special institutions for their care and reformation.

Table 3.1   Legislation supplying industrial schools.

Legislation	Offence	Age
Industrial Schools Act 1866		
Section 14	begging	7–14
	wandering	
	destitute and orphan	
	frequenting company of thieves	
Section 15	convicted of felony (first offence)	12–14
Section 16	child as uncontrollable (parental consent)	7–14
Industrial Schools Act 1880		
	residing in brothel	7–14
	frequenting company of prostitutes	
Prevention of Crimes Act 1871		
Section 14	mother convicted of crime (if only guardian)	7–14
Education Act (Scotland) 1872		
	truant from school	5–13
	wandering	
Industrial Day Schools Act (Glasgow) 1878		
	truant or misbehaving in day school	5–13

Source: calculated from PP SC, 1897, p. 9.

Youthful Offenders Act 1854

Mounting public pressure combined with the findings of the 1852 Select Committee on Criminal and Destitute Juveniles induced the government to support C. B. Adderley's Youthful Offenders Bill of 1854 for the regulation of reformatories. Under the conditions of the Youthful Offenders Act judges and magistrates could sentence the guilty under the age of 16 who had completed a preliminary 14-day prison term to the reformatory for up to five years. This distinguished it from earlier practices because residence in a reformatory ceased to be voluntary. Moreover, recalcitrant and unruly inmates could be sent back to prison for up to three months. The Act advantaged reformatories because parents were deterred from trying to get their children released and the maintenance costs were met by the state (unless parents could be made to pay), thus making reformatories less dependent on the charity box.

Although the Youthful Offenders Act 1854 was heralded as a victory by many, it also had its critics. The disadvantage was that as residence was no longer voluntary it was difficult to get rid of unruly inmates. Even those who were sent back to prison would eventually reappear, perhaps more unmanageable than before. This cycle could continue until the five-year sentence had elapsed. The coming and going of some inmates disturbed the others; it also called for stricter discipline as break-outs became common.[41] Another disadvantage was that it increased the proportion of inmates with criminal records to that of the voluntary cases that continued, under special circumstances, to be admitted. In 1850, for example, only 12 out of 36 girls in the Glasgow House of Refuge had been admitted under court order, whereas by 1858, 35 out of 39 inmates were admitted from prison.[42]

Dunlop's Act 1854

In addition to the Youthful Offenders Act, which applied to reformatories, the findings of the Select Committee in 1852 also resulted in the passing in Scotland of Dunlop's Act (17 & 18 Vict. c. 74) in 1854 (extended to England in 1857), which dealt with industrial schools. Named for its author, Alexander Murray Dunlop (1798–1870), a

Liberal Member of Parliament for Greenock, it enabled magistrates to send vagrant, homeless and neglected children under 14 (raised to 16 in 1908) to any industrial school, reformatory, parish home or private residence until their fifteenth birthday (raised to 18 in 1908). The sentence was not preceded by imprisonment, the only charge being vagrancy. The cost of maintaining the child was charged to the parents where possible, or to the parish.

The most significant consequence of the Act was that industrial school residence ceased to be nonresidential. It had been the distinct philosophy of early Watson and Guthrie schools that children should return home in the evenings, but dormitory accommodation was implied under the Act; the children had been sent under magistrate's warrant, after all. This fact, plus increased competition between schools for inmates, forced many schools to reconsider the question of dormitories. By the mid-century many schools were so desperate for financial aid that they complied with the terms of the Act in order to qualify for a grant.[43] Residential industrial schools in Ayr, Aberdeen, Edinburgh, Glasgow and Kilmarnock were certified in 1855, Arbroath and Paisley in 1856, Perth in 1857 and Stranraer in 1858. Dundee, Rothsay and Falkirk followed in 1861, 1864 and 1867 respectively.[44]

Reformatory and Industrial Schools Act 1866

The statistics for Scotland reveal that the total number of children admitted or transferred to industrial schools jumped from 378 in 1865 to 1,003 in 1868.[45] According to historian Margaret May, taking children into industrial schools as "vagrants" proved difficult to negotiate as the charge was not clearly defined.[46] In 1866, however, a consolidated act was passed that specified more clearly which children were regarded as at risk and how they should be dealt with. The Reformatory and Industrial Schools Act 1866 consolidated industrial schools and reformatories in Scotland and England under the same administrative body. Institutions in both countries were expected to submit their rules to the Secretary of State, which appointed an inspector from the Home Office to oversee their administration. The inmates were required to undergo at least 18 months' incarceration, and they were to be 14 years old and ideally to have reached the third standard in school before they were eligible for the parole system called licensing. The Act specified the three classes of children requiring custodial care: vagrants, felons and children beyond parental control.

The vagrant child was regarded as "any child under the age of fourteen found begging or receiving alms . . . wandering, and not having a home or settled place of abode, or any visible means of subsistence, or [who] frequents the company of reputed thieves". Begging, vagrancy and wandering cases were dealt with under section 14 ("at risk") and were tried in the burgh court. First offenders of any age and repeat offenders under 12 were charged under section 15 of the Act and were dealt with in the police court,[47] except in Edinburgh where cases such as housebreaking were dealt with in the burgh court.[48] Classified as felons, first offenders and children under 12 were sent to industrial schools, whereas children over 12 were sent to reformatories.[49] Section 16 of the 1866 Act[50] created a new, controversial offence for children. It was used in cases where a child was brought to the burgh magistrate court by the parents, who testified that their son or daughter was beyond their control. The child was then sent to an industrial school. After 1872, section 16 was also used in truancy cases. It was the only clause that required prior consent of the parent.[51]

Industrial training ships

By the 1860s the rapidly increasing populations of areas like Lanarkshire and neighboring areas in the west of Scotland, especially Glasgow, and Edinburgh and the coastal ports, were reported to be producing disturbingly high rates of "crime and destitution".[52] Industrial schools became residential and, with few exceptions, inmates were committed by magistrates and could not return home at night, so there was no longer any necessity for the institutions to be situated near the children's homes.[53] Hence, the trend in the 1860s was for such schools to be removed to sites (thought healthier) in the outskirts of the cities. One manifestation of this trend was the appearance of certified industrial training ships for boys charged under section 14 of the Reformatory and Industrial Schools Act. The concept of a naval training ship as a method of educating young men was popularized after the Crimean War, when the extent of British naval unpreparedness was revealed. The system was established in 1860 by the Admiralty Office of the Royal Navy for cadets who would in the course of time become midshipmen and officers.[54] The idea of ship schools was quick to catch on and by the end of the decade it had expanded to the class of boys who were being put into residential schools. Each boy remained on board the ship for a period averaging one year and nine months.[55] By 1869 Scotland had two training ships: the *Mars*, situated on the Tay near Dundee, and the *Cumberland* (replaced by the *Empress* after a fire in 1889), near Dumbarton: the ships were dry-docked in these ports until the 1930s. Both came within the scope of the Industrial Schools Act.[56] The industrial training ship attracted a special breed of Scottish philanthropist, retired Royal Navy officers and industrialists with interests in shipping, whose philosophy of reform revealed their strong belief in rugged individualism, strict discipline and the acceptance of hierarchies of authority. According to the captain of the *Cumberland*, "It is true [that] . . . the Reformatory and Industrial Schools had been in operation for a number of years, and . . . the ship . . . would supply an important desideratum outside the legal scope and fair expectations of the Reformatory and Industrial Schools."[57]

Lochburn Home (Glasgow Magdalene Asylum)

In addition to "boy only" institutions, it is important to emphasize that magistrates continued to depend on female rescue homes for a special class of girl. Convicted girls over the age of 12 were usually sent to reformatories under section 15 of the Reformatory and Industrial Schools Act, and vagrants, who were seen as neglected and uncontrollable children, were charged under sections 14 and 16. The Act of 1880 declared that magistrates could send any child under 14 found in a brothel or residing with reputed prostitutes (including their own mothers) to industrial schools.[58] In practice, industrial school managers hesitated to take brothel cases when girls were involved. It was feared that they would be "corrupting others in the school".[59] School board members of the 1930s saw the dilemma in the following way. One inspector stated that he did not like putting a doubtful girl of 16 or 17 in the same school as a quite decent girl of 12 or 13, particularly when we remember what influence older scholars can exert on younger scholars in residential schools. The same argument applies to boys, though I think to a lesser degree . . . I think that sexually depraved girls should be kept apart from others.[60]

A representative of the Scottish Board of Education put it in these terms: "The circumstances in the case of the depraved girls, possibly with a strong sex instinct are different and I am in complete agreement with the opinion that it would be undesirable to have 8 or 12 of that type closely associated together in small [mixed] homes."[61]

Under the Reformatory and Industrial Schools Acts there were two grounds whereby residential school managers could refuse admission to a child sent by the court: "infectious diseases" and "moral considerations".[62] The latter was rarely applied to boys, but girls who were suspected prostitutes, found living in brothels, victims of sexual assault and incest, or suffering from venereal disease were frequently rejected.[63] These girls were referred to as penitentiary cases. Throughout the late nineteenth and early twentieth centuries such girls were transferred to magdalene homes in Edinburgh and Glasgow; after 1930 they were sent almost exclusively to Lochburn Home (formally called the Glasgow Magdalene Institution),[64] a practice that continued until Lochburn Institution was closed following a riot by a number of inmates in 1958.[65]

In spite of frequent invitations, Lochburn Home never became certified under any industrial or reformatory schools act.[66] The managers believed that they would be more effective if they remained outside of the statutory system, but this did not stop them from admitting teenage girls who were under magistrate warrant. They accomplished this under sections of the Reformatory and Industrial Schools Act which stated that children under 14 found in immoral surroundings could be licensed to the guardianship of private individuals. This permitted the Juvenile Delinquency Board to license girls into the personal custody of the various matrons employed at Lochburn. After the passing of the Probation of Offenders Act in 1907, girls on probation might also be placed in Lochburn if the court considered their homes unsatisfactory. In these cases the warrant of probation stated "with place of residence" and Lochburn was specified as the residence where the girl had to live.[67] Lochburn was an integral part of the child-saving movement and the managers had the same legal control over their inmates as did those of certified reformatories and industrial schools.

Industrial Day Schools (1878) Glasgow Delinquency Act

As the child-saving system developed and expanded, more classes of children were swept into its net. The clearest example of this process is the appearance (or reappearance) of the certified industrial day school after the passing of the Education Act in Scotland in 1872. This was an important piece of legislation in that it created another new category of deviant: the truant. Board of Education and police office statistics demonstrated that a great deal of "delinquency" was committed during the daytime by children who were truant from school. In the late 1870s the newly created school boards turned their attention towards controlling truancy, which they considered to be the fault of careless and neglectful parents. Ironically, as Mary Carpenter was quick to point out, "the same experiment was tried a quarter of a century ago by Sheriff Watson in Aberdeen, and Dr Guthrie in Edinburgh, and with entire success".[68]

The Education Act (Scotland) 1872 made school attendance compulsory for children between the ages of 5 and 13 (in 1883 the leaving age was raised to 14). It was felt that this legislation could be amended to save young children from parental neglect, and the first Industrial Day Schools Act was passed in Glasgow in 1878. The wording of the Act required that any child found wandering the street or neglected by parents should be brought to the attention of the Glasgow Board of Education and the circumstances of the case taken before a magistrate. The philosophy of the day school was that it should be a place of protection "where children would be looked after" and not a "form of punishment".[69] The process of committal, however, required a court appearance by the child. As one industrial day school girl in the 1920s recalled, "you went to a court . . . you sat some place with the janitor . . . and they [put] you in the school. When you were leaving that school you had to go back again to the same place, to the court again."[70] The schools were intended for truancy cases, but they were also used by single parents who had to work and therefore could not guarantee their children's regular attendance at school.[71] Attendance was compulsory and the students were confined to the school from 6 am to 6 pm. Many children were sent to these schools who in former days would have been sent to residential schools. Conversely, children could be sent to residential schools for misbehaving in day schools. After the Day Industrial Schools (Scotland) Act, 56 & 57 Vict. C. 12 was passed in 1893, each school board in Scotland obtained the power to bypass the day school and send truancy cases directly to industrial schools, where the court considered it to be in the best interests of the child.[72] One of the contradictions of the system was that the 1893 Act set the punishment for truancy at three months' detention in an industrial school, whereas the effect of an action brought under sections 14 or 16 of the Act was four to five years in the industrial school. One of the abuses of the system was the tendency to charge troublesome truancy cases under sections 14 and 16 to ensure a much longer period of incarceration than truancy brought. A former inmate of Guthrie's Girls' School in the early 1950s recalled the circumstances of her truancy case:

> I began to take more days off school mostly when I was sick and somehow my medical certificates I got from my doctor never reached the education authorities and a senior school inspector called Mr Micourt came up to see my father about it. You knew when Mr Micourt came up to see about school reports it was trouble and so I appeared at the juvenile sheriff court and although my father paid five pounds for a solicitor called Mr Walsh it didn't do me any good. The sheriff or judge said to me I was to be sent to an approved school for three years. Approved schools were what you would call List D homes today . . . Little did I know then I would be away from my family until I was seventeen.[73]

Edinburgh was the first Scottish city to request the power to set up industrial day schools financed by the rates. This power was granted to the English school boards by the 1876 Elementary Education Act but it was not extended to Scotland until the Day Industrial Schools (Scotland) Act of 1893. In Glasgow, by contrast, amendments were made to the Glasgow Juvenile Delinquency Act. The following industrial day schools opened in Glasgow after 1878: Green Street (1879), Rotten Row (1882) and Rose Street (1889) and four other schools by 1911. The Edinburgh Board opened St John's Hill Day Industrial School in 1898. Other Scottish towns did not take up the idea as quickly, however; presumably, as Ralston suggests, this was because their small populations enabled the poor children to be more easily absorbed into ordinary board schools.[74]

The protective era, 1885–1932

Once the system was in place the uses for the schools expanded and many significant pieces of legislation concerning child welfare were passed between 1885 and 1932. These covered the employment of children, the probation of young offenders and the creation of the children's court. Essentially, late-nineteenth- and early-twentieth-century legislation demonstrated the goal of protecting all children from "adult work, legal processes, and adult cruelty and from some of the worst effects of adult poverty".[75]

Employment of Children Act 1903

By the late nineteenth century the first experience of work for thousands of Scottish children was an after-school or Saturday job "that could be either gruelling or fun".[76] The Education Act of 1872 made school compulsory, though numerous exemptions and provisions were made for "half-time" work. After 1883 children between 12 and 14 years of age were allowed to work as half-timers if they had reached standard III in reading, writing and arithmetic, and were permitted to leave school altogether if they reached standard V. In 1903 the Employment of Children Act was passed to regulate street trading by boys and girls and to improve the working conditions of those employed by shopkeepers and tradesmen. This enabled local authorities to pass by-laws, under school board administration, for the regulation of employment by persons between 14 and 16 years of age.[77] Section 2 applied to street trading. Activities such as hawking newspapers, matches or flowers, shoe-blacking and similar occupations, and busking (performing for profit), which it was feared led to juvenile delinquency, were regulated.

Scottish magistrates framed by-laws absolutely prohibiting girls under 16 and boys under 12 from street trading. Boys between 12 and 16 were permitted to trade in the streets only if issued with a licence that stated the hours during which trading could take place. A contravention of the by-laws meant an appearance in the sheriff court and a 20 shilling fine; a subsequent offence might mean an industrial school. But, as the Chief Criminal Officer for Glasgow pointed out, case loads were so heavy that would-be traders knew the chances of being prosecuted were slim. A survey taken by the Scottish Society for the Prevention of Cruelty to Children in 1909 uncovered 232 unlicensed boys trading.[78] Although girls were barred from obtaining a licence, large numbers were frequently found selling flowers and matches in the streets. According to the Chief Criminal Officer, "as an illustration of the evil of such a life for girls . . . great numbers, frequently before they reach the age of 14 years, are found to be suffering from venereal disease".[79] He revealed that under the Prevention of Cruelty to Children Act and section 58 of the Children Act the police and officers of the Society for the Prevention of Cruelty to Children had succeeded in committing many of these girls to industrial schools.

Children Act 1908

The late nineteenth and early twentieth centuries also saw the emergence of new philanthropic organizations and Scottish branches of the National Society for the Prevention of Cruelty to Children and the National Vigilance Association. The Society focused on children and the Association dealt with teenagers and women. Throughout Britain campaigns for the protection of young girls began several years before the Criminal Law Amendment Act 1885 raised the age of consent to 16 and set harsher penalties for brothel-keeping and pimping. They were offshoots of the social purity lobbies against the state regulation of prostitution under Contagious Diseases Acts in parts of England and Ireland in the 1860s and 1870s.[80] With the abolition of the Contagious Diseases Acts in the 1880s, attention turned to child prostitution and the traffic in young girls. In 1889 the National Vigilance Association founded the International Bureau for the Suppression of the Traffic in Persons (1885), which, according to Gorham, made "the issue of child prostitution and the traffic in young girls . . . an institutionalized social problem".[81] The initiatives of local branches of the National Vigilance Association and the

Society resulted in the passing of a succession of statutes culminating in the Punishment of Incest Act of 1908 and Herbert Samuel's Children Act 1908.[82]
Legislation such at the Children Act of 1908 (which came into operation in Scotland on 1 April 1909) was designed for the protection of all children. Thus, those who offended and those offended against were all entitled to certain forms of protection. This was achieved by the move beyond reformatory treatment. It involved the assertion of new powers of state intervention in parent/child relationships. The Act consolidated the law for the protection of children from cruelty, danger, exploitation and neglect, and standardized methods for dealing with juvenile offenders by consolidating into one act of Parliament the provisions of nearly 40 separate acts. According to one contemporary, "the aim of this Act is prevention – to save children from falling into habits of criminality and immorality, and to ensure their being adequately provided for and *protected* from criminal and neglectful parents and guardians".[83] It included legislation to combat baby-farming, cruelty to children and juvenile smoking, and further regulated reformatory and industrial school administration. Section 108 required the establishment of a juvenile court so girls and boys could no longer be tried in an adult court. Unfortunately, most cities and towns handled this by scheduling children's hearings in the regular courtroom before or after hearing the other cases.[84] This Act is of particular significance because it was the violation of many of its sections by both parents and children that landed the children in residential and day schools.

Probation of Offenders Act 1907

Amendments to the 1866 Industrial Schools Act under Lord Leigh's Act of 1893 abolished the preliminary prison sentence for convicted children sent to reform schools and raised the age of detention to 19. The links with the adult prison system were finally severed. In 1907 the Probation of Offenders Act was passed, marking the introduction of the final institution for the protection of children. According to Mary Hill, JP, the first female probation officer in Scotland, the probation system "introduced a new era in penal treatment, because it recognizes man as an intelligence to be reformed by methods directed to the inner self, rather than a machine to be tinkered at externally".[85] Probation was generally offered to a first offender who "has a good record for school attendance, a good home and respectable parents". As one court official revealed, "If the offender has been previously in trouble he is sometimes whipped, sometimes sent to an industrial school, or reformatory, depending on the nature of the crime."[86] The placing of juvenile offenders on probation entailed that the child be placed under a "bond of caution" and the supervision of a person named in the order for a period of three years. Children who violated the probation order could be placed in residential schools under section 15 (convicted of a felony) of the Industrial Schools Act. [87]

Probation is obviously not an institution in the physical sense, but it does constitute a far-reaching institutionalized system of custody and surveillance, which people at the time regarded as more extensive than residential school custody because its effectiveness required that the probation officer observe the activities of the entire family. According to a former headmaster, "It is not too much to say that the family is equally on probation . . . the parents might also be put on probation thus ensuring that treatment was being extended to the whole situation."[88] Probation gave the court and authorities a chance to find out about the home. As one female probation officer reported, "I find that in some cases children who come from bad homes do not keep their probation, they usually get into trouble then I think an industrial school would be a good thing."[89] The role of the probation officer was "to visit, advise and befriend",[90] which required her to cultivate a personal relationship with the entire family. Ideally the probation officer would have other social responsibilities, perhaps as a Sunday school teacher, or "someone in connection with the Boy Scouts, Boys' Brigade, Girl Guides, or some other club, so that the officer may have his ward as much as possible under his care, and give him the best possible attention".[91] When offenders were allowed to remain in the home, the family also became involved, which clearly increased the responsibility of the probation officer. According to one probation officer in 1925, "It often happens that a child is put on probation and the probation officer has to shoulder the whole family."[92] Thus, under the probation system, surveillance clearly did not stop with the offender. "There is frequently a reacting benefit to the other members of the household and a higher sense of responsibility introduced into the home. It is frequently found that there is a laxity of parental control in the home and the visits of the probation officer tend to strengthen the control."[93] Probation was also preferable to fines for young women charged with soliciting or prostitution-related offences. According to one probation officer, "Fines are always paid by undesirable people . . . . In the case of the street girl (under 20), the fines are always paid by their companions who are also on the street."[94]

By 1910 probation became a major scheme for diverting young offenders from the prison and residential school systems. Criminal returns for Glasgow for 1910 reveal that of the 634 boys who appeared in court, 134 were put on probation, 31 were sent to industrial schools and 54 were sent to reformatories.[95] In 1925 a female probation officer revealed that the majority of young women on probation between 14 and 20 were on probation for prostitution.[96]

Children and Young Persons (Scotland) Act 1932

In the 1930s another consolidated act – the Children and Young Persons Act – was passed. This legislation was directed towards individuals under the age of 18. It dealt with all aspects of child care, including the prevention of moral and physical danger and cruelty to children, the employment of minors and the children's court.[97] Juvenile courts first established under the Children Act 1908 were improved, and the distinction between reformatory and industrial schools was abolished; these were grouped under the title "approved schools". The term signified an establishment set apart for the residential training and education of children who were either juvenile offenders or non-offenders regarded as pre-delinquent, neglected or beyond parental control. It was hoped that the new name would signify the beginning of a new era, where these institutions would be perceived by the public as schools and not penal institutions, and would reduce the stigmatization formerly suffered by inmates. Technically, the designation "approved school" simply indicated that the school in question had been approved by the Secretary of State for the purpose of receiving and training children sent by the court under the Children and Young Persons (Scotland) Act 1932.[98] The most significant effect of the legislation was that the administration of the school was transferred from the Home Office to the Scottish

Education Department, thus the formal association between the reformatory and industrial schools and the prison system was terminated.

Conclusion

The modes of intervention designed to save convicted children from the adult criminal justice system resulted in the expansion of the entire control system, which began to include more children as it affected a greater age range and more types of offences. With every major new piece of legislation new offences were identified and a new class of offender was created. The early-nineteenth-century campaign for the juvenile offender to be treated in a separate system from adults resulted in the development of certified reformatories, industrial schools, industrial training ships for boys, special voluntary rescue homes for girls and certified industrial day schools for truants, and the system of probation. The Reformatory and Industrial Schools Act enabled the court to send convicted children to reformatories, and vagrant and neglected children, and those beyond parental control, to industrial schools or training ships. The Industrial Day Schools Act enabled the court to send truancy cases to certified day industrial schools by the late 1870s. These measures "provided an alternative to the imprisonment of children . . . rather than ending it . . . [T]hey marked official recognition that children had different needs, and the state an interest in their condition."[99] Young offenders would never again be punished as little adults. The newly emerging juvenile court system was not primarily concerned with punishment, but with welfare and training. The gravity of the crime was a secondary consideration, the emphasis being on rehabilitation.

A theory of the juvenile criminal career was produced, whereby the child would move from stage to stage unless stopped.[100] It is at this point, however, that we see the emergence of the diverse treatment of boys and of girls by reformatory and industrial school authorities. This suggests another dimension to the hypothesized moral or criminal career for girls, the connection between crime and sexual promiscuity, which was absent for boys. A double standard in the treatment of juvenile offenders produced a new category of female delinquent: the magdalene, who was set apart and sent to the magdalene asylum for her sexual behaviour rather than her crime. Each new institution supplemented rather than replaced existing institutions and each evolved experts who established monopolistic claims over a select population of clients. In fact, in 1896 in their report to the Secretary of State for the Home Department, the Committee on Reformatory and Industrial Schools revealed that these reformatories and industrial schools were actually competing with each other for inmates.[101]

Chapter 4

☙

The child-savers:
the terrain of contestation

The child-saving movement was part of a larger programme, if an apparently piecemeal one, to remake delinquent youth into ideal citizens. An adequate understanding of this process, however, means examining how the inmates, staff and volunteers each participated in the process. Scottish child-savers were not united by a single organization or movement, but represented many branches of local government and voluntary initiatives to aid the poor. The interest groups involved in child-rescue can be divided into four general categories: the parish or parochial board, the school boards, charity homes set up by voluntary agencies, such as the Scottish National Society for the Prevention of Cruelty to Children and the National Vigilance Association, and the certified reformatories and industrial schools themselves. Even where they shared a common ideology, such as the explanation of the cause of juvenile delinquency being an unsatisfactory family, or a vision of the ideal institution, at no time between 1850 and 1932 did they ever make up a unified body of authorities. Nor did they make up a single coherent system, although that was the impression they wanted to give the public.

The social has been defined as a space midway between the private world of home and family and the public sphere of work and commerce. It emerges where social integration appears the least secure. Its power lies within the administration, ideology and discipline of its mode of intervention. The two critical points to remember about the social are, first, that its emergence is closely linked to the rise of a professional class of expert who administers it, and secondly, it is the site where rival interpretations and discourses about people's needs are produced and played out. Jacques Donzelot indicates that new professional experts were not attached to a single institution but scattered throughout the existing apparatuses of the judiciary, social welfare and the education systems. The mode of intervention followed the contours of the less-favoured classes. "Within these . . . [they focused] on the pathology of children in its dual form: children in danger – those whose upbringing and education leaves something to be desired, and dangerous children, or delinquent minors."[1] The first part of this chapter will examine the late-nineteenth- and early-twentieth-century debates about the appropriate methods for targeting and treating the child "in danger" and the "dangerous" child. The remainder will examine the patriarchal aspects of these social institutions more specifically by examining the contradictory position of women in the child-saving movement. Just as there was debate within and between schools about the best treatment of inmates, at the administrative level the interests of the various groups involved in child-saving also came into conflict. Intraprofessional rivalries, divisions between branches of government, and suspicion between voluntary workers and state authorities all played a part in determining the nature of the services offered.[2] What was at stake was control over the grey boundary: the social. Who had the right to intervene in private life? Was it to be state bodies, like the parish or the school board, or voluntary bodies like the Society for the Prevention of Cruelty to Children, or philanthropic citizens disillusioned by the existing situation?

The unstable alliance: evil aspects

In their earliest phases industrial schools and parochial boards worked in close co-operation, but this was not to last. The ragged and industrial schools of the 1840s conformed to the traditions of the Scottish Poor Law and the premiss that charity would corrupt the poor. Therefore, early industrial schools cautiously defined the types of children who would receive "free schooling and meals".[3] These were children who had no claim to poor relief. Traditionally the Scottish authorities had been reluctant to institutionalize children in workhouses; orphans and foundlings[4] were "boarded-out" with rural parish families, where it was hoped that the children would blend in and be adopted by the community, thereby escaping the corrupting influence of the overcrowded cities.[5] Unlike England, Scotland had no union schools attached to the workhouses and this gave Scottish parochial boards "very extensive discretionary powers . . . in the administration of the relief to the poor".[6] After the passing of the first industrial school acts in the 1850s, parochial autonomy was threatened as control over a major area of child welfare was passed to the industrial schools; though children continued to be boarded-out, more and more were placed in industrial schools and paid for from the revenue of the Poor Law assessment.

The parochial board expressed its resentment in an attack on residential care, arguing that children placed in institutions would be deprived of the intimate parental care that was bestowed on children who were placed in foster homes.[7] Boarded-out children had all the freedoms of home life and could attend an ordinary parish school. They might even be apprenticed to local merchants so that at the age of 14 the foster-children would be indistinguishable from other children of their class and region. In residential schools, where children were herded together for years on end, they grew ill-accustomed to life on the outside. "They are very much like a ship without a rudder, they do not know which direction to take and where to go, and they are very frequently wrecked."[8]

The reformatory and industrial schools responded to this attack by arguing that the country life promised by the parish was not superior to life in the city for the class of child involved. The superintendent of Dundee Industrial School argued that country life was "not the refined nice thing that you are apt to think of in towns".[9] Children boarded-out in the country had few opportunities to experience the varied vocations provided in a large town.[10] Furthermore, the class of people who accepted parish children were "coarse" and "mercenary". In Scotland it was difficult to "get the best of our country people to take such children into their homes". The person who would take street beggars or pickpockets and lodge them among their own children was not the "sort of person who really exercise a good influence over it".[11] An industrial school matron in the 1920s maintained that girls were

> very much better protected and better cared for in an institution . . . I know what I see visiting in those outlandish places where they have parish children, and I would not have any of my girls under the same circumstances . . . They are most

uncared for, their clothing is very scant and poor. They just look as if they are growing up wild.[12]
Residential school officials asserted that their trained and educated staff were in a better position to deal with children than an "inferior class of working people".[13] Foster-parents could not provide the education and industrial training or discipline necessary to remove the "bad habits that led the child to the courts in the first place".[14] The industrial school could also take a more active interest in the children after they had left institutional care. The only case where foster care was recommended was where very young children were found in brothels or with prostitutes, and this was as much for the school's protection as the child's.[15]

The promise of the industrial day school, which re-emerged in the 1870s, was that it would keep the family together so the parents would be subtly influenced through their children's education. For certified industrial day school supporters, "the oldest training school was still the best". No institution could replace the home. As the Reverend Thomas Guthrie, the founder of the Original Ragged School, explained, residential provision "assum[es] the rights, and undertakes burdens and responsibilities which do not . . . naturally belong to a school". Separating the parent and child relieved the parents of their duty and their burden. "It loosens all family ties, prevents the growth of domestic affections and makes the object of its care a mere cosmopolite without love of home or country."[16] Certified industrial day school supporters upheld the right, however, to place recalcitrant children into residential care if the day school teachers concluded that "a child was doing no good, and the home influence at night was bad". In such cases "we would try to get such a child committed into Maryhill or Mossbank [Industrial] Schools".[17] Thus, for many children the day industrial school stood half-way between the family and residential care.

The Society for the Prevention of Cruelty to Children was a charity that had been formed in England and became active in child-rescue work in Scotland in the 1880s. The Scottish National Society for the Prevention of Cruelty to Children was also critical of the practices of the residential schools. It was the Society's policy never to take children from their parents. Their mandate was to warn, admonish, and punish parents, but never to break up families.[18] Their special agents watched over the community, to listen and to learn of acts of "cruelty". When an agent came across children begging, sleeping rough or misbehaving in other ways the first step was to take the child to the Temporary Children's Shelter. The second step was to inform the parents and to investigate the home environment. After two warnings the Society took legal action against the parents under the most relevant section of the Reformatory and Industrial Schools Act or the Children Act. Representatives of the Society saw themselves as the only child-welfare agency that actually endeavoured to aid families. Their agenda was much larger than simply getting children admitted to industrial schools. "The reason we scour the streets is not so much for getting children sent to industrial schools as to get into their homes to find out other cruelties."[19] They complained that industrial school agents and truancy officers were too quick to pick up children and toss them into the schools.[20] Removing children from the home did not necessarily punish the parents, certainly not the way court appearances and fines did.

The only instance where the Society for the Prevention of Cruelty to Children supported immediate residential or foster care was where girls were found in brothels. Unlike Flora Stevenson of the Edinburgh School Board, who argued that all children should be removed from "immoral surroundings", the Society agents maintained "that boys can look after themselves", but not girls. "I have seen some [girls] . . . at nine as developed in vice as plenty would be at twenty."[21] Boys need not be removed even if the home was a brothel.[22] In addition to their complaints about industrial schools the Society also criticized the certified industrial day schools because they left children unprotected out of school hours and no provision was made for young people over 14 years of age. A female inspector for the Society expressed her "personal opinion . . . that there are a considerable number of children who would be better in a residential school than in a day industrial school" because "the day industrial school only provides for them during the day".[23]

> In the case of widowers who are not able, either from circumstances or character, to look properly after their children, sending the children to a day industrial school does not really deal with the whole situation . . . [A]t night, and during the school holidays those children are exposed to many dangers – more especially the girls . . . Sometimes we arrange for such children to be sent to the ordinary industrial school.[24]

Between 1885 and 1896, 1,653 children were sent by the Society for the Prevention of Cruelty to Children to industrial schools.[25] Critics of the Society complained that, contrary to its protestations, it was a major cog in the system.[26] A Justice of the Peace in Glasgow estimated that the Society averaged "three cases a week".[27] A Home Office agent reckoned that about 50 per cent of the cases were sent by the Society: "I am objecting to them almost, if not daily, weekly."[28] The Society was observed to work willingly with truancy officers. In fact, many of its members were school board and local council members, which indicated a conflict of interest.[29] The paid Society agents, or "the cruelty men", as they were called by the local people, who "patrol the streets by night, [to] take up waifs and children of that description",[30] were accredited with getting them committed to industrial schools. The Home Office agent quoted above declared that if the Society truly wanted to help, it should send children to its own shelters and not make them expensive wards of the state. In serious cases, where a parent was prosecuted for child neglect and imprisoned for 30 days, the child would be detained in the industrial school until the age of 16 and no opportunity would be granted to the parent to demonstrate whether imprisonment had worked a reformation or not.[31] This caused "monstrous hardship on the children to be shut up for a long term of years [and] for the parent, who perhaps had been reformed".[32] An opposing view, however, was that the Society waited "too long before prosecuting [and] . . . the children suffer as a result".[33] A probation officer described the Society's methods as a "cruel game of cat and mouse".[34] The continual surveillance, inspections and threats to prosecute go "on for months or years and it is always hanging over their heads . . . I often hear fathers [in court] saying, 'I am glad it's over.'"[35]

After the Probation of Offenders Act came into effect in 1907, in many respects probation replaced the certified industrial day school as the first step in the network of child-saving institutions. Probation officers argued that all a young delinquent needed was a good probation officer. Incidentally, the members of the family of the young person on probation also had to comply with the probation officer's wishes. Supporters of probation, like police court sister Mary Hill, stressed that "education in its deepest, highest sense, education of the heart and character, can never be communicated by any system. This is always a question of personal influence."[36] She claimed that "[a] good probation officer . . . is the best sort of person to look after the child who has gone wrong, not the parents who might 'make light' of the offense".[37] The exception, again, was for girls found in brothels and young women on probation for soliciting and prostitution-related charges. In these cases, it was preferable to encourage the girls to enter rescue homes or magdalene asylums during their probationary period, to "allow them to learn something and improve their character".[38] It was acknowledged that when the probation system broke down, which was often the case, blame lay on the "continued failure of parents". In these cases a residential school was the best place "to send on probation children from vicious homes".[39]

Lady child-savers and the street children

The advent of the social as a sphere between public (economic and political) and private (family) life required a new breed of experts to administer it. But examining the ambivalent position of women experts within the network of agencies and institutions is a relatively new area of historical scholarship. In Scotland the women in the child-saving movement were privileged in terms of class, relative to those whose lives they administered, but positioned as the subordinate gender in the institutions they were expected to run. The main paradox of the system was that while work in child-saving institutions emancipated certain middle-class women from domestic routine, they were leaving their own homes to preach the gospel of domesticity to working-class mothers and daughters. Their regime was based on familial ideology that insisted on a domestic role for working-class women. Although the child-savers recognized that an exclusively domestic role was unnatural for themselves, they did not see it as unnatural for working-class women. They acknowledged, however, that it required skills that had to be learned. This entailed isolating reformatory school girls from their own neighbours and kin by placing them in exclusive contact with women of a higher class who would train them in nurturing skills and housewifery. This ambiguous positioning produced a women's discourse that was marked by a certain sympathy for the lives of their clients, even though they never fully subverted the class-power relations on which the movement was predicated. The purpose of this section is to examine the patriarchal aspects of the social more specifically by examining the contradictory position of the middle-class women in the child-saving movement.

A great deal is known about the heroes and the occasional heroines of the child-saving movement, particularly Thomas Guthrie, Sheriff Watson and Mary Carpenter. Much less is known about the hundreds of middle-class women fund-raisers, school visitors, social workers and teachers who were the driving force behind the day-to-day administration of these schools. Since the early nineteenth century upper-class Scottish women had been active charity volunteers in a range of "philanthropic" institutions, including hospitals and prisons, and homes for destitute children, juvenile offenders, and prostitutes. In 1800 the wives and daughters of merchants, professionals and prominent clergy united around the plight of the "fallen females" of Edinburgh by forming the Ladies' Committee of the Magdalene Asylum, one of the first of its kind in the United Kingdom. When the directors of a similar institution in Glasgow announced their need for volunteers in 1860, 100 women immediately offered their services as home visitors, tutors, and fund-raisers.[40] It was assumed that middle-class ladies would grace the homes of the underprivileged the way they graced their own homes.[41]

The language of class and gender was an integral part of the mid-nineteenth-century child-saving movement. It was the natural calling for upper-class "ladies of culture".[42] A maternal discourse was written into the new ideologies of penology and the institutions for decarceration like those intended to divert young offenders from the adult prison system. Women were seen as the "natural caretakers" of renegade boys as well as wayward girls. For many of the wives, widows and independent women, child-saving was a sacred duty, a moral mission, supported by the contemporary belief in women's moral superiority.[43] Drawing inspiration from women like Elizabeth Fry and Florence Nightingale, women who "caused revolutions, not by the vote, but by their humble untiring, faithful following of our Master's example", Lady Griselda Cheape of Edinburgh, wrote: "Be we married or not, we women can influence the little children . . . if every woman in this country would take one family and look after them and bring them and themselves to Christ's feet, we should have a better and happier world."[44]

Praising the superintendents' wives, one commentator remarked, "They sweeten the atmosphere . . . they soften the discipline; and, without their husbands realizing it . . . everything important and everything good really emanates from their clever and tactful brains."[45] It was a deliberate point of school board policy that the industrial day schools should be totally under the management of women, as a school board member, William Mitchell, pointed out: "The effect of female influence upon boys is marvellous . . . The most rebellious, stubborn natures are subdued, and truants become quite reformed."[46] In 1897 the Royal Commission on Industrial Schools and Reformatories concluded that "women have special qualifications for the supervision of such institutions . . . There is the further advantage to girls, who have been under the care of refined and educated women, in having a friend of their own sex on whom they may depend in after life for sympathy and guidance."[47]

This is just one point of view, however. In contrast to this rather stereotypical view of the Victorian "Lady Bountiful", not all of these women were volunteers and their activities were certainly not limited to Bible-reading and fund-raising. By the late nineteenth century a great many earned their livelihood as superintendents, teachers, probation officers and social workers in these institutions, which provided an outlet for the growing middle-class female labour force. Through rescue work and child-saving institutions, Scottish women mobilized around a wide range of social issues such as child labour laws, Poor Law reform, compulsory education, and sanitation and housing reform. They also acquired first-hand knowledge of the struggles of working-class women and girls and some sensitivity to the danger that poverty and life on the streets posed for unprotected women. Linda Gordon's study of Boston feminist reformers demonstrates how early feminists spearheaded public recognition of the need for charitable and professional intervention into family life. They campaigned fervently to get the problem of domestic violence, incest and rape on to the public agenda. These feminists recognized that these "family oppressions" were problems shared by women across class lines.[48]

Early-nineteenth-century philanthropists like Elizabeth Fry were the inspiration for the Scottish branches of Fry's British Ladies' Society for Promoting the Reformation of Female Prisoners, established in Edinburgh, Glasgow, Aberdeen, Greenock and Perth, and rescue shelters for women and girls. Many, like Dean Bank Rescue Home (1832), Perth Ladies' House of Refuge for Destitute Girls (1843), Dundee and District Female Rescue Home (1876) and Greenock House of Refuge (1853), became members of Mary Carpenter's Reformatory and Refuge Union and some were certified as industrial schools and reformatories in the 1850s. In 1911 branches of the National Vigilance Association were formed in the east and west of Scotland.[49] These organizations were responsible for a great deal of late-nineteenth- and early-twentieth-century social work in Scotland.

Work within the child-saving agencies provided many of these women with a way out of their traditional domestic responsibilities and a way into the political sphere. Scottish women strongly supported Josephine Butler in her battle against the licensing of prostitutes in England and Ireland under the Contagious Diseases Acts, and Scottish branches of the Ladies' Association for the Repeal of the Contagious Diseases Acts were formed in the 1870s.[50] At a repeal conference in Glasgow in 1874, Mrs Duncan McLaren of Edinburgh, who had marched with Elizabeth Fry through the dungeons of Newgate, spoke of the "imperative duty of women to become informed of the state of society in order that they might stand on the defensive against the inroads of immorality".[51] In 1878 the Ladies' Committee of the Edinburgh Magdalene Asylum attended a public forum "to see what could be done for the protection of newspaper girls and older girls who are exposed to great moral danger".[52] In 1898 the Ladies' Committee also signed a bill in favour of "Habitual Inebriates being dealt with by the Home Secretary".[53] Many women, such as Louisa and Flora Stevenson, became popular platform speakers at national meetings of the Social Science Association; others testified in the Royal Commissions on reformatories and industrial schools, and they influenced the shape of child-welfare policy in Scotland.

Leonore Davidoff and Catherine Hall argue that all social institutions are gendered.[54] Although Scottish women child-savers were instrumental in establishing and administering many institutions, there was certainly no equity in administration practices. Like institutions today, the reformatory and industrial school stood as a microcosm for the roles of women in the society at large. Hence, the lady child-savers had to fight for recognition of themselves as "professional" child-care workers, while male school officials appreciated them only for their maternal qualities. For example, the Glasgow Juvenile Delinquency Board in 1897 stressed the importance of schools employing a female superintendent in order to "mother" the children. "A mother, certainly, looks after the children better than a father . . . a woman is much more capable of entering into a child's feelings than a man."[55] Board members admitted that the question of women sitting on the Board had "never entered into our head", things having "worked so well hitherto".[56] Although there were no constitutional rules to actually prohibit women from sitting on the Board, they confessed that they did not think it "advisable" or "necessary".[57]

The general barriers of institutional sexism meant that women were marginalized or simply ignored by their male counterparts. Yet unmarried women also found that their private lives were the subject of scrutiny. Fear of potential sexual immorality was expressed by one training ship captain who admitted that he "strongly objected"[58] to having a matron on board his ship because "such a woman", if not "an officer's wife", would "have to live with the officers, or she would have a place by herself; she would do any amount of mischief".[59] The only women he allowed on board were his own wife and sister.[60] In contrast to the dangerous sexuality of the single woman was the concern that if a woman had no sexual involvement, or no heterosexual relations, this might also inhibit her ability to perform her job. As comments by a former headmaster reveal:

Most of the women in the girls' schools were frustrated spinsters, to start with . . . Oh there were some corkers! . . . There really were some of the most corkingly frustrated women themselves and they were determined that if they couldn't have anything these girls wouldn't either . . . they really were the most dramatic people.[61]

Evidence suggests that many women fought to improve their position in reformatory and industrial schools, at both the administrative and institutional levels. As early as 1843, feminist opposition to the notion of a women's sphere could be heard. Marion Reid of Edinburgh wrote: "Let us hear no more of female influence, as if it were an equivalent to the rights which man possesses."[62] But, unlike the men, the women did not form a unified body in their own right, even where they came into conflict with male governors, directors and superintendents. There may have been points of tension between the "volunteers" of certain ladies' committees and female staff. For example, Lady Cheape's belief that women could cause revolutions by love rather than by the vote would certainly not have been shared by the two Scottish feminists who used the occasions of their testimonies at the 1896 and 1914 Parliamentary Commissions on Industrial Schools and Reformatories to get "sexual politics" on to the public agenda. In 1896 Flora Stevenson, of the Edinburgh School Board and a member of the National Society for Women's Suffrage, demanded the right of women to sit on the management boards of certified industrial schools. "I think that in the interests of the schools women should be eligible as directors or governors."[63] In 1914 Catherine Hunter-Crastor, the former matron of Chapelton Girls' Reformatory, demanded equal pay for female matrons and superintendents.[64]

In addition to protesting against the double standard, many women were also critical of certain institutional practices. Mary Burton, a member of the Edinburgh School Board and of the Parish Council, opposed the residential schools provided for vagrant children under the Reformatory and Industrial Schools Acts. She offered the following testimony at the Royal Commission on industrial schools in 1896: "These industrial schools do no good whatever to the children. That is an important thing because people are apt to say: Well, we cannot have the children neglected; but I think the children are none the better, but a good deal worse because of it."[65] In her involvement with an association for ameliorating the conditions of the poor, Mary Burton had become frustrated by the lack of power to affect any real change, so she purchased her own slum property where she "could do exactly as I liked".[66] She believed that the industrial school system "demoralized" both the parents and the children. Mary Burton maintained that industrial schools did not teach boys the appropriate manly values and work ethic. "Roughing it is good for children."[67] Her ideas, however, were not based on an analysis of political economy, but on a staunch Calvinist disdain for charity and government intervention in social problems. The Royal Commissioners thought it appropriate to remind her that "the object of schools is not to provide you, or ladies like you with servants".[68]

In 1876 Miss Kent, a female missionary to aid the fallen, was dismissed from her position by the Edinburgh Magdalene Asylum because she was caught "paying out money for the inmates at their request and carrying messages for them, thereby infringing upon one of the rules of the institution".[69] Her actions indicate that she regarded those rules as too strict and unreasonable. In 1914 Dr Anne Watson, medical inspector of Aberdeen Female School of Industry, a position she had held for ten years, lost her job because of her damaging testimony at the Royal Commission. She revealed that the girls from Aberdeen Female School of Industry whom they "sen[t] out at sixteen years of age to farm situations in the country are rather knocked about, and the result is a considerable amount of immorality . . . There is a Ladies' Committee, and I have spoken to them about it, but they all seem to shirk the difficulty."[70]

It is not easy to characterize Scottish women child-savers as feminists; certainly, only a few of them would have identified themselves as such, even where they were raising questions that are now called issues of sexual politics. The women child-savers of the 1850s struggled against the constraints of their prescribed social-class and gender roles by breaking out of the suffocating domestic sphere through appropriate charitable work, such as helping children, one of the few avenues open to "respectable" women of their class. By the end of the century many women were earning their living as superintendents, teachers, probation officers or social workers. The influence of the lady volunteer was declining, replaced by a more professional ethos requiring training in rescue and reform work. As staff and employees of child-welfare institutions, they had to fight for professional recognition, equal wages and the right of full participation at the executive level, even if larger feminist goals caused tension between themselves and their nonfeminist and working-class sisters.

Conclusion

By the early twentieth century, in spite of their opposing views and criticism of each other's methods, an unofficial alliance had formed between the members of the school boards, the residential schools and the Scottish National Society for the Prevention of Cruelty to Children. These organizations all employed agents "to gather up children".[71] The industrial school agent, the cruelty officer and private citizens all worked very closely with the truant officers; "too closely", critics remarked. "Where there is any difficulty they bring the School Board to their assistance, and between them they manage the committal."[72] The school boards did not restrict themselves to handing out three- or six-month detentions for truancy under the Industrial Day Schools Act but took advantage of relevant sections of the Reformatory and Industrial Schools Act to charge the parents of truant or "wandering" children with "want of guardianship" or "neglect".[73] Incidentally, having truants incarcerated in long-term residential care in industrial schools also got "troublesome children . . . off their hands" and relieved the truant officer of the burden of "recalcitrant families" who were an "irritant to most inspectors".[74] While contemporaries criticized the alliance and the part it played in child-saving agencies, they all agreed that it was "in the child's best interest".[75] In the words of the Secretary to the Scottish Education Department, there were probably certain "evil aspects" to the alliance, but nevertheless, "it [was] an important and healthy relationship".[76]

Despite their agreement on the causes of juvenile delinquency, what prevented the child-saving movement from co-ordinating was the belief that each institution was the true champion of the family. The parochial council argued that the ideal family could be replicated only in a humble pastoral setting. In contrast, advocates of the residential school system claimed that this was impossible given the "class" of people involved. For them the imaginary family of the institution was the only acceptable surrogate for the inmates' own anti-social families. On the other hand, the Society for the Prevention of Cruelty to Children, the industrial day schools and probation officers each believed that there was no substitute for the child's own natural parents and that the best means of dealing with a child was to work with the entire family. All were free to evoke the discipline of the reformatory when their best efforts failed. Despite their rivalry, the parts of the system made up a whole; each supplemented the efforts of the other. Children who misbehaved in day schools could be placed in residential schools; children on probation were only a couple of warnings away from being taken into custody; while many maintained that the reformatory was the last resort, it was frequently resorted to.[77]

Chapter 5

❧

Child-saving institutions

> The only thing you didn't get was education . . . We learned Britain owned the world, and all the red bits belonged to Britain .[1]

> You learnt what discipline was. You learnt that things that didn't belong to ya, were to be left there.[2]

> When you got to be twelve the girls were taught how to keep house . . . Taught to clean, taught to work, to scrub.[3]

By the late 1850s most Scottish cities had at least one industrial school or juvenile reformatory. The official goal of the child-saving institution was to educate and train children at risk before they fell into a delinquent lifestyle. While the bad family was identified as the chief cause of deviance, the cure was doses of education, training and discipline in the juvenile reformatory. What was thought to be fit education for girls and boys was closely marked by class and gender. According to one director, the reform school was "the Rugby and the Eton"[4] of lower-working-class education. In contrast to the official version, however, former inmates, as indicated in the quotes above, remember another "education". This chapter develops further the assertion that the power of the social rests upon its modes of intervention, in this case the disciplining of class and gender in the reform school. It considers, first, the recruitment practices, and, secondly, the formal curriculum of education and industrial training offered to girls and boys. There follows an examination of how the preceding modes of intervention were supported by a system of military discipline, and of the licensing or parole system offered to inmates who were ready to be released.

Recruitment: families on trial

Children were usually brought to the notice of the courts by the police, the school board, the Society for the Prevention of Cruelty to Children, concerned neighbours, "anonymous letters" or occasionally their own parents. The Reformatory and Industrial Schools Act 1866 provided only very general guidelines as to eligibility for admission to industrial schools and reformatories. By and large, the decision as to whether a child was sent to a reformatory, an industrial school, a day school, a refuge or a temporary shelter, or placed on probation, was based on the magistrate's perception of the child's immediate circumstances, which necessarily involved an assessment of the character of the child's parents. Throughout the entire court proceedings, no plea was taken, no warrant was issued, no attempt was made to verify the evidence, and the witnesses were not under oath.[5] Consequently, the court had a great deal of discretionary power and "there [wa]s a great divergence of practice in the different courts".[6]

While it was expected that a parent would be present to speak on the child's behalf, when the parents were unavailable it was not unusual for an older sibling to stand in for them.[7] The way a case was decided frequently depended on where the hearing took place. For example, because of their heavy case loads urban magistrates were forced to be more lenient than those in the villages. City children therefore were given more warnings before they were finally committed; while country sheriffs could afford to be more severe on first offenders, "to set an example for the area . . . In Glasgow kids would get a longer run for their money."[8]

The inspectors of the reformatories and industrial schools were appointed by the Secretary of State under the Home Office. It was their responsibility to gather information and provide statistics for the annual reports on every child admitted to a certified institution. These included whether the parents were legally married, the financial circumstances, and whether either parent had a criminal record. Between 1861 and 1898 approximately 60 per cent of the reformatory and industrial school girls and boys were orphans or semi-orphans (one parent dead or absent) or had been deserted by their parents.[9] Statistical data collected by the Inspector of Reformatory and Industrial Schools indicate (Table A.1) that 14 per cent of industrial school girls and boys were under warrant for begging, 9 per cent were destitute or orphaned, 16 per cent were found in brothels or in the company of thieves or with persons of "disreputable" character. By far the most common offence was wandering and sleeping out at night: 49 per cent of the children were sentenced under this statute.[10] All of these "delinquencies" were ascribed to the character of the child's parents.

An analysis of the available data reveals a distinct gender pattern in admission practices. Forty-one per cent of the reformatory boys were first offenders and 59 per cent were repeat offenders before they were taken into the reformatory. In contrast, 70 per cent of the reformatory girls were first offenders (Table A.2). Taken into consideration with the statistics for age of admission, the incarceration trends suggest that, although reformatory girls were slightly older than reformatory boys,[11] only 30 per cent of the girls had ever been charged with a criminal offense. In the case of industrial school children (Table A.3), 26 per cent of the boys and 48 per cent of the girls were under ten, indicating that industrial school girls were, on average, younger than industrial school boys. Ten per cent of the reformatory and industrial school girls and 5 per cent of the boys had parents who were described as being involved in "disreputable" activities or in prison. Girls were taken up more quickly and sent to reformatories for first offenses.[12] Eighty-seven per cent of the reformatory girls, compared with 77 per cent of the boys, were over 12 years of age (Table A.4). Approximately 30 per cent of the girls and 59 per cent of reformatory boys had been convicted of a minor criminal offense (Table A.2). The majority of industrial school girls were incarcerated for begging, wandering, as homeless or orphaned, uncontrollable at home, frequenting the company of thieves or residing with their mothers in brothels.

Under certain clauses in the Reformatory and Industrial Schools Act both boys and girls found in brothels could be sent to industrial schools, but in practice boys were taken to temporary shelters run by the Scottish Society for the Prevention of Cruelty to Children and then handed back to their parents. This was not the case for girls, who were more likely to be committed to a residential school; this might mean five years in custody and three years on licence. This practice could still be observed in the 1920s. The matron of a girls' industrial school revealed that the majority of her girls had been "found wandering, and having a parent who does not exercise proper guardianship, or is living in circumstances calculated to cause, encourage, or favour the seduction or prostitution of the child".[13] As Schlossman and Wallach point out in their North American study, "[t]his so called chivalrous attitude leads to earlier intervention and longer periods of supervision" for girls who are seen as especially "vulnerable to evil and temptations".[14] Regarding the situation in Scotland, a former residental school headmaster observed that the court was more strict with girls, "because girls were supposed to have higher standards . . . The [court] would have argued that they were going to be made into loose girls . . . and so in the sense of being more severe more quickly, they were really trying to protect them. That was their idea of protection."[15] Many of the girls and young women who were not placed in reform schools were encouraged to enter the magdalene asylums in Edinburgh and Glasgow.

Available statistics from magdalene institutions suggest one-third of the inmates were under 18 years of age. Although they had not been charged with any crime they were expected to undergo a two-year detention period. The annual reports of these magdalene homes also published information on the family background of the inmates. Eighty-two per cent of the inmates in the Glasgow Magdalene Institution were orphans, or semi-orphans.[16] The directors stressed the devastating effect for a girl of the loss of a parent, especially a mother, during her early teen years. They argued that semi-orphaned girls were more often in a "more desolate and dangerous condition" than the orphan, because orphans "were more readily cared for by charities", and therefore protected from "scenes of temptation and the grasp of the seducer". Children from broken homes were "cast on the care of relatives or hired keepers".[17] It was argued in the official reports at the time that delinquent girls were harder to reform than boys, especially if they had been prostitutes. Historian Steven Humphries suggests that this was because they had taken a more drastic step in defying convention, and found it harder to conform.[18]

These statistics support the contemporary view that residential school children were not serious offenders.[19] Even section 15

offences, such as theft, were attributed to character flaws: the per-
petrator's lack of forethought, a craving for excitement, dodging
school or a sweet tooth. "It is dense ignorance and want of training
more than criminality that is the cause of their offending . . . The
older they get the more difficult they are to teach, of course."[20]
According to one boys' reformatory superintendent, "It is not those
who are sharp in crime that we usually get; those who are sharp in
crime are sharp enough to evade the police." Reformatories were
more likely to be sent the "bungler in crime".[21] They explained that
the children, who in "nine out of ten cases . . . [were] more sinned
against than sinning",[22] should be removed from their families and
placed in residential care. In fact, they suspected that many parents
purposely neglected their children in order to get them into these
schools.[23] Even after the probation system was introduced in 1907,
the home environment continued to be an important factor in determining the sentence. According to the Chief Constable in Edinburgh
in 1925, "I have little hesitation in stating that the home environment should be the deciding factor as to the method of dealing with
the young offender."[24] The child-savers did not look upon their
schools as penal institutions: "We do not look upon it as an infringe-
ment of the liberty of the child, the liberty might be its ruin . . . we
look upon it as an institution to guide the children, and bring them
up to a better life."[25]

The residential school: the "family home"

By the end of the nineteenth century it was argued that the only
difference between reformatory children and industrial school children was that the latter were "caught younger".[26] There was no
substantial difference between industrial school and reformatory
education, training or discipline beyond that appropriate for the differences in the inmates' ages. There were basically three models of
residential industrial schools and reformatories: the training ship,
the residential school and the family cottage.

The training ship was designed to provide "a home, a refuge, a
school, and a workshop to hundreds of boys who were fast drifting
into vice and misery".[27] The certified industrial training ships in England were the *Southampton* at Hull, which accommodated 179 boys;

the *Wellesley* on the Tyne, which accommodated 200 boys; and the *Formidable* at Bristol which held 219. The industrial training ships in Scotland were the *Mars* at Dundee, which accommodated 219 boys, and the *Cumberland* on the Clyde, which was replaced by the *Empress* after some inmates set fire to the *Cumberland* in 1889. This ship had a licence for 350 boys, which made it the largest industrial training ship in Britain. The daily routine was designed to emulate sea life as closely as the boys' strength and maturity would permit. The directors were not concerned about the large numbers of boys on the ships; the goal was training for the Navy or the mercantile marine, and ships in full commission carried crews of 700. Thus, the more boys on a ship the more complete their training would be.

Residential schools ranged in size from 30 to over 200 inmates. They consisted usually of a single barracks or institution with dormitories, workshops and classrooms and a dining room, which in less affluent institutions might also serve as the school's chapel. In contrast, the other model of school was the cottage, which was less common because they were more expensive to administer. Modelled after William Quarrier's Orphan Homes at Bridge-of-Weir, the "family home" was regarded by some as the most progressive style of residential school. According to Quarrier: "Institutional life under any form is an evil, and if you can bring more of the home life to bear upon the children, then you will have the greatest results."[28] Following this philosophy, Maryhill Industrial School for Girls in Glasgow, which had 200 inmates, was constructed on the "family cottage system". There was lodging for 120 inmates in the main building and the remaining 80 were divided between eight cottages, each with its own foster mother. In each cottage, along with the foster mother lived eight senior girls of "good character" and 12 junior girls.[29] It was believed that small cottages provided a better opportunity to train girls for domestic service than large institutions, where food preparation was on an institutional scale.

In contrast to those who favoured the family cottage were the critics who regarded it as harmful. They complained that cottage inmates lost the benefit of the "responsible eye of the superintendent". The problem was with the character of the foster mother. For the regime of moral rehabilitation to work, many argued that the "children should be under persons of a very much higher class than themselves or their parents". By implication, then, "when you get down to the class of people who will accept situations of [fifteen pounds] a year", which was a house mother's salary, "they are people with no particular qualification . . . [Many] of them have no tact in dealing with children, who in consequence are exposed to the too frequent use of the tongue, and are made sulky and sullen and unfitted for after life."[30]

The daily routine varied little between institutions or from decade to decade. With the exception of the training ship, which was modelled upon the training necessary for a career at sea, life in a residential school was designed to mirror that of an efficiently run home, and to emulate the respectable family life of the households of the directors; or, more accurately, the life of a servant in one of their homes. Because all certified reformatories and industrial schools were run as joint ventures between government and charity, the facilities varied enormously from school to school. Chapelton Reformatory for Girls was "beautifully situated in Bearsden" near Glasgow. It was ideal for picnics and long country strolls.[31] Fechney Industrial School for Boys near Perth had "good premises": a playground, workshops, gymnasium and swimming pool.[32] The Duke of Argyle permitted the *Cumberland* training ship boys to use the estate grounds of Rosneath Castle for cricket, football and hiking.[33] However, other schools were less fortunate. The playground at Aberdeen Female School of Industry was a sorry sight, described as "simply a square gravel yard with two open-fronted sheds and a trunk of a dying tree in the centre".[34]

The reformatory and industrial school inmates were described as coming from the "lowest" ranks of the population and the school medical officers confirmed that their heights and weights were below national averages for the labouring classes of Britain. According to these authorities this was "due to hereditary causes, or to neglect at home during early childhood".[35] Dr Anne Watson, medical officer at Aberdeen Female School of Industry in 1914, described the inmates under her care as "thin, somewhat spare children rather deficient in the round fatness of an ordinary child".[36] This fact, however, might have had something to do with the institutional diet. In 1857 a matron at a Glasgow industrial school declared that institutions "are not places where gastronomy should rise beyond the level of a necessity". One did not want to run the "risk of unduly stimulating appetite . . . The simplest meals, like the cheapest pleasures, are the best."[37] Dr Watson described the steamed fish served at Aberdeen as the most "insipid and monotonous" dishes imaginable. It must be stressed, however, that some industrial school children were better clothed and fed than they would have been in their homes in times of crisis. One boy, who was in for neglect, was most impressed by the standard of living in his industrial school: "We had three meals a day, dead on time . . . and sheets!"[38]

The disruption of family ties

At the root of the residential school discipline lay the conviction that character could actually be shaped by education, but this required, first and foremost, a receptive child. The first step in the process of moral reform was incarceration, or to get the child away from the parents and other unsound influences. Put sociologically, separating inmates from family members and the community served the larger purpose of resocialization. The goal of restricted access to family was clear. The institution's primacy had to be accepted by the inmate. "The school had to become a microcosm of the larger society in the child's reality",[39] not his or her family or their old neighborhood.

Residential school children would have to internalize the values of the school if they were to succeed after they were released. The contemporary debate about whether inmates should mix with the general community was often raised and it illustrates the logic of incarceration, or what was known in the late nineteenth century as the "asylum theory". Those who endorsed the asylum theory supported these institutions because they protected children, and it was their belief that vulnerable children would be better off in institutions than their home.

While boys' school superintendents acknowledged the concern that weekend outings would have negative ramifications for the local community, such as increased vandalism, petty theft and loitering as dozens of industrial school boys with nothing in particular to do invaded the town centre, those who favoured it stressed the importance of allowing a boy to "keep in touch with other lads", especially "superior lads to himself".[40] By the later decades of the nineteenth century it was considered to be important for a boy's development to have outside contacts. In Dundee Industrial School, for example, the directors apprenticed boys over 14 with local tradesmen during the day. Many boys' schools also allowed inmates to attend football matches or to visit their parents on Saturdays.

The opposing view of the asylum theory was that the school's role was to protect the community from bad or potentially bad children; thus this view supported the institutions because they protected the community.[41] It was almost universally agreed that because of their vulnerability, girls should not have any contact with the community.[42] Protecting girls might prevent them from becoming prostitutes at the same time that it protected the community.

To ensure that the good work of the institution was not undone by the corrupting influence of relatives and friends, nor the inmates tempted to return to their old ways, relatives merely wishing to visit their children were required to make an appointment and visits were restricted to specified days and times. Visitors were also put under surveillance. With few exceptions, incoming and outgoing mail was censored. School directors maintained that inmates were more likely to internalize the reformatory's teachings about how they ought to behave if they were isolated from contradictory examples while in the institution. This applied particularly to inmates with family and friends whom the institution regarded as troublesome. Despite their strict controls, school officials confessed that the inmates' families continued to be a problematic force to be reckoned with. They reported that visiting days made inmates "impertinent and very defiant".[43] The parents "just come in with all the sordid tales of their homes . . . Always after visiting day we find the effect . . . They very often undo what we have been doing when they visit."[44]

Education: hewers of wood and drawers of water

Supporting the asylum theory were the two pillars of moral rehabilitation: education and industrial training. In 1868 the Reverend Mr Robertson of Kilmarnock Ragged and Industrial Certified School stated that he hoped "the day will soon dawn when education, in at least the three Rs and the Bible, will be the heritage of every British born child".[45] Historians have since suggested that residential school "principles paved the way for compulsory education".[46] The compulsory education of the "respectable" classes, however, would follow 20 years after the "compulsory" education was imposed on the needy, destitute and vulnerable children of the "unrespectable" poor by the reformatory and industrial school system.

Through the Reformatory and Industrial School Acts, the state stood *in loco parentis* to the inmates. Once a child entered an institution, therefore, the managers assumed all the legal rights and responsibilities which were normally vested in the parents. They took on "all the duties of good parents":[47] to feed, clothe, educate and rear the child. New "scientific" studies of criminology developed in the nineteenth century documented a connection between crime and literacy, and it was hoped that a general education would raise children's intellectual faculties and increase their ability to judge between right and wrong and resist temptation.[48] The act of Parliament for industrial schools and training ships stipulated that at least four hours of general academic education be provided to residential school children. The act relating to reformatories, however, did not, but the model rules recommended that the inmates in all types of school receive between four and six hours of general education.[49] With the rest of the day partitioned out to industrial work there was little time for more than the "three Rs". Children under ten received full-time schooling under section 5 of the Education Act 1878, but they were also expected to do productive work. Light occupations, such as match-box making and wood chopping, were provided for little boys, and polishing boots was offered to keep little girls "from idleness and weariness during the hours not devoted to school or to drill or play".[50] Inmates between 10 and 14 were educated on the "half-time" system, which ensured them four hours' academic instruction daily. Formal education ended when girls passed the third standard and boys passed the fifth or in special cases the sixth standard.[51] The school day was divided between early morning and late afternoon, the middle of the day being devoted to productive work.

From the outset in the 1850s reformatory and industrial schools provided inmates with a general education, ranging from basic reading and writing to geography, arithmetic and music after 1872, in compliance with the standards set by the school board. A comparison between reformatory and industrial school education and ordinary elementary school education reveals that, although children were expected to be at the same level, residential school pupils were generally older than their peers on the outside, and they were taught a smaller range of subjects. Reform school teachers had very low expectations for their students and described them as "intellectually dull", "totally ignorant" and "backward". The superintendent of the St Joseph's Industrial School reported that the boys between the ages of six and ten he received were "nearly totally ignorant".[52] An annual report for the Glasgow Boys' House of Refuge revealed that "upwards of two-thirds were in a state of deplorable ignorance"; 244 of the 294 boys "knew nothing of arithmetic".[53] This continued until after the Second World War; as a headmaster explained, the boys were "never going to be skilled operatives, but [acquire] menial skills".[54] Another elaborated: "Nearly all of them, by virtue of their intelligence levels, predispositions and local cultural patterns, are destined to be hewers of wood and drawers of water. Our aim therefore is to equip them for these callings in such a way they can draw satisfaction from their daily work."[55] To the statement "Bees make honey", a reformatory girl in Chapelton had responded: "That's not true, mum. The bumblebee makes nae honey; it is John Buchanan that makes honey in his factory." Her matron explained that "some [girls] could neither read nor write", but she added that Chapelton girls "have a fine command of language of a certain kind".[56]

Recent historical and sociological research has explored the numerous ways in which schooling is involved in the process of legitimation and the social reproduction of class relations. The public utterances of teachers concerning their reformatory and industrial school students' ability, therefore, must be interpreted cautiously. Rosemary Deem has remarked that mass education has been marked by three crucial divisions: class, ability and gender.[57] According to Nell Keddie the notion of "ability" merely provides an acceptable way for educationalists to talk about social class, whereas it is in fact a social construction. She postulates that it is "derived largely for social class judgments of pupils' social, moral and intellectual behaviour".[58] Nevertheless, negative evaluations of "ability" have been inextricably linked to working-class boys and girls, as "some teachers appear to use social class as an explanation of educational performance".[59] There also may have been certain material interests behind their assessment of the children's intellectual ability. Presenting children as "backward" enabled the teachers to mask their own failure to teach them while it also supported their demand for increased allocations to their education budgets, which would attract the more qualified teachers. Unlike Oakbank Industrial School, where all the teachers were certified,[60] the superintendent of Parkhead Reformatory testified he had a great difficulty in getting qualified teachers. "Good men will not come, or if they do, they only take the place for a stop-gap until they get something else . . . I have had to put up with anything I could get."[61] Another factor, recognized at the time, that contributed to pupils' school performance was that the classrooms were too large for proper attention. "These boys are the incorrigibles from the other schools, and require more expert disciplinarians, and better teachers to instruct them than would be required for a school outside." [62]

Despite these structural constraints, it was intended that every child should get a plain but substantial education. Children were not encouraged to continue in school, they were not expected to take qualifying exams and the majority were too old to transfer to other schools after they were released. Oakbank Industrial School taught general courses in geography, history and grammar "so far as to enable them to write a decent letter".[63] But overall it was dedicated to turning out farm labourers and boys specialized in market gardening.[64] On the *Mars* training ship, where only the head teacher was certified, boys were given special classes in geography. Singing on the *Mars* was discontinued in 1897 because the boys' voices were "at the cracking stage" making the results not "very good".[65] In contrast, Fechney Industrial School boys, who were younger, participated in a strong singing programme.[66] The superintendent of Dundee Industrial School offered his boys special classes in botany.[67]

While an academic education may have been underemphasized in boys' institutions, it was thought to be almost totally unnecessary in girls' institutions. Consequently, girls were not taken to the same level as boys or offered the same range of courses. After the age of 14 little attention was paid to girls' education.[68] According to one official, the great aim of the girls' education curriculum was to "train intelligence . . . with domestic service in view".[69] The matron at Chapelton Girls' Reformatory mocked a male inspector's suggestion that she should teach decimal fractions and geometry to her girls.

I said I would be quite pleased to teach them how to boil a potato in the time they were teaching geometry . . . [Many a] good wife had existed who did not know how to read very

well. Many a good mother has admirably brought up a family without any great literary knowledge.[70]
The lady Home Office Inspector in 1896 recommended that girls, regardless of their education, should "concentrate on domestic matters, because she was very likely to earn her living by housework".[71] A former industrial day school girl between 1901 and 1906 recalled, "They didn't encourage cleaners . . . we did most of the cleaning . . when you got to be twelve the girls were taught how to keep house . . . [We] peeled potatoes by the pail . . . if you peeled so many pails of potatoes . . . you got half a slice of bread."[72]

Industrial training: a game not worth the candle

The act of Parliament for certified industrial schools required that industrial training be provided. The act relating to reformatories, though it mentioned the training of offenders, did not specify that the training had to be industrial in nature. But the general rules required industrial training for both kinds of schools and stipulated provision in reformatories four to six hours per day and in industrial schools at least four hours per day.[73] It was generally accepted that "knowledge of a trade" was the prerequisite for an honest and industrious life. Years of experience had convinced the boys' school directors that "till you can put a young man in the way of earning an honest livelihood for himself you can do little for his reformation".[74]

According to the official rhetoric, industrial training benefited the inmates in two ways; first, it would keep them occupied and accustomed to labour and, second, the trade would provide a means of earning a living when they left the school. Conversely, industrial training also benefited the school by making it eligible for Home Office grants and of course generating a profit.

Trades were a very central part of the boy's instruction; the Glasgow Boys' House of Refuge, for example, offered a wide range to suit individual tastes, such as tailoring (school uniforms and clothing for the County Police), shoemaking (they made shoes for a number of charity schools and the Female House of Shelter as well as private customers), smithing, baking, coopering, printing, bookbinding and woodcutting. Carpentry was offered to boys who planned to enter the furniture trade. Finally, for boys who hoped to emigrate to

Canada an extensive garden was maintained (by spade labour) to introduce boys to farm labour so "when sent to the colonies they will be thoroughly fitted for agricultural employment".[75] In addition to nautical training limited industrial training was also offered on the training ships. Everything used on the *Cumberland* in the early 1870s had been made on board, including tailored clothes and other sewn items, binding for books and of course cooked food.[76] "Tailoring", which included the sewing of uniforms, towels, underwear, mess bags and nightclothes, was cut from the programme in 1873, but reintroduced in 1895 because the ship had trouble finding berths for all boys willing to go to sea. The ship directors had to find the boys positions in town and tailoring skills made them more marketable.[77] Mossbank Industrial School boasted that their baking programme was superior to any apprentice system offered in town.[78] The convener of Mossbank School also reported that a large number of the "stronger lads" became miners and they were practically adopted by the mining families about the countryside. The director of the Dundee Industrial School tried to place his boys in trades rather than the mills because the pay was better in trades, the opportunities for men in the mills were fewer and family culture among mill workers violated his perception of familial ideology.[79] "A man earning 13s to 14s a week is not in an equally good position as he would be if he were a tradesman . . . The result is that the wife has to work . . . The [children] are more or less neglected, and while the father and mother work, the guardian of the home, in many cases, is a child of 10 or 11 years."[80]

Judging by the variety of subjects and trades that were offered, industrial training, like education, appears to have been taken more seriously in boys' institutions than in girls'. In girls' schools industrial training was confined to housework, laundry and sewing.[81] The child-savers seldom approached the girls as anything other than potential agents of domesticity, as future maids or mothers.[82] In 1914 a female Home Office Inspector claimed: "I think it is quite natural for girls to be fitted for domestic service. It is the natural thing for the girls to care for the house."[83] She believed that it was more important to "get some housework than school work, because [a girl] has very likely to earn her living by housework".[84] Boys' institutions, on the other hand, rarely trained inmates as household servants. One headmaster reported that his efforts to train industrial school boys as pages in "gentlemen's houses" had been largely unsuccessful, because when the "servant girls" discovered that the boy came from a home they "make a pet of him . . . and when he begins to take in the situation, gets self-willed, and will do nothing but what pleases himself, the result is that the master sends back the boy or sends a complaint about him and we are obliged to take him back".[85]

Individual schools varied greatly in their ambitions regarding laundry work. Some institutions ran large, fully commercial laundries or did laundry for neighbouring boys' schools, while others did only the laundry for the school. Sheets, blankets and uniforms gave the girls experience in "rough work", and "fine work" experience was acquired doing the matron's and superintendent's personal laundry.[86] It was recognized that this practice would not prepare inmates for high-wage work in commercial laundries, but they could begin as "under-laundresses in a private house", thus they would be suitable "little maids in any man's house".[87] Younger girls were taught to knit and large portions of the day were spent knitting hosiery for the institution. By the age of 12 they were given a needle and began the important task of making an outfit for service. In some schools girls received small wages for their labour and this money was kept in a bank account for them so that they would learn the value of honest labour, thrift and financial management. According to the superintendent at Kilmarnock Industrial School in 1909, "Like the happy nation with no history, girls who save money, get happily married and become mothers of a healthy family have a meagre record, but none the less satisfaction on that account."[88]

Discipline

The programme was strict and the rules numerous. The superintendents expected a high standard of behaviour from inmates. Although they were intended to be non-penal institutions many relics of their penal ancestry survived. There was solitary confinement, and obligatory silence in workrooms and at mealtimes; the buildings were surrounded with walls. Between 1850 and the passing of Lord Leigh's Act in 1893 boys and girls sent to reformatories had to spend a fortnight in prison.[89] There was a great deal of debate about the most appropriate level of discipline. For many the transfer to the reformatory was intended to symbolize the end of punishment and the beginning of rehabilitation. The superintendent of an industrial school in Dundee maintained that they were not penal institutions and that the children were perfectly free to abscond, but he admitted that "there is always an amount of supervision going on".[90] Others argued that "a reformatory is a prison; you may call it what you please, but it is a prison under a different name".[91] This criticism reveals one of the greatest sources of debates among contemporaries surrounding the true purpose of these institutions: was it punishment, education or treatment?

The regimes of discipline and control varied greatly from school to school and were more likely to reflect the individual superintendent's management style than any school board or the Home Office rules. The use of corporal punishment had decreased by the mid-nineteenth century. Lighted and ventilated "isolation rooms" replaced old dark "cells", and new approaches to rational punishment with elaborate systems of positive reinforcement and behaviour modification replaced older "faster" forms. It is debatable whether the modern system of punishment was less cruel or humiliating to children than five lashes with the leather strap. Michel Foucault argues that the transition from punishing the body by means of physical torture to punishing the "psyche" or character by means of prison discipline, education and training was a product of rational humanitarianism. This trend could be observed in all major institutions by the late nineteenth century. Authorities in schools, hospitals and factories established panoptical rules and regulations concerning the efficient use of time, attention to labour, proper deference, dress, cleanliness and sexual decency. Panoptical discipline produced "docile bodies", obedient women, men and children.[92]

In the 1850s the matron of Glasgow Girls' House of Refuge introduced a somewhat macabre system of justice into her school, which illustrates the fine line between rational discipline and cruel punishment. Under her system of "substitutionary suffering", girls who misbehaved stood before a disciplinary tribunal composed of their peers. In one case, for example, a girl was judged "guilty of striking a companion" and two inmates were elected from 70 volunteers to "suffer the punishment in her stead". According to this matron:

> Such discipline has a most salutary influence. Substitutionary suffering in another, appeals to the better feelings and moves

deeply and with greater lasting effect than personal pain would. For the common good must be order, and among the wayward there may be one means only for securing it, that of constraint.[93]

Two generations of Maryhill superintendents used positive reinforcement in that school. In 1896 the good girls under Mrs Cameron's care could be distinguished from bad girls by their red or blue hair ribbons.[94] Bad girls wore unflattering brown hair ribbons. In 1914 Superintendent Catherine Dow maintained that a good system of merit marks and rewards (umbrellas for older girls and dolls and beads for younger), backed up by the threat of food deprivation, made corporal punishment unnecessary. She reserved the right, however, to use isolation (not in excess of three days) for outbursts of bad temper. She reported that it

had a good effect on girls . . . if she will not do what she is told. She simply refuses and defies you . . . or is impertinent to a teacher before class, you could not allow that. If she would apologize and say she was sorry that would be the end of it, but if she will not do that you must do something with the girl, and I myself always put her into the isolation room . . . I take her there and speak to her quietly and tell her she can remain there and think about herself.[95]

Neither superintendent objected to reporting unmanageable cases to the magistrates' court, where they would be sent to reformatories, and the girls were warned that if they "ever ran away" their hair would be cropped short "so they would be known at once".[96]

Most superintendents preferred to emphasize positive reinforcement rather than punishment. In some institutions good conduct badges carried with them a monetary reward. Badges earned for good conduct brought with them 1s 2d to 1s 6d per month. Good conduct boys were also granted leave. Unlike the girls, boys were allowed to return home for short visits as a reward for good behaviour. The superintendent of Dundee Industrial School permitted every boy at the school to see his family for one afternoon[97] every other month after spending a probationary year in the school. The good conduct boys, the boys wearing badges and acting as serjeants and monitors, were allowed out once a month.[98] Perth Industrial School permitted groups of boys to go to town on Saturday afternoons. The superintendent testified, however, that he was careful "not to flood the town with them".[99] At Aberdeen Industrial School well-behaved boys were permitted either to go home or to Saturday afternoon football or cricket matches.[100] In some schools trustworthy boys were allowed to carry money or pocket knives. So as not to tempt fate, however, these controversial items were banned in other schools. On the subject of boys carrying money, one superintendent stated that he was against it, because they had no need for money, "and then they play pitch and toss with it if they have it, or they give it to other boys to keep for them . . . [It] leads to accusations and theft . . . It is a temptation to others to take it away from them or at least to bully."[101]

When liberal therapeutic methods failed, teachers were quick to resort to a firmer disciplinary stand.[102] The Home Office rules regarding punishment were not formalized until 1918. Regarding corporal punishment they stated that:

> In girls' schools corporal punishment may be inflicted only on the hands and the number of strokes shall not exceed three in all . . . In boys' schools punishment may be inflicted only on the hands or on the posterior over ordinary cloth trousers, and the number of strokes shall not exceed . . . [for boys under 14] 2 strokes on each hand or 6 strokes on the posterior. [For boys over 14] 3 strokes on each hand or 8 strokes on the posterior . . . No scholar shall receive punishment in presence of other scholars . . . . Boys must never be employed to hold an offender while he is being punished.[103]

The rules for residential schools also stated that a record of all corporal punishment of any kind be recorded.[104] But the superintendent of Fechney Industrial School refused to record a punishment of only one or two strokes, claiming that it was unrealistic and unprofessional to expect teachers to record every single "palmy": "It is demoralizing to ask a man to record every stroke he gives a child . . . There is nothing more humiliating to me than to present that book of punishments to my directors once a month."[105]

The daily routine and discipline were intended to instil a sense of duty in these youths that would help them adapt to the expectations of the world outside the institution. According to the captain of the *Cumberland*, when a sense of duty was instilled, "they are bound to grow up better citizens and better men".[106] While the majority of offences were regarded as boyish pranks, discipline on board ships was maintained by corporal punishment. In 1887, for example, there were 100 "boyish offenses", including stealing, pilfering and breaking into the storage rooms. Additionally, 84 cases were dealt with by the withdrawal of privileges or of leave, or with extra drills. The possession of tobacco was a continual problem, as smoking was prohibited by law under the Juvenile Smoking Act 1908. It had always been regarded as a breach of school rules. The annual report of the *Empress* training ship for 1891 revealed that "the possession of tobacco appeared to be rather a stumbling block to many". Apparently "a great deal of this contraband is due to parents and so-called friends"; it was also reported that "a man . . . has been known to row about the ship and throw tobacco to the boys".[107] Very serious discipline cases were referred to the magistrate and offenders were sent to a reformatory, such as occurred on the *Cumberland* in 1892 when the captain was obliged to send seven boys to the magistrate for trial, two for detention, one for "incorrigibility" and four because they attempted to set fire to the ship.[108]

The *Register of offences and punishments* of Mossbank Industrial School for 1893–1924 reveals that boys received between 6 and 12 "stripes" or "strokes" with a light cane or strap on the behind and over their trousers for a variety of offences such as bad language, lying, deception, neglecting duties, noisiness and disorderly conduct, general carelessness, idleness, unexplained absence from work, quarrelling, absconding, smoking cigarettes and chewing tobacco. In October 1894 three boys were handed over to the police and later sent to reformatories for "setting fire to three mattresses in dormitory number 6". On 15 October 1922 Norman Rosenberg and Henry Weinberg were "given 8 strokes on posterior over trousers" for absconding to participate in a Jewish festival (there is no evidence that Jewish holidays were observed in any of the schools). In February 1923 three 14-year- old boys each received six "strokes with a strap over trousers" for smoking in their dormitory. For workroom and school faults such as errors in lessons or disobeying instructors, between four and six "palmies" were the appropriate punishment given. Special privileges such as a Saturday afternoon leave were also revoked when appropriate.[109]

In contrast to the "gentle" approach used at Maryhill, the matron of Chapelton Reformatory believed strongly in the preventative powers of whipping. Some young women, she explained, "require

whipping, and are the better for it".[110] In 1894, out of an average
of 39 inmates, 36 had been whipped ("on the hand mostly"). "Thoroughly bad girls", like those who swear "dreadfully",[111] were taken
to bed and stripped and beaten. "We put them to bed . . . It is always
done before two teachers, and sometimes if the girl is a very bad girl
. . . I have a girl to hold her hands while she is being whipped." She
reasoned that these beatings were necessary because the girls, "many
of whom were young women between sixteen and eighteen, were
accustomed to it and saw no degradation in it".[112] They justified this
form of punishment by suggesting inmates were either from abusive
homes or transfers from other abusive institutions and did "not
understand anything else".[113] Matrons reported that girls came in
"from the outside black and blue with thrashings". In one case a
matron always reminded the girls: "My whipping is nothing compared to the whipping your father has been accustomed to give you
. . . It is the disgrace that goes with my whipping that is the punishment . . . I make it as a very great disgrace."[114]

A former inmate of a girls' school between 1945 and 1955 remembers being subjected to the "holding therapies" that were popular at
that time. She recalled that as a little girl she misbehaved regularly
just "to get close to the matron", but during her early teens she
would get extremely angry, as many teenagers do. Her matron handled the situation by enlisting older girls to pin her against the floor
until the tantrum passed. "I remember laying on the floor when one
or two of them was on me, and I was in a temper." She recalls
screaming at the matron: "When I get out of here I'm going to marry
a Teddy Boy and I don't care what you say, I'm going to marry a
Teddy Boy!"[115] Clearly she intended to hurt the matron's feelings
and this was the cruellest threat that a girl who had been in a children's home since the age of five could think of to say.

Former industrial school boys also recalled harsh punishment even
though corporal punishment was not allowed. A former inmate of a
Roman Catholic reformatory between 1927 and 1934 recalled that,
although they were frequently given "extra prayers" as punishment,
"it was not just extra prayers you were getting, [the Brothers] all carried straps, and the straps were well used". Recalling the events surrounding the particularly severe beating he received after his parents
refused to allow him to return to the school after one of his Sunday
visits home, he revealed:

My father was just the same as a lot of other seamen, so when he came home all he could think about was drink . . . my mother [was the same]. So you see . . . it's the usual drunken caper . . . and him and my mother decide I'm not going back to the school. I say: "I have to go back or else I'll get a doin'." They say: "You're no goin' back!" You have to do what they tell ya; they're the parents. So I don't go back that night. By the time they sober up on Monday morning they decide . . . we'd better get him back before the police come . . . Now my mother was very small, like the typical Glasgow women . . . So she goes in [to the headmaster's office] and sees this benign looking old gentleman . . . Brother–. A nice old man, supposed to be . . . on the face of it, that is what he looked like. He says right, Andrew just come in and wait here . . . I'm standing at the door listening to the patter and of course my mother cannea be content just letting it go at that. She starts tellin' him: "Now you've no ta hit him . . . you've no ta this, and no ta that." And he's just sitting there, "It's all right Missus we'll look after him." By the time she is finished a "roddin' and bawling" at him, he comes in and shuts the door and says to me: "Just go up to the dormitory and take your clothes off." I go up and two boys come up behind me . . . and I put a night shirt on . . . but the night shirt doesn't do you any good . . . So Brother– comes up and by the time they'd finished I was in my bed for 9 days, I just couldnae get out. And I got kept in [the school] for 18 months.[116]

A Protestant industrial school inmate of the same period also remembered harsh punishment used in his school. "Boys were put over [gymnastic] horses . . . They used to tie the boy's feet to each leg. There was plenty of leather." Ironically, he confessed that it was fear of hunger and not fear of the strap, that kept him in line. He had been put in the institution for "neglect" and he claimed that he followed the school rules because he was "dead scared of getting put out [of the school] to rake the bins for food".[117] Finally, a former industrial school boy in the 1940s recalled that boys were made to wear thin plastic pants, so the marks from beatings would not be evident to the school inspector, and an interview with a former residential school headmaster verified this. This headmaster knew of colleagues who "used to shave the trousers thin . . . and the reason was that if [you beat the boy] over a heavy pair of moleskin or corduroy trousers . . . You were wasting your time . . . You were making a fool of yourself . . . Some would give them gym shorts [so you wouldn't mark the bottom]."[118]

Ironically, most institution staff found it justifiable to replicate the abusive behaviour that so many child-savers found reprehensible in the children's parents and that might have been the occasion for removing children from their homes. According to the captain of the *Mars* training ship, "It is perfectly impossible, with the class of boys we get, to do without this little corporal punishment on the hands, many of them are so apathetic and lethargic. I believe in very little of it, but you must have it."[119] Another school superintendent agreed that "I do not think you can manage a school perfectly without punishment."[120] Reliance on pressure from other inmates to induce compliant behaviour may also be problematic because forms of retaliation by children on other children are often undetected or overlooked by school authorities. Peer pressure can be particularly devastating when children are exposed to it 24 hours a day. In the residential school there is no escape.[121] As one former inmate recalls, "It was fight, fight, fight. You know, boys would fight with boys . . . There were a lot of weak boys and a lot of strong boys. There were boys who you wouldn't need to raise your voice to them and you'd see the tears comin' . . . They should never have been in the place."[122]

One common survival strategy was to develop dormitory subcultures as psychological defences against the repressive regime and to resist school authority. Many of the boys recalled that the gangs they formed inside the institutions were similar to those outside the institution. One Glasgow boy claimed that his group "hated people from Edinburgh".[123] There is a history of rivalry between these two Scottish cities. Humphries argues that such subcultural "psychological support was highly insufficient, in the long term, to enable most to withstand powerful pressure to conform".[124] Many interviews with former inmates revealed that they had feelings of powerlessness within the institutions. As the following former inmate recalled: "If you were covered with bruises . . . nobody bothered to ask. It was your own fucking tough luck."[125]

It might be objected that the harsh discipline documented in this chapter was basically no different from that which existed in the state schools of the day, but it should be noted that alternative methods for educating this class of children had been experimented with since Robert Owen set up his schools in the early 1800s. The first Infant School Society (1824) was established in London under the supervision of James Buchanan, who had come from Owen's New Lanark Infant School. The philosophy of the movement was that children should be ruled by love, not fear. Although this movement was in decline by the 1840s,[126] education historian Brian Simon argues that there was a similar movement among socialists against the use of corporal punishment in state schools around the turn of the century.[127] Although it is true that harsh discipline has always been used in state schools, few residential school administrators could legitimately claim to be ignorant of alternative models. During the 1850s Robert Owen frequently addressed meetings of the National Association for the Promotion of Social Sciences and in the early twentieth century the socialist and education reformer Margaret Macmillan presented papers at meetings of the Reformatory and Refuge Union, as did the early childhood education pioneer Maria Montessori.

Licensing

By common law a parent was not entitled to claim control of a son after the age of 14 and a daughter after the age of 16. The Reformatory and Industrial Schools Act prohibited parents from inducing a child to escape licence, and children who ran away were taken into custody when caught; thus by the time children were free of custodial care the parents had no legal right to interfere with their placement.[128] Inmates were usually kept in the industrial schools and day schools until they were 14 and in reformatories until they were 16. Penitentiary cases were expected to remain in the magdalene asylums for two years, unless they were under magistrate's warrant. The power to license was at the discretion of the school managers.[129] Inmates and magdalene cases were "licensed out" to a pre-arranged employment. For girls this usually meant domestic service and for boys a position was found with a local merchant or a berth on a merchant ship. They were not technically free until their licences expired at the age of 18 (19 after 1893). The consent to be licensed was required from the child but not the parent. The only exception, if it was an exception, was in cases of emigration, where the Secretary of State was required to consult the parents before sending the child away, but their objections were not necessarily taken into consideration.[130]

The purpose of the licence was to provide children with supervision while they readjusted to the community. In the case of an industrial school child who had been in the school since the age of six or seven this was a major adjustment. Children on licence were regularly visited by the superintendent and those sent to other districts were visited by local clergy and volunteers. They were expected to keep in touch with the institution via the post for the first three years following release. A parish inspector from Edinburgh had observed that residential school children needed a great deal of help adjusting; he noted that they showed a "curious ignorance of common things".[131] Dr Anne Watson, a more vocal critic of residential schools, argued that very little was done to prepare children for the trials of life, consequently they were hopelessly "ignorant of the ways of the world". She knew of cases where "girls . . . [had] taken their wages to the women they were staying with after leaving the Industrial School and [asked] 'How much is that?' "[132] In fact, there was a great deal of debate about the correct age at which to release children from these schools. According to the superintendent of the Fechney Industrial School it was best to keep boys in the school until they were 16. Twenty years of experience had taught him that licensing out at 14 led to "a good many lapses".[133]

Regarding the best age to release girls, George Greig, Parish Inspector for Edinburgh, testified that 14 was the best age for girls to be sent to service, but release depended very much on her circumstances. "If the girl showed sickness at the time we would retain her a little . . . I mean the change at that period of life. Or we would generally arrange with the mistress to who she was sent that she should really look after her and attend to her."[134] According to the superintendent of a girls' industrial school, "We keep them out of harm's way while we have them, and then we give them a good domestic training and bring up their education, and by precedent and example show them the right thing to do."[135]

It was hoped that by the time the licence expired the individual would be too settled in their work to abandon it to return to "parents, uncertain futures, and bad environments".[136] Table 5.1

Table 5.1   Residential school discharges, 1861–1900.

Discharges	Boys %		Girls %	
Family:				
Reformatory	1,777	19.47	603	27.22
Industrial	5,773	24.29	1,723	22.70
Work:				
Reformatory	5,829	63.89	1,168	52.73
Industrial	10,156	42.73	4,678	61.63
Emigrated:				
Reformatory	296	3.24	107	4.83
Industrial	217	0.91	212	2.79
To sea:				
Reformatory	158	1.73	–	–
Industrial	4,307	18.12	–	–
Enlisted:				
Reformatory	89	0.97	–	–
Industrial	366	1.54	–	–
Sent to hospital:				
Reformatory	121	1.32	37	1.67
Industrial	460	1.93	129	1.69
Sent to prison/reformatory (incorrigible):				
Reformatory	26	0.28	24	1.08
Industrial	340	1.43	58	0.76
Discharged (Special Order):				
Reformatory	–	–	–	–
Industrial	181	0.76	136	1.79
Transferred:				
Reformatory	221	2.42	84	3.79
Industrial	551	2.31	142	1.87
Died:				
Reformatory	287	3.14	71	3.20
Industrial	912	3.83	404	5.32
Absconded:				
Reformatory	319	3.49	121	5.46
Industrial	500	2.10	108	1.42
Total:				
Reformatory	9,123	99.95	2,215	99.98
Industrial	23,763	99.95	7,590	99.97

Source: calculated from annual reports of the Inspector of reformatories and industrial schools, 1861–1900.

provides information regarding the placement of the 32,886 boys and 9,805 girls who were discharged from reformatory and industrial schools between 1861 and 1900. Approximately one-quarter had to be directly returned to their families, which raised the fear that they would be "dragged back into vice or crime by evil influence".[137] It appears that just over half of the reformatory and industrial school inmates were placed directly into employment, but this percentage is artificially high. Fifty-seven per cent of the superintendents surveyed in 1896 revealed that where girls and boys quit their jobs and returned home immediately after their detention expired, the cases were still entered in the school registers as "sent to employment"[138] and it was well known that the majority drifted home in the months and years following their release. Nevertheless, the licence was supposed to be insurance against the interference of disruptive parents and although the parents had no right to the child, the child-savers had a great deal of difficulty keeping newly released children and parents apart.

Conclusion

The precise evidence regarding the background of inmates in Scottish reformatories and industrial schools and rescue homes will never be known,[139] but it is possible to construct a rough social profile of the girls and boys who were admitted to these institutions in the late nineteenth and early twentieth centuries. The children most likely to be taken into care were from what magistrates and other court officials regarded as problem families. Girls, on average, were taken up earlier, and were less likely to have a criminal history than boys, and more girls than boys were taken up for wandering, destitution, residing in brothels and for first offences. Once admitted to an institution, the daily routine varied little. What also differed between girls and boys was the education and vocational training offered. Although the residential school children were not given the same calibre of education that other children received in public and state schools, residential school boys were offered a better education and a wider range of vocational choices than were girls. Regarding magdalene cases, the incarceration of girls and adolescent women indicates that sexual practices were the key marker of their "delinquent" status, in the same way that criminal activity marked boys. This analysis demonstrates how legislation for the prevention of juvenile delinquency and the reformation and protection of children at risk was used in the targeting, training and disciplining of inmates and their families: it also demonstrates the link between the disciplining of gender and class, and the productive nature of the social.

Chapter 6

✦

Sexuality and the gendered delinquent

> See ragged and rough, young Indolent stands,
>   his hair uncombed, and dirty his hands;
> And crawling and creeping he goes a snail's pace,
>   he's always too late, and so in disgrace.
> Indolent Dick, Indolent Dick, O' what will become of
>   poor Indolent Dick.[1]

The reformatory and industrial school systems were linked by the elaboration of a theory of the genesis of delinquency. As illustrated in this tale of poor 'Indolent Dick', the fictional industrial school boy, who could have been any one of the inmates in their pre-incarceration days, the purpose of the residential schools system was much more than just recruiting idle, wayward and delinquent youth, or a daily regime of elementary education and moral instruction. Measures of success were not confined to admission and discharge rates either. Success was demonstrated by the manner in which former inmates went out in to the world. Being reformed involved much more than simply applying the rules learnt in the classroom to one's daily life without the intervention of outside authorities. The goal was the making of a "new" person. Class, gender and sexual subjectivities were constructed for boys and girls through training and discipline that were designed to change their inner selves. "That was the very interesting thing", a former headmaster remarked. "Many [children] would go back and reject . . . the standard in which their parents were still living . . . Partly due to the training . . . they were no longer ready to accept the standards their own parents still probably lived by."[2] This chapter will look more deeply at the hidden curriculum of the reformatory and industrial school, how the programme proceeded with regard to sexuality and work, and where these themes came together in a recasting of the ideal proletarian family.[3]

The management of sexuality

In 1859 an Edinburgh physician wrote: "Oh, that some magic power were given to the moneyed and respectable classes, so they might have but one brief comprehensible glimpse of all the frightful orgies that are transacted, night after night, in the squalid lairs of the sunken and depraved."[4] This passage illustrates the concern for the "moral state of the nation" which was a dominant social issue from the mid-nineteenth to the early twentieth century. Mariana Valverde argues that, in discourses of national degeneration, the fragile nation was seen as subject to the organic process of decay that could "only be halted if individuals, the cells of the body politic, [took] control over their innermost essence or self". Sexual desire itself was perceived as a "dangerous force, a threat to civilization . . . which most needed taming".[5] According to Michel Foucault, concern about children's sexuality was constructed as part of the problem. Since the eighteenth century it had been recognized that "children indulge or are prone to indulge in sexual activity" and this was both "natural" and "contrary to nature" because of the "physical and moral, individual and collective dangers" it posed. The solution was the "pedagogization of children's sex". The wide concern about children's sexuality is evidenced by the proliferation of a body of literature published on the subject throughout the eighteenth and nineteenth centuries. Parents, educators, doctors and eventually psychologists "would have to take charge . . . of this precious and perilous, dangerous and endangered sexual potential"[6] and channel it in socially useful directions. The Victorian rhetoric of national decline that was deployed to generate support for the child-saving institutions drew widely on images of the "excessive sexuality" of the lower-class children. The specific sexual activities targeted for control in reformatory and industrial schools were, for boys, masturbation lest it lead to homosexuality and, for girls, precocious sexuality lest it lead to prostitution.

Girls: from assaulted girls to dissolute women

More girls than boys were taken up for wandering, destitution, residing in brothels and first offences. There was also a significant minority of girls who had been sexually assaulted. They represent the dark side to this readiness to intervene, which illustrates most clearly the contradictions of familial ideology in relation to girls. Historian Linda Gordon has argued that the patriarchal authority structure of the nuclear family expected girls to be dependent, obedient and sexually pure until marriage. The assumption that the family was a safe haven, guaranteeing a girl's purity and protection, presented a problem for girls who could not stay home, and it explains why residential care was favoured over probation, day schools or evening curfews as a means of keeping girls off the streets.

A girl was expected to stay home, obey her father and submit to his will and protection,[7] an expectation fully endorsed by the majority of child-savers. Frances Hepburn of the Scottish National Society for the Prevention of Cruelty to Children encountered many girls who "contracted the habit of wandering" because they were "afraid to remain in the house alone with father at home";[8] they preferred to sleep on stairs and in alleys. As one female probation officer testified in 1925, "I am afraid there is much more incest then ever comes to the surface."[9] An examination of the Maryhill Industrial School for Girls Register indicates that in the periods 1914–16 and 1920–25 "wandering" was a convenient charge for girls suffering from a variety of forms of physical and sexual abuse. These little girls were described in the admission books as "shockingly neglected", "verminous" and "badly knocked about", which explains why girls eight, nine and ten years old would prefer staying out all night, roaming cold, dark streets and sleeping rough on stairs or in toilets rather than remaining at home. It was agreed that these girls should be sent to industrial schools.

Reference to actual or suspected sexual abuse in the case notes of various agencies was usually indirect prior to 1920. It was generally couched in terms of concern about the girl's wandering or the number of beds in the house. It was the policy of the Society for the Prevention of Cruelty to Children not to disclose the details of such cases in their widely circulated annual reports.[10] When Helen McDonald (13 years old) was picked up for wandering in 1914, it was recorded in the register that as her house had only "one bed in a single apartment for 2 grown up girls and a son (20), the moral upbringing was very much against [Helen] getting a chance in life".[11] By 1920, however, the case notes on the girls are much more explicit about the nature of the assault and whether charges had been laid.

> Jane Peterson (13) and Mary Brown (6) [stepsisters]. Father in Duke Street Prison charged with incest. The stepdaughter has not been to school since December owing to parent's behaviour. He was out of late drinking very heavily. The family lived in a one room house, and the girls slept with their father.[12]

> Betty Scott (13). The mother is dead. The father is of drunken habits. An older sister was admitted to Stobhill [hospital] recently. She is pregnant and her brother 18 years of age is responsible for her condition. He has been apprehended on a charge of incest. The girl is 16 years of age. The two girls with the brother and father occupied the one bed. The father says he did this because of the cold weather.[13]

> Mary Thompson (10). The girl was today discharged from . . . hospital where she was under treatment for gonorrhoea. Allegations are made by her that the stepfather had assaulted her on different occasions.[14]

Certainly, even when a male household member was prosecuted for incest, it would not always have been possible for a girl to remain at home. There was often no home remaining to shelter her. Although a desperate girl might take refuge in an institution she was expected to undergo a process of moral rehabilitation in order to interrupt her otherwise inevitable decline. Mrs James T. Hunter, founding member of the Scottish branch of the National Vigilance Association and Lock Hospital director, predicted that "many of them, when assaulted as children, grow up to be dissolute women".[15] The authorities, nevertheless, committed these girls for "wandering" even after the circumstances of cases had been disclosed in court. This, presumably, was the only way they had of protecting the girls concerned from further abuse. It does, however, implicate them in the conspiracy of silence that other writers have argued has historically surrounded sexual abuse, thus keeping it "the best kept secret".[16]

It must be emphasized that the victims of sexual abuse composed only a fraction of the total population in girls' residential schools at a given time.[17] The cases have been cited, however, to illustrate one of the most extreme contradictions of familial ideology. Recent studies of modern sexual abuse reveal that the incest "taboos" are not as effective as has previously been believed. In fact, incestuous abuse is currently widespread. There is no reason to assume that this has not also been the case in the past. Nevertheless, the incest taboo was as strongly held in the nineteenth century as in any other period. It was punishable by the death penalty in Scotland until 1887.[18] Its violation "suggested disease at the heart of what Victorians regarded as essential to the moral, religious, social harmony of their society: the virtuous Christian family".[19] Gordon argues that historically society has dealt with the contradiction by shifting the locus of sexual abuse outside the home, thus enabling the victims to be cast as delinquents and the perpetrators shift from being male relatives to strangers, johns and "dirty old men".[20] This lets fathers and male relatives off the hook, but not mothers. Posing the problem in terms of "moral neglect" rather than incest made it by definition a mother's crime[21] because she should have been able to stop it. It was argued that whenever girls went "wrong" their mothers were chiefly to blame. According to a female parish inspector in Glasgow:

mothers have a mistaken idea that ignorance is innocence and leave the matters at that . . . Very often when a mother is spoken to after her girl has gone wrong, the answer one gets is, "but I did not know". I feel I would like to punish every woman who says "I do not know" when she is asked where her girl or boy goes in the evenings.[22]

Like public discussion, the private admission practices of individual girls' institutions also indicate a concern with the mother's moral character. Between 1920 and 1925, 18 per cent of the girls in Maryhill Industrial School had been found living in brothels or "circumstances calculated to encourage seduction or prostitution".[23] Although the school treated them as girls at risk and were reticent about calling them prostitutes, they had no such reservations about their mothers. In fact, girls were frequently incarcerated because their mothers (and sometimes aunts and sisters) were said to be generally unfit, prostitutes, brothel-keepers, drunkards, immoral, mentally deficient, cohabiting with men and having too many illegitimate children or illegal abortions, criminal inclinations or venereal disease. On the subject of prostitution and motherhood, in 1925 one female probation officer testified that "

> no matter how much they want to be good and nice to the children, I don't think you can reconcile the two occupations . . . After all, except for the dinner hour time, night time is when these people's duties begin, and that is the time the children are mostly at home and see what is going on and understand what is going on. You will get little people of five telling you all about it sometimes.[24]

The child-saver's desire and duty to protect such girls was at odds with their allegiance to familial ideology and it was by and large the mother's and daughter's behaviour and character rather than the ideology that was reinterpreted. The threat of sexual assault on girls, then, is used to restrict their movement and to bind them more tightly to their homes.[25] This logic was observable in Scotland, where public outrage focused on juvenile and amateur prostitution, a phenomenon that was located safely outside the home. Insofar as family members were implicated, it was the mother who was to blame for not keeping a closer eye on her daughter.

This climate supported conferences in 1911 on Social Evil in Glasgow and Public Morals in Edinburgh. The publication of Lock Hospital statistics by Mrs Maitland Ramsey, MD, the surgeon at the hospital, revealed that 34 girls under 16 had been admitted for venereal disease in Glasgow alone.[26] The shock and outrage resulted in the formation of the Glasgow branch of the National Vigilance Association, the pressure group dedicated to the protection of women and girls through the enforcement of the Criminal Law Amendment Act 1885. The sensationalistic exposés of casual sex, street-corner boys, parental neglect and female precocity produced by the Scottish Council for Women's Trades at their Glasgow conference in 1911 suggested that the brassy and unremorseful 15-year-old laundress quoted below was typical of many of the independent working-class girls who spent their evenings flirting with boys and listening to gramophones in the Italian ice-cream parlours.

> I am sure it was A.B. I got the trouble [syphilis] from, as he had connection with me on a Thursday night, and on the following night, he had connection with my chum . . . A week afterwards,

we both felt something wrong. We both bathed ourselves with Condy's fluid. She got better, but I got worse, and was not able to walk. [My grandmother] got the doctor to examine me, and he sent me to the Lock Hospital. I never importuned on the streets, and I did not get money from any of the lads .[27]

The Council for Women's Trades concluded that these ice-cream shops were the "first pubs" for boys and girls.[28] "They were the dens from which boys learned to gamble and steal" and young girls exchanged their "virtue" with soldiers for "chocolate, trumpery scarves [and] cheap jewellery".[29] The Council joined the National Vigilance Association in supporting the enforcement of protective legislation such as the Criminal Law Amendment Act 1885 and the Children Act 1908 which "protect[ed] girls by criminalizing the men who exploited them".[30]

For the most part it was the sexual promiscuity that these independent working-class girls displayed that was the greatest source of anxiety and alarm. Reformers believed that early sexual experience (abuse or seduction) led to prostitution. The case notes on several girls reveal, however, that few were passive victims. Girls such as the following presented a problem because they had not been drugged and seduced by strangers but seemed willingly to enter into relationships with men of their own choice. Lizzy Dunlop (13) went to "picture houses and begg[ed] money from men";[31] Hannah Montrose (11) also went to the pictures and let a man keep "her out late at night";[32] Sarah Walters (13) and her friend Joan McCall (13) were found on the banks of the Clyde with men "who gave them money for immoral purposes";[33] Sarah McCann (15) was "running wild and not willing to work";[34] Annie McCormack (15) was "running absolutely wild in with a set of girls [and was] caught with sailors and soldiers".[35] One child-saver stressed that such a girl needed to be taught "that she carries a priceless jewel in her honour – however plain her person – however humble her rank may be – which, without the deepest shame and detriment, she dare not give away".[36] According to the headmistress of Guthrie's Girls' School in 1925, it was "absolutely necessary to remove little girls from a degrading home environment if they are to become decent citizens and future mothers of the race".[37] The solution to the problem, then, was to catch girls at risk early and to channel them into an appropriate regime of moral rehabilitation in reformatories or industrial schools, depending on their age.

Sex and the street-corner boys

The sexuality of both girls and boys was perceived as a dangerous force. But, unlike girls, boys were not often placed in residential schools for precocious sexual activity and there was no equivalent to a magdalene asylum for them. The contradiction in the case of boys, recognized at the time, was that boys' sexual "deviance", such as masturbation and homosexuality, was more likely to occur in a single-sex residential school than on the outside. The goal of replicating "the family" in a residential school was therefore complicated in the case of boys' institutions by two concerns: first, the physical danger to little boys of being bullied by the big boys and, second, the "moral" danger common to all single-sex institutions of sexual "corruption".

Most superintendents of boys' institutions believed in principle that boys of all ages should be in the same institution and that senior boys should take on "big brother" and mentorship roles.[38] However, they also feared that the "little boys would get corrupted" by bigger boys,[39] especially in "a reformatory, where boys are detained till, in some cases, almost manhood".[40] Interviews with former inmates and staff of a boys' residential school reveal that "indecency, fiddling about, [and] mutual masturbation" were frequent among the inmates.[41] By the 1920s masturbation, or what was called "self-abuse" among adolescents, was regarded, "not so much as an abnormality, but as a normality, which, under certain conditions, and in certain environments develops as a temporary habit which, if it continues may cause undesirable and abnormal manifestations to appear".[42]

> Modern scientific investigation seems to point to the fact that every individual goes through a stage during which this habit, and its companion homosexuality may or may not develop . . . To illustrate my point I will refer again to the boys at the Public School, because there one is dealing with the everyday normal child, not with the "social problem child" who . . . [is] found in Homes and Institutions . . . [I]n all Public Schools there are a few boys who practise self-abuse; in most instances it has been developed as the result of lack of knowledge regarding sexual matters and intensified by coming into contact with other boys who are experiencing the same difficulties . . . When they leave school, the environment which caused the habit to appear comes, automatically, to an end.[43]

A former headmaster of a residential school confirmed that while masturbation was regarded as a harmless "part of every young boy's upbringing", he admitted that occasionally a "bully kind of boy would sneak into a soft boy's bed, even with a night watchman about".[44] These were incidents, if discovered, which the headmasters punished very severely.

Consequently the sexual surveillance of boys in residential schools was one reason why large dormitories or "barracks" were maintained throughout the late nineteenth and early twentieth centuries. This supports Foucault's thesis, developed in *The history of sexuality* (1980), where he argues that on the surface sex was not spoken of in institutions for education.

> But one only has to glance over the architectural layout, the rules of discipline, and their whole internal organization to see that the question of sex was their constant preoccupation . . . the builders considered it explicitly. The organizers took it permanently into account. All who held a measure of authority were placed in a state of perpetual alert, which the fixtures, the precautions taken, the interplay of punishment and responsibilities, never ceased to reiterate. The space for classes, the shape of the tables, the planning of the recreation lessons, the distribution of the dormitories (with or without partitions, with or without curtains), the rules for monitoring bedtime and sleep periods – all this referred, in the most prolix manner, to the sexuality of children. What one might call the internal discourse of the institution . . . was largely based on the assumption that this sexuality existed, that it was precocious, active, and ever present.[45]

Scottish child-savers exhibited a similar preoccupation with illicit sex among inmates. Mossbank Industrial School, for example, was built on the "pavilion principle": an open air design which provided the night watchmen with a clear view of the sleeping boys.[46]

In 1928 the discipline on the *Mars* training ship was at a very low ebb and the Home Office received more complaints about "trouble of a certain kind on the *Mars* than . . . any other school in Scotland".[47] In December 1928 a special enquiry revealed that the ship was still understaffed following the war, run by an aged headmaster, and the boys were "addicted to depraved and immoral practices of a very grave nature"; in other words, homosexual activities, which, to quote Sir George McDonald, applied to "every boy on ship".[48] The Board of Education was assured, however, that steps had been taken to "rectify this unsavoury situation" and "immoral conduct was speedily dissipated". The solution the captain proposed was to seal up all "obscure holes and corners". Next, he appointed duty officers to make "surprise visits to every part of the ship after working hours and during the night". Thirdly, he divided the boys into age-segregated working and sleeping divisions so there would be no more mixing as the divisions would sleep on different decks. Finally, and most importantly, "sports and games were organized and freely encouraged". In summer and in winter "competitions including drawing, essays, draughts, dominoes etc. were introduced without cessation". Happily, the boys' other "interests were soon aroused . . . [having] no time for unclean thoughts. Turned in comfortably tired, [to] fatigue induced sleep . . . "[49]

An interview with a former residential schoolmaster confirmed the thesis that sexual surveillance was one of the reasons why large dormitories were maintained.[50] Despite the "special care", however, the punishment books suggest that boys were frequently caned and strapped for sexual misdemeanours, euphemistically described as "extreme perverseness", "gross irregularity", "filthy habits" and "intemperance".[51] An approved school inmate from the 1940s paints quite another picture of illicit sexual activities in at least one reform school to set against the official view of "inappropriate" schoolboy sexual experimentation described by the superintendents before and after the Second World War. This former inmate confirmed that

in a place like an industrial school where boys are [together] you get to the stage where you love a boy . . . You can get a thing for a boy just as much as you can for a lassie. You grow out of it as you get a bit older and a wee bit more intelligent, you go to different places and see how the world is. And you say to yourself: "That was wrong" . . . It was an affair you could have with a boy . . . some boys could get over it and some boys couldnae.[52]

However, it was his perception that "most of the pupils became 'perverted' through the teachers". He observed, from moving through the junior approved school, the senior approved school and, finally, the Borstal (for young adults between 18 and 21) that "three-quarters of the boys" were sexually assaulted by the staff.

I was sexually abused myself . . . When it was forced upon ya
. . . it could affect ya for the rest of your life . . . In the approved
school [the hard part about it] . . . was that it wasnae voluntary,
it was adults forcing themselves upon kids . . . some of the kids
in [my school] came from junior schools . . . they were used to
it. A lot of boys were bullied into it [and by senior approved
school] it became a way of life.[53]

Hidden curriculum: moral regulation and familial ideology

A familial ideology may be reproduced through social institutions,
either directly or indirectly, through institutional ritual and practices.[54] Consequently familial ideology can be embedded in seemingly nonfamilial institutions such as residential schools, rescue
homes and industrial day schools for girls and boys. According to the
testimonies of the women and men at the Parliamentary Commissions on reformatories and industrial schools in 1852, 1896–8,
1914–15 and 1925, the appropriate feminine and masculine values
could be taught to girls and boys outside the structure of the nuclear
family. It was hoped that girls and boys would learn these roles by
emulating the women and men who governed the institutions. The
imaginary family of the institution, ironically, might be a better
teacher of family values than the real, anti-social family of the young
delinquent.

The organizational structure of residential schools was based on
a paternalist model of the family. The "fatherly" male directors
reigned supreme as the chief disciplinary officers, followed by a
ladies' support committee and female staff and servants, who were
expected to play tutelary, service and expressive roles. They taught
basic literacy, read scripture and sang hymns, nursed the sick, and
cooked and scrubbed. In addition, male staff introduced boys to
basic manual trades. The means used to reform inmates was a com-
bination of academic and moral education, industrial training, and
"military discipline"[55] or the leather strap or "tawse" as it was called.
When successful, this formula was intended to exercise a reforming
influence on both male and female inmates.

Considerable attention was paid to the character of the staff who
ruled the schools. In some institutions inmates were not allowed to

mix with the servants[56] and the Home Office inspectors were known to be critical of institutions where the "instructors were really people of the domestic servant class and therefore of a very rough and ready character".[57] In boys' institutions the real work of moral reform fell on the male teachers and workshop instructors. As the superintendent of the Glasgow Boys' House of Refuge in the 1860s reminded his staff, the boys' "minds are volatile. They need line upon line, and precept upon precept. They look to *you* for instruction."[58] The younger male staff were required to participate in and supervise games. "It benefits the boys very much to have persons of that stamp along with them to supervise their play."[59] They were all instructed to "continually impress on the children the importance of valuing their present opportunities for improvement".[60] It was the particular responsibility of the workshop instructors to impress upon the boys the dignity of honest labour and "the necessity of combining honesty and integrity with proficiency".[61] In the words of a former headmaster in the period following the Second World War:

One of our tasks is to teach our students the nobility of labour
. . . To work alongside a skilled tradesman and to discover and capture some of the joy which that man finds in his craft. I want him to see conscientiousness, punctuality and honesty in action, in the hope that he too will acquire these characteristics.[62]

For training ship boys, it was argued that "no life for them could be more manly, healthful, or independent" than a seafaring life.[63]

Women played a peripheral role in most boys' institutions. Outside the limited contact they were permitted with their mothers, the women with whom the boys had the most contact were the lady volunteers who came in for scripture readings and the headmasters' wives and patronesses, like Princess Louisa, for example, who presented Scottish training ship boys with their merit badges in the 1890s. Presenting these upper-class women in their perfume, silk and lace as the feminine ideal must have been confusing to many boys whose own unworthy mothers drank, cursed and pawned their shoes.

Historians examining the gendering of education have gone beyond the early view that "masculinity could be left to look after itself" and that "the learning of masculinity, unlike femininity was not thought of as the central task of the school".[64] What was thought to be a fit education for boys and girls was closely related to their projected roles in a division of labour marked by class and gender. Reformed class and gender subjectivities were not constructed only through gender-appropriate sexual behaviour, but also through work, which could be demonstrated by what you do in the world, your labour; thus, girls and boys had to be presented with the right sort of work to do.

Residential schools had a formal, explicitly taught curriculum (as outlined in Chapter 5), comprising reading, writing, arithmetic and industrial training. Besides this, however, they also had what social scientists call a "hidden curriculum", in which there is a set of values, attitudes or principles that are implicitly conveyed to pupils by teachers. According to S. Bowles and H. Gintis, the hidden curriculum promotes social control at school and in society at large by training people to conform and to obey authority, teaching them to regard social inequalities as natural and ensuring cultural reproduction.[65] In reformatories and industrial schools inmates were expected to acquire the skills and values – punctuality, discipline and obedience – thought appropriate for working-class youth in the industrial labour force.

The relationship between work and moral reform of inmates represents a number of class- and gender-related contradictions. Even though the notion that children should be sheltered from work and adult responsibility by deferred entry into the labour force was a dominant theme of the rhetoric of the child-saving movement, and the basis of their major criticism of the working-class family culture,[66] reform schools expected children to work – and to work hard. There were three ways in which the school resolved this contradiction. First, inmates were trained for approved trades that (unlike street trading) were appropriate to their gender and class position. Secondly, the children did not receive wages, but might be given just a few pennies, little presents or merit points which, at best, served as rewards for good behaviour. Finally, approved forms of labour were imbued with a moral significance. Thus inmates were becoming not merely workers but citizens. In this environment "industry" indicated both a certain type of occupation or job and an attitude of diligence and application brought to any endeavour. The ambiguity, as the case of the street-trader illustrates, lies in the fact that although employment was said to be the remedy for pauperism – providing an income and a check on the habits of idleness and indigence, which were held to be at the root of vice – precocious employment or the wrong sorts of employment might be an early warning sign of the predictable descent into vice and crime.

Training in Christian manliness

Boys' residential schools were modelled on the public school regime familiar to the majority of directors. Basing education and training on public school principles, however, resulted in conflicting ideas of working-class masculinity and leadership. The main challenge involved the acquisition of an appropriate work ethic for working-class boys. The unskilled and undisciplined juvenile street-trader was held up as the antithesis of the disciplined skilled worker. It was street trading rather than the labour market that was perceived as the "cause of unemployment and casual employment".[67] On the street, these boys were "to a great extent their own masters". They could "do as they please[d]"[68] and a shrewd trader could earn twice the income of an apprentice. Consequently, many found it difficult to conform to the demands of wage labour, accustomed as they were to a higher income, and they quit their apprenticeships, even though in the long run a trade promised higher wages and more security. In other cases, by the time they realized the value of a trade they were too old to be taken on by a tradesman. When the street pedlars "left the streets" their earning power was no greater than it had been when they were 14 years of age.[69] Thus it was concluded that street trading rendered boys undisciplined and unfit for "regular employment", and that without the proper values and work ethic these boys became the next generation of wife- and child-deserters and were a great moral and economic cost to the state.[70] According to the chief of the Glasgow police in 1909: "They usually become street sellers of toys and flowers, bookmakers, touts, hangers-on at railway stations, loafers, and thieves. If in the later years they take to work at all, it is only of a casual sort . . . Frequently they are found living off the immoral earnings of prostitutes."[71]

The goal of reformatory and industrial school education was to enable boys to escape from an otherwise vulnerable position in the labour market. However, the institutions still depended on the income generated by the boys' labour to meet their operating expenses. The benefit of a large school was that it could generate income adequate to employ qualified instructors and purchase quality tools and equipment.[72] Smaller industrial schools were often unable to employ a full-time workroom instructor so boys were given only a few hours of training per week. Many argued that a boy could not learn a trade under these conditions;[73] very few stayed with the trades they were supposed to have acquired and despite the years of training they were unable to get employment above the rank of apprentice. "For all their training, in the end, boys had to begin at the beginning upon their release."[74] This frustrated the boys.

The majority of residential schools focused on shoemaking, carpentry and tailoring. The problem of training boys as shoemakers and carpenters was that it required a considerable outlay for materials with the risk that they might be wasted. Consequently many schools were forced to resort to work that was inexpensive and described as "uninstructive", "repetitive", "sedentary and unhealthy" for the mental and physical development of growing boys. It was the blunt opinion of one critic at Oakbank Industrial School that tailoring was a suitable trade only "for a lame boy".[75] He argued that the best form of employment for growing boys was gardening, "where the boy can run about, and get developed".[76]

The most "unproductive" but profitable trades were matchbox making, wood chopping and hair teasing, all of which were very popular during the later part of the nineteenth century and most likely to be given to the youngest children or found in the poorest schools. In 1897 a Lanark sheriff demanded government regulations to assure "uniformity of management, discipline, and punishment" and more importantly a more systematic training in trades.

> The question of making profit is one largely looked to in the present private system. Lads are put to unhealthy occupations such as baking without proper regard to their physique: government would, I think, see that nothing but healthy trades were taught; and again, wood chopping, paper-bag making, and occupations of that kind, which do not qualify for a trade for a full grown-man, would not be allowed.[77]

Concern about unproductive labour also addressed its effect on the children's health. Throughout the late eighteenth and early nineteenth centuries a series of Factory Acts had been enacted to restrict child labour, especially in what was regarded as the "dangerous trades". One such trade was match making. The handling and washing of white and yellow phosphorous, sulphur and other chemicals used in the manufacture of "Lucifer matches" caused phosphorous poisoning or "phossy jaw", a particularly painful and disfiguring disease which could have a fatal outcome.[78] The side-effects of phosphorous poisoning were influenza-like symptoms, toothaches, the swelling of the jaw, and eventually necrosis: the destruction of tissue and bone growth. There was also the danger of fire. The manufacture of Lucifer matches was declared a dangerous trade in June 1892, but it continued to be the principal occupation of the boys in Oakbank Industrial School until 1895. In 1893 the Inspector for the Home Office began warning the directors that Lucifer match making was "unsuitable for an Industrial School", but his efforts to have the production discontinued met with great opposition from "interested parties in Aberdeen". He wrote to the Home Office on 22 January 1894: "I do not think match making should be allowed in this school. It must be attended with a certain risk to health. It is not work calculated to improve the intelligence of the children or to help them to make a livelihood in after life. Only it *pays* the manager [£250 per annum]."[79]

In their own defence two members of the Board of Directors protested that, since the Factory Acts had been passed, match making had been abandoned by ordinary manufacturers in Aberdeen and the nearest factory was in Glasgow. They argued that match making had been practised safely and "profitably" in the industrial school for the past six years. It was their opinion that the health of the children had actually improved during this period and they stressed that the only dangerous element to match making was the "'dipping' [which was] done by a paid dipper from outside . . . All the children have to do with phosphorus is that they carry the frames with matches from the dipping to the drying room."[80]

On 31 January 1894 the Inspector informed the secretary of the industrial school that "I am directed by the Secretary of State to warn you that he cannot allow boys under your care to continue to be employed in match making" and he granted them six months to find another trade. Seven months later they were still stalling and refusing to comply with the order. They informed the Inspector that they intended to "make a representation to the Home Secretary for a further continuance as it has been found impossible as yet to procure another industry sufficient to employ the boys. Our scope of industries in the North is very limited."[81] The Inspector responded by expressing his "great distrust of the chairman of the Board of Directors" of the school. The private files of the Reformatory Inspectors reveal that match making at Oakbank Industrial School was still in progress on 17 September 1895.

The fact that this industrial school was able to persist in manufacturing matches despite the Schools Inspector's opposition, warnings and repeated attempts to have it stopped is consistent with what Karl Marx argues in *Capital*. Marx indicates that while the passing of the various Factory Acts might have been a victory for the working class, this was not necessarily the case, because industrialists were able to undermine the acts by taking advantage of certain loopholes.[82] In the case of Oakbank Industrial School the loophole was that shop work in reformatories and industrial schools fell outside the ordinary jurisdiction of local factory inspectors, so inspectors had no mandate to regulate what went on within them.

Another example of the contradiction between the goals of the residential school and the labour market is found in the relationship between the industrial training ships and the Royal Navy. While many believed that the class of boy found in the industrial school would make an ideal sailor, the Royal Navy did not accept industrial school boys as recruits. They refused boys who had been charged under sections 15 and 16 of the Reformatory and Industrial Schools Act and those who did not meet their strict height and weight standards. All but a few residential school boys were described as "too wee" to pass the physical examination. Despite constant appeals, the Navy blocked entry of industrial school boys to its training school. Consequently, training ships had no outlet for their boys other than the merchant service,[83] where the demand for industrial school boys was high because the standards of the commercial sector were far less rigid. Thus the certified industrial training ships served the private interests of the numerous industrialists who were their strongest supporters,[84] although critics noted that the boys had been trained at the public's expense. The majority of the ships' boards of directors were Clyde shipowners. The captain of the *Empress* stated that his entire board of directors were "shipowners, and they take as many boys as they can".[85] For them the certified industrial training ship was not just a refuge for boys but "a valuable nursery to the mercantile marine of the Clyde".[86]

While trying to teach the boys the value of an honest trade, industrial schools remained at odds with many trade unions. From the outset many trade unions attacked these schools on the grounds that they did not pay wages and they interfered with, or increased competition in, the labour market. In Glasgow in the 1840s "a large body of Chartists congregated, and carried a motion in opposition"[87] to the passing of the local Industrial Schools Act. An official from the Boys' House of Refuge maintained that it was Chartist opposition to the Glasgow House of Refuges Bill in 1841 that assured "our getting the Act, because it looked perfectly absurd, an opposition by a class who were not likely to pay the assessment".[88] Chartists were not enamoured with the philanthropically conceived moral education of the poor. "Educationalists", said the Northern Star in 1848, were "the pretended friends, but the real enemies of the people".[89] Chartism embraced "versions of democracy and education as worked and conceived from below; philanthropy's alignment was with forms of democratic rule such as might be imposed from above".[90] It was also revealed by the Royal Commission in 1894 that the shoemakers' unions blocked entry of boys into that trade as did some other "branches of trade".[91] Between 1909 and 1920 the managers of female refuges fought the repeated efforts to have institutional laundries included in the Trades Board Acts.[92]

Where the appeal of the British public school model was that it "promised to turn small boys with well-to-do parents [into] acceptable members of the upper-middle class",[93] it was not intended that reform school boys should aspire to the rank of "gentleman"; and certain bourgeois values, such as entrepreneurship, were castigated when manifested in the juvenile street-trader. Residential school boys were not being trained to run their own businesses, but simply to work punctually and diligently for others.[94]

Emphasis on games and athletics was an important part of this character-building process. In public schools team sports were identified as the most important experience of character building, in a process "comprising ethos of loyalty, team spirit, patriotism, pluck, and manliness . . . games and physical exercise which supposedly built national character and thereby contributed to the Empire's greatness". In residential schools the value of sports was to "train not simply the muscle and the eye, but . . . the judgment and also the alacrity of resources".[95] Sportsmanship training was "part of the development . . . it was intended to develop a bit of a competitive edge as human beings, again to help them move up through the pile".[96] But it also taught them to accept defeat.

> To accept the referee's decision . . . to applaud a rival who has played . . . well . . . [To] sink one's individuality for the good of the team . . . Sportsmanship can't make a bad boy good . . . [but] accepting the referee's decision and self-control in thwarting situations is carried over . . . to the larger life outside.[97]

In the late nineteenth century the Inspector's Cup was introduced and inter-school football competitions were established.

By the 1920s most residential schools had some affiliation with Boy Scout troops, Rovers (a senior branch for boys over 17) or the Boys' Brigade (Mossbank had a large Brigade Company). Regarding the objectives of the Rover troop in Barlinnie Prison, Glasgow, in 1924 the troop leader stated that

> the object is to help lads towards good citizenship and good parenthood, and the root idea is service for others. Instruction and information is imported in an elementary manner on such subjects as Parliamentary Government, Government of the Empire, Municipal Governing, simple laws of health and sex hygiene.[98]

Recent studies of the working-class youth movement suggest that organizations like the Boys' Brigade, which were a part of most residential schools by the early twentieth century, "introduced working-class boys to codified sports and games, extending what had hitherto been public school *esprit de corps* to a much wider social spectrum".[99] The Boys' Brigade was especially appealing to residential schools because it recruited its members largely from the working class, from which the majority of juvenile offenders were also found. It was hoped that the habits developed in the Brigade would "continue in after life and the young man devotes himself to healthy interests all his life".[100] Consequently many Boys' Brigade officers were also voluntary probation officers and some used their personal influence to intervene with the court when Brigade members got into trouble. Therefore there was a link, albeit informal, between these boys' clubs and the criminal justice system. Regarding his own membership in the Mossbank Industrial School Boys' Brigade between 1924 and 1933 one former inmate recalled, "We had the hat and everything."[101]

Girls: the dis-budding of flowers

In girls' institutions the female staff played a very important role. It was stressed that the matron should be of "a social class superior to [the inmates'] own mothers",[102] as she would mould the inmates in her image and thus "the wrong done in the home"[103] would be corrected. It was hoped that under the watchful eye and maternal guidance of the matron the girls would learn the domestic skills necessary to become good little maids and mothers. In the 1930s the matron's role was reinterpreted to conform to psychoanalytic theory that redefined the causes of female juvenile delinquency. Social workers continued to argue that girls were harder to reform than boys, but this was no longer simply because they had strayed farther from the path of virtue. In the psychoanalytic discourse female maladjustment was caused by the girl's impaired ideal-ego-formation brought on by the cruel or neglectful behaviour of a mother who did not return the infant daughter's love and admiration. The result was that "their personality has not developed to the same extent as have their instinctual wishes".[104] The first stage in reformatory treatment, which one social worker referred to as "the dis-budding of flowers, which makes them finer",[105] was to help the girl to forget that she was almost grown-up. "In the institution we emphasize the dependence of childhood" in order to develop a retarded ideal-ego-formation. The love of their superior

> [the matron], the powerful representative of the early childhood mother, will be the reward for suppressing their excessive instinctual wishes . . . Girls who become prostitutes have never really experienced sexual satisfaction. They do not want a man; their desire and longing is unconsciously directed backwards toward the love of their own mother. That is one of the reasons why a good mother-matron can do them such a lot of good. The profoundest analyses of prostitution-fantasies mostly bring up the longing of the girl-child to be protected by her mother, the fear of being alone, which drives her from one man to another – just for the sake of money or food or clothes.[106]

For her part, in her dual role as disciplinarian and nurturer, the matron became both the "strict father . . . and the loving mother".[107] Through the process of transference the inmates learned that in the reformatory matron they now had a "good mother", one "who would not act as their own mother had done".[108] Through their incarceration, infantilization and domestic training the inmate would "gradually . . . soften from sophisticated young women to teachable school girls again. They begin to feel immature again. They wear school uniforms and have their hair cut short."[109] A former headmaster remembering reformatory girls recalled that they "were always unattractively dressed . . . [They wore something] like smocks, grey or dull colours, drab colours, no shape, like a sack cut to fit them. They were all lumpy stout girls."[110]

The second stage in the girls' reformatory rehabilitation was to provide them with a settled, secure environment: "Security as to food, shelter and clothes [and] regular hours for food and sleep". The inmates were then taught "all that goes into home-making: cooking, housewifery and laundry".[111] The economic importance of laundries among rescue homes did more than help to cut the cost of an inmate's confinement. There was a moral, psychological and practical dimension to the tasks the girls learned. Laundry work in particular had a symbolic importance, teaching the virtue of spiritual as well as physical cleanliness. It was intended to "drive home the fundamental importance of cleanliness and order". According to Lady Griselda Cheape, "The first moral medicine is 'discipline' . . . Washing is good, it gives regular work and teaches cleanliness of body and soul."[112] It was also held to be particularly suitable for the "rougher" sort of girl who found it irksome to sit still and be quiet as she sewed. In 1877 the directors of the Glasgow Magdalene Institution imbued laundry work with great moral significance. It was not only more "healthful and more remunerative" but, in its moral tendencies, far superior to needlework. Even as late as 1931 the directors of the Edinburgh Magdalene Asylum applauded the "moral" virtue of those patrons who "by entrusting their washing to the Institution . . . make a real contribution . . . One of the most difficult social problems of the day . . . [it] engenders a feeling of independence and tends to the restoration of self-respect."[113]

Unlike boys' institutions, it was believed to be in the moral interest of the older girls to have little children of their own sex in the school to "mother". In industrial schools, where the girls ranged in age from 6 to 15, the senior girls were appointed to look after the little girls.[114] In reformatories like Chapelton, where the majority were over 14, former married inmates were encouraged to visit and to bring their babies to the school. The advantage of having former inmates back to the school to show off their tidy clothes and healthy babies was that "really nice old girls coming about the school as a success themselves, talk to the girls and reason with them, and thus they form ideals".[115] The superintendent of Chapelton, herself a trained nurse, instructed inmates in physiology, health nursing and bandaging techniques. She found that the girls were "very good to each other when they were sick". By nursing each other, she explained, they would acquire "a knowledge that they will carry with them in after life. They will forget the poetry and the grammar they learn, but they will not forget the bandaging, and the attention, and the poultice-making that they do in a practical lesson with me."[116]

Particular emphasis on a girl's moral rehabilitation was laid upon her future role as mother. Sex education was formulated through a language of maternal prospects but, whereas a precocious interest in sex was held to be improper, an early interest in motherhood and child-care was fully endorsed. According to a matron who followed this new therapeutic approach of the 1930s: "I talk to them of the baby they might have some time in the future. One day you will have a baby, and think what it will mean to you."[117] Of course they never mentioned the men with whom the girls had had their sexual experiences. This logic parallels the splitting of sexuality and maternity that Eileen Yeo has identified in the thinking of pioneer feminists, social scientists and reformers. For example, the childless woman (a matron or lady child-saver) could be a moral, if not biological, mother to orphans, replacing the absent or inadequate birth mother.[118] The maturity of their female inmates was measured on the basis of the girl's readiness to embrace maternity without showing undue interest in, or familiarity with, the process by which it would be achieved.

Familial ideology regarded the mother as the linchpin of the family; her influence and labour, for better or worse, was what could make the difference between rough and respectable status for the working-class family. According to Mrs Hunter-Crastor, girls were considered to be morally reformed when they had "learned to be of use to somebody".[119] The bourgeois doctrine of separate spheres proscribed employment for women, yet this was an ideal (even if it was shared) that was simply unrealistic for the majority of the working class. Working-class women, at least before marriage, would have to be able to earn a wage, and this doctrine was reinterpreted to include employment so long at it was supervised and suitable. The guidelines were that it should not encroach on men's province or usurp men's prior right to work, and was compatible with women's culturally prescribed role as wife and mother.[120] The job that best fitted this typification was domestic work. As a servant, a young woman laboured in private: she was a dependant in someone's home; she was not in competition with men; she was subjected to close personal control by a supervisor; and she was engaged in appropriate "women's work". The residential school matrons were confident that respectability was within the grasp of any girl who could learn self-control, discipline and above all chastity. The stigma of her reformatory past need not hold her back but, just to be sure, Mrs Hunter-Crastor cautioned her girls against telling others where they had been. She did advise them, however, "in every case to tell their husbands before getting married".[121]

If each generation of wife and mother could be educated to a proper domestic competence, the lure of the streets and pubs would be so much less for those they nurtured, and the cycle of deprivation would be broken. Thus, central to the regime of moral reform was the expansion of working-class women's domestic role. Reformed girls would see themselves as more than contributors to the family economy through their paid work; they would be a true source of emotional support and comfort.[122] From exercising domestic skills as maids in someone else's house they would progress to become the role models of women of their class – neighbours and daughters – and agents who would lead husbands and sons off the streets, out of the pubs and more into line with their own "manly" roles.[123] As a Scottish clergyman wrote:

> I feel persuaded that one of the best methods of making the allurements and excitements of the public house less attractive to the hard-wrought artisan . . . is to increase the attractions of his fire-side by educating help-mates for him, instead of the tawdry, thriftless, ignorant wives that are too commonly met with.[124]

The child-savers recognized that their regime did not enable all inmates to escape the cycle of poverty, and as the decades passed, the reformatories, industrial schools and the Society for the Prevention of Cruelty to Children dealt with a significant number of children whose parents had been through the system.[125] Reflecting on the girls' training in residential schools, a former headmaster confessed that

> in a sense the girls . . . had a less good opportunity in "out-there life" of being able to come up through the pile . . . Girls were trained for catering, sewing, for working in hotels, farms; the more menial female jobs . . . They were trained to be cooks and sewing maids, pantry maids . . . And many of the kinds of jobs that the girls would go into: hotel work, restaurant work, were the very kind, where they were open prey to the male of "that kind". Many would have illegitimate children or very early marriages.[126]

In response, in the 1920s the Glasgow Magdalene Institution set up a home for unwed mothers and the Society for the Prevention of Cruelty to Children established social schemes, mothers' meetings and girls' clubs to assist poor young mothers "to struggle on".[127] They held baby competitions with prizes for well-tended babies, and home employment schemes for mothers:

> The object . . . is to keep the mothers more in their own homes during their spare time, which is so apt to be spent hanging about the closes gossiping with their neighbours – a great temptation to fall back into their former bad habits – and to give them some wholesome interest to occupy their minds [piecework sewing], so that they may feel that by their own industry they can add a little to the husband's weekly wages.[128]

After the First World War the Young Women's Christian Association established St Katherine's Girls' Club in Aberdeen, which recruited its members from among the factory girls and fish workers between the ages of 14 and 16. According to Bella Walker, the club director, "we try to get the roughest".[129] "We have arranged our membership so that all the girls come from the poorest part of the city. It would be easy to fill the club with middle class girls. Our girls are chosen for low physical condition, bad homes, or difficult working conditions."[130] She divided the club members into seven categories: young offenders, headstrong girls, girls of bad parentage, girls without homes, vicious girls, subnormal girls and girls on probation. The club's goal was to teach every girl housewifery and homemaking skills and to develop in her a sense of "responsibility as good Christian citizens . . . [and] self-respect".[131]

The appearance of St Katherine's Club and similar schemes illustrates another contradiction of the residential school system. Aberdeen "fish girls" were described as "mostly very high spirited and difficult girls, very rough and very wild. They are similar to the Dundee jute workers."[132] By the 1920s, however, it was also recognized that this "wildness" and similar "unfeminine" behaviour was a reaction to their "monotonous jobs".[133] Margaret Irwin called this "industrial fatigue": "I have often been struck with the terribly depressing character of the girls' work. It is very simple work and demands no intelligence whatever, it is tiring physically, and there she goes at it all day, and no wonder she breaks out at night."[134]

In the 1920s the Scottish National Council of Juvenile Organizations also observed high rates of offences committed by girls who worked as domestic labourers. They attributed this tendency to the acting out of work-related tensions. "By her very nature she is prone to forget the drudgery of the day in any pleasure, sometimes in any excitement, which comes her way."[135] But rather than training them for more satisfying jobs the remedy the child-savers proposed was an intensification of the gospel of domesticity. The child-savers regarded these girls and young women as "unfeminine". They associated mannerisms which offended bourgeois norms – rough voices, garish dress, drinking and swearing – with another: sexual promiscuity. Of course this is just one view. It is the middle classes' perception of these women's behaviour. Oral history suggests that fish girls and factory workers had their own definitions of respectability and that what may have appeared to middle-class observers as unsettled or rebellious behaviour was really very closely controlled. Margaret Buchan's interviews with East Coast fish girls, for example, reveals that although they earned their living by following the herring, and lodged in digs, they always shared with female relatives, stuck very closely together and were usually under the informal supervision of the older women.[136]

It was hoped that the right sort of values and priorities would fortify these young Scottish women against temptation. In the case of girls from St Katherine's Club this did not mean "cultivated labour" like the household servant. With a club girl "the mention of something superior, like a table maid, would rather annoy her. She would not want that."[137] The director admitted that she "was thinking more of the very dirty and unkempt girl who could be taken down to the clothes cupboard and shown a nice coat and a hat, and told that she would look very smart in those".[138] According to her, the "only safeguard that a girl is going to have" against going astray is "if she has a strong instinct for homemaking . . . some of us are very much convinced that we cannot over-develop the womanly side of the girl. We don't even mind if a girl powders and paints."[139] Regarding residential school girls, a former headmaster explained that they were "preparing them for being able to be a good mother, in the sense that they would be able to cook, and keep a house and make clothing . . . though technically it was to enable them to make a living until these things came".[140]

Residential school directors and magdalene asylum directors both hoped to find places for inmates as servants wherever possible. As servants, inmates could act out their femininity in paid employment, which also enabled bourgeois women to protect their own femininity by freeing them from housework. It was seen to be of the utmost importance for their moral rehabilitation "to have an outlet for the young women, as domestic servants, especially into Christian families, who will care and watch over them".[141] Throughout the decades the directors were always hesitant about placing inmates in factories, shops and warehouses, and favoured country service over the city because in a rural setting inmates would be "free[r] from temptations than those in large towns".[142]

Although industrial training to prepare inmates to enter skilled employment such as dressmaking or teaching was generally unavailable to girls in residential schools, most could boast a success story or two regarding an extraordinary or atypical girl. As the lady Home Office Inspector revealed,

> there have been just a few cases where girls have shown exceptional aptitude, and then the managers have sometimes been good enough to send them for special training, but those are quite isolated cases . . . Training is mainly devoted to fitting them to be domestic servants.[143]

Girls were not apprenticed the way boys were. They generally were sent to domestic service and lived under the roof of their employers, so finding accommodation was not a problem for the school directors. In 1904 a reformatory school matron stated that it was an "absolute fact" that:

> the [domestic] service girl makes a much better wife than the

factory girl. . . [I]t is also a fact that fully 98 percent of our girls
marry . . . I can hardly imagine any calling better fitted than
domestic service to develop out of the reformatory girl, that
choicest of God's gift to man – a good wife and mother, the
most reliable bulwark a nation can possess.[144]

She also stated that while they did occasionally meet with "excep-
tionally clever girls" they did not give them the education or training
needed to qualify them for high-ranking domestic positions such as a
governess, or a school teacher. She explained:

I could never see that the game was worth the candle . . . What
parent would desire to hand over the moral and intellectual
training of his child to a young woman – however clever she
might be – who, he knew, had run the gauntlet of common
lodging-house life, or, even while living with respectable parents, had associated with the criminally disposed of a class,
perhaps lower than her own . . . [Why] let them risk ruining
their health with over-study, introduce them into a sphere
which they might be neither happy, nor successful, and into an
already overcrowded profession?[145]

It was hoped that female inmates would shake off their "lower
class" taint by restricted access to their families, but no Eliza
Doolittles would be found in girls' residential schools. It was not
intended that girls should rise above their "natural" stations in life.
One headmistress testified that "there are certain limitations to our
work and our powers. We cannot turn out a refined child."[146] The
matron at the Glasgow Girls' House of Refuge refused to teach
"crocheting or fancy work . . . It unfits for more useful occupations,
and has a dissipating tendency upon the mind."[147] Another matron
reported that she would not dream of "training [inmates] as clerks,
typewriters, and that sort of thing . . . It would not be possible to
make a highly paid governess out of a reformatory girl."[148] They
concluded that there was little point in training girls for any profession because the majority lacked suitable homes to return to and it
was pointless to train relatively homeless girls for day jobs. In her
semi-autobiographical account of her residence in a children's home
in the 1920s in Aberdeenshire, the Scottish author Jessie Kesson
remembers the ambivalent reaction of the staff when she announced
her plans to study poetry rather than becoming a farm servant.
Although the majority of inmates left these institutions as servants, a

few did go on to work in trades as book-folders, dressmakers and mill-workers,[149] but service was favoured well into the twentieth century "because it was easiest".[150]

Recasting the proletarian family: the fire of pure love

The child-savers were not alone in their attempts to reform working-class masculinity and femininity. The goal was also shared by late-nineteenth- and early-twentieth-century socialists, feminists, trade unionists, evangelical Christians and the founders of various youth organizations, even where they differed as to the means or ideals. Historical analyses of working-class culture have examined how reformers often risked presenting the masculine ideal as "effeminate". Men's right to spend their leisure time and money as they chose, on drink and gambling, for example – targeted by all reformers – allowed them "to define and display manliness at a time when the periodic, seasonal and poorly paid employment available to proletarian men undermined their status as rightful heads of household".[151] Reformed femininity was less a violation of existing values than an economic problem, because of the necessity of employment before marriage and possibly after marriage. In this respect, the reformers often met with more success in their dealings with women, who recognized that particular aspects of men's behaviour harmed them and their children. A certain instrumental alliance between the classes and between women is evident in working-class women's recourse to the child-saving agencies.

Like other reformers, the child-savers attempted to tackle the question of reforming gender and sex roles by emphasizing how their ideal subjects were more "manly" and "truer" women than the rowdy and undisciplined real subjects whom they confronted. For residential school children and adolescents, moral education consisted of conveying lessons on the appropriate behaviour both for a dependent minor and for future adults. We have seen something of how this programme proceeded with regard to education, work and sexuality, and will focus in this section on how these themes came together in a recasting of the ideal proletarian family.

Central to the regime of moral reform was the expansion of the working-class domestic role for both boys and girls. While the ideal future role of working-class girls was to become domestic servants and laundresses and eventually mothers, when industrial school boys grew up they would become defenders of the hearth and home, either through wage labour or training and membership in the Naval Reserve. Like girls' schools, boys' institutions operated in what sociologists call the "long shadow of work", basing their regime on training in deference and subordination; qualities the inmates would need as reliable labourers. Boys were not given an education that would enable them to enter secondary schools and thus to rise above their class. Neither were they encouraged to develop an entrepreneurial spirit that might enable them to set up in business on their own. The development of a class consciousness, either through kinship loyalty or participation in class politics such as trade unions or socialist Sunday schools, was also discouraged. Instead, they were encouraged to join politically conservative organizations like the Boys' Brigade or the Scouts. They were becoming not only "workers" but good citizens. According to an industrial school boy, between 1924 and 1933, "You learned to sing 'Rule Britannia' . . . you were brought up strictly as a pure Britisher."[152] Thus, even where a superintendent was willing to admit that he failed to turn out fully qualified apprentices, he was able to argue that the training his boys received corresponded to the larger needs of the economy. The reformed boy was a "Jack-of-all-trades" who could turn his hand to anything. According to one training ship official, "Technical training ought to be planned as to lay a foundation on which any trade may be built; it matters little what one does for a living so long as he is a good citizen."[153]

This does not mean that the moral instruction of the residential school had no immediate domestic role for boys. Boys were definitely encouraged to strike out on their own. On training ships:

> as soon as the boy has learned so much of the calling of a seaman as is sufficient to enable him to act for himself, or be useful on board ship, a berth is found for him . . . it removes the boys . . . from the foul atmosphere and association in which they have either degenerated or been brought up, and cuts them loose from the advice, example and control of their vicious parents.[154]

According to a former residential school headmaster, "These children were being brought up, not to deliberately reject their homes, but they were being brought up to stand totally on their own two feet, that is what was behind it all."[155] Ironically, there is another side to the familial rhetoric. While a bad family had been the cause of delinquency and separation from it was essential, the boys were brought up to be loyal sons. One of the values the regime promoted was a man's responsibility for his female kin, especially his mother. According to Leonore Davidoff and Catherine Hall, by the nineteenth century masculine honour was increasingly equated with independence and this had both political and sexual connotations. "Manhood also implied the ability and the willingness to support and protect women and children."[156] Resolving this was achieved by imagining a special kind of success story. There was, as the annual reports proclaimed, no greater testimony to moral reformation than the training ship boy, "the gallant young tar",[157] who once at sea instructed the captain to forward a portion of his wages home to his widowed mother. "Many a widow's heart sang for the joy that her 'Boy in Blue' had been placed the right way, and was able to earn an honest livelihood for his mother and himself."[158]

Since working wives and mothers were seen as chief causes of delinquency, one of the goals of the boys' institutions was to teach boys to fulfil their manly role as sole providers for their future families. The question of marriage among the working class reveals a class contradiction for much of the Victorian period. It had been observed that while marriage was deferred among the upper classes until men had achieved a comparatively affluent financial status, the very opposite occurred among the lower classes. "Young people, little other than children, without character, without means, without principle, without thought rashly link themselves as man and wife."[159] Marriage was said to be "the normal state of the healthy adult man", but in this health was equated with wealth. In "the better ranks, if two young loving hearts can see their way . . . let them marry . . . It would raise the tone of character of our young men . . . It would draw away all frivolity and effeminacy."[160] While middle-class manliness was equated with early marriage, fatherhood and domestic routine, working-class youth were encouraged to forget about marriage and concentrate on building up a savings account.

> Let the operative class avoid the hasty premature unions . . . as fraught with little else than evil to themselves and others; but

when they have arrived at the marriageable age – say 20 to 25 – when reproduction of the species may be normally performed; when they meet with a loving partner in life in all respects "equal;" and when, by honest industry, they can secure a home for themselves and family . . . Let them marry too, expecting, not in vain the blessings of their betters. To look forward to such a happy lot, nerves the young man's heart to stem the world's tide; and the fire of his pure love will burn too hotly, to brook beside it another flame of mere animal lust. Let young men learn, in sober industry, to fit themselves to be good husbands; and let the community at large help the young women to become good wives, by teaching them . . . household duties, of which the vast majority are deplorably ignorant, but which are quite essential to happiness and security in the married state. Before marriage, let both sexes learn to be industrious and chaste; afterwards they will choose honest labour still, while loathing personal defilement and dishonour.[161]

What such commentators failed to realize, however, was that putting off marriage in favour of saving probably would not have made much difference in the overall standard of living of a family. Another view of the "marriage question" expressed by Fabian Maud Pember Reeves in 1905 was that if marriage was postponed working-class men might become too used to a certain standard of living as bachelors and would be less likely than younger men just moving out of their parents' overcrowded homes to sacrifice it to support others.[162]

Conclusion

The recruitment practices and daily routine suggest that the school administrators were not interested only in producing ideal proletarian subjects from undisciplined inmates, or even proletarian subjects reconciled to their subordinate status; they were producing *female* and *male* proletarians who were to take up quite distinct positions in the class and gender order. These institutions offered a bourgeois model of the "ideal" proletarian family culture, and class-specific ideologies of childhood and adult femininity and masculinity, which were intended to make recalcitrant and saucy girls into docile, submissive daughters and servants, and rough, renegade boys into industrious labourers and loyal sons. Reformed subjectivities were constructed for girls and boys through sex education and work. The way the schools functioned, their power to confine and discipline, their day-to-day management, their programme for moral rehabilitation and the selection of suitable subjects exemplify the value of Foucault's perception that this sexuality was not just condemned or repressed "but managed, inserted into systems of utility, [and] regulated".[163] The problem of sexuality, however, differentiated between boys and girls. There was little overt concern about lesbianism, and boys were not put into institutions to protect them from becoming prostitutes. In boys' institutions the solution to the problem of excessive libidinous energy was not to pathologize it by transferring them to special institutions or refuges, as was the frequently suggested alternative for girls. For boys the solution was sports, youth clubs and sex education. As we have already seen, the problem "of a certain sort" was solved on the training ship by heavy doses of team sports, games, contests and competitions. Boys should be "kept constantly on the go, healthily and happily occupied".[164] Another solution was to get boys involved in youth clubs like the Boys' Brigade or Scouts, or "some healthy pursuit, such as the cultivation of a hobby".[165] It was hoped that by following Scout laws, which encouraged good citizenship, self-reliance, loyalty, thoughtfulness and hygiene, boys in poor areas would stay "out of trouble".[166] According to Frank Mort, "This is the point of entry for militarized conceptions of male sexuality. Obedience to command, rational control over mind and body."[167]

The solution for girls was quite the opposite; for them the outside world was perceived as the danger rather than the solution. Girls' sexuality was seen in almost totally negative terms. "When girls had already become bold and flighty . . . [they had to be] isolated from their friends in order to prevent contamination. Once a girl had 'fallen' there was little to be done other than to contain the danger."[168] The only positive remedy, inherent in her sex education, was preparation for motherhood. Girls were promised definite joys and satisfactions if they conformed to their maternal role. Thus, the schools discouraged precocious sexuality while encouraging a precocious interest in motherhood. In the words of a former residential school headmaster, it was "a very stern Christian, prudish, Victorian motherhood".[169]

Behind the institution's programme of education and training lay the contradiction between the material reproduction of the institution itself and the moral regulation of working-class youth. The strategy the directors followed to resolve this contradiction was to attach a moral significance to work. The directors assigned a moral meaning to certain forms of male and female labour; thus they created not only girls and boys fit for work, but work fit for girls and boys. Although the explicit goal of the child-saving movement was vocational training, this implied an equally important goal: the acquisition of appropriate working-class gender roles. This meant being taught the right sort of work for their class and also their gender. In some areas both the perception of problems and proposed solutions were the same for male and female inmates; they were all regarded as lazy, dishonest, slothful, ignorant and unruly. They all had to act positively, presenting good examples, learning new work habits and self-discipline; however, the work role differed for girls and for boys.

A reformed subjectivity could then be demonstrated in the inmates' outward behaviour, especially in their attitudes towards their families. In the institution's view successfully reformed young people did not go back to their parents unless the authorities approved of their character. Ideally, the reformed girl accepted her place in domestic service, where she would be under the observation of a respectable employer, while the reformed boy struck out on his own, maintaining loyalty to his family without living off them. It is ironic, then, that while the school encouraged girls and boys to reject their real families they were to remain bound to the ideology of familialism.

Chapter 7

❧

Conclusion:
policing gender, class and family

The child-welfare agencies separated children at risk from their parents on the grounds that the home was intolerable. Nevertheless, the statistics from reformatory and industrial schools indicate that almost 30 per cent of the inmates in reformatories and industrial schools returned to their parents following their detention, and hundreds of others drifted home in the years following those spent in the institution. The child-savers admitted to trying to discourage this. One stated that he told a boy on the eve of his release after four years: "Your father doesn't want you, he simply asks you to come to him that he may have your wages."[1] To another boy he said: "You know your father and you know your mother; you know how badly they behaved to you. I do not want you to go to them."[2] A girls' reformatory matron explained: "I can generally talk to the parents . . . and try to make them understand that the girls will do better among strangers than in their old environment."[3] The child-savers were severely disappointed when they learned that an inmate had gone home. While they attributed the decision to "parental interference",[4] this concluding chapter will return to the suggestion that we must think of the institution as a social system of domination and resistance ordered by complex rituals of exchange and communication.[5] The goal of this chapter is to place the foregoing analysis of the child-saving movement into this broader perspective.

The great gulf: the meaning of the street

Have you got children?
"Why, yes, we've at present got three,
And them brats, if they live,
    will all grow up brutes like me;
Their unnatural father ne'er gave them a meal,
They've been bred up from babies, to beg and steal."[6]

The residential school system rested on a great gulf between middle- and working-class subcultures, in particular the middle class's understanding of the working class's way of life. This is illustrated by their tendency to call "pathological" anything that deviated from a very artificial familial ideology. For example, there was the tendency to equate with dishonesty many poor parents' efforts to borrow clothes and furniture from neighbours in order to conceal from various school inspectors and agents their absolute poverty, rather than to recognize this as a struggle to keep their children from being taken into care. On the subject of the behaviour of working-class girls, one female probation officer stressed that they were dealing with a *different* culture, not merely the absence of one; nevertheless, she was unable to resist condemning it, eliding courtship with, if not actual prostitution, "promiscuous intercourse".

If you were out late among young people . . . you would realize they go about together in sort of squads, companies, and they all know perfectly well they are accessible for this abominable purpose, and then they pair off . . . but there is no soliciting. It is a sort of mutual consent. It is really a form of pastime. They don't do it for money but they get boxes of chocolates and things of that kind, fish dinners and nights at the theatre and bits of finery and that sort. It is all very revolting, but it is so. They do this sort of thing for fun.[7]

In discussions of the overcrowded houses of the poor the child-savers were quick to equate the number of beds in a house with incest rather than poverty, which reveals their tendency to believe the very worst about the living habits of the poor. More sympathetic female child-savers cautioned, however: "You have to be very careful that you are not unjust to them."[8] According to Dorothea Maitland the problem was to do with the "housing question"; where a large family is forced to live in a single room "they cannot all have separate beds".[9] A probation officer, Mary Hill, stated that "Even if there is a large family, some of them, although they are very crowded and that sort of thing, are taught from the very beginning about truth and honesty."[10] A female inspector for the Society for the Prevention of Cruelty to Children also understood the twin problems of poverty and alcoholism sociologically. She recognized the existence of a poverty cycle. According to her, the social problems were due less to drink itself than to "unhealthy and unsanitary living conditions"; in other words, the "conditions" in which people drank. Excessive drinking was only a symptom of a larger social problem. She predicted that as long as "slum areas" continued to exist one would find a "vicious circle".[11]

Archival data and oral testimony support evidence from other studies of working-class culture that the working class was perfectly capable of making distinctions between "rough" and "respectable" class cultures. Linda Gordon argues that traditional forms of social control (community gossip or private intervention) were no more tolerant of individual liberty or deviance than the modern bureaucratic state and its professions.[12] In a brave effort to "protect them from the cruelty of others"[13] it was frequently the parents, and especially single parents, who initiated their daughters' committal to these institutions. In 1880 15-year-old Mary Louise was sent to the Edinburgh Magdalene Asylum by her widowed mother, who claimed she had "lost control of her".[14] In 1920 Lizzy Fuller's mother, whom the school register described as a "drunkard", took her "dirty . . . verminous" young daughters down to the police station, and reported that someone had been sexually assaulting the eldest of them. Little came of the charge, but her six-year-old was placed in an industrial school until she was 16 years old and thereby protected from an environment that her mother realized was unsafe.[15]

The poor had their own definitions of acceptable and unacceptable behaviour, and these differed from those of the middle class. As Sean Damer has recently pointed out, the Scottish poor "knew perfectly well what was wrong with their existence". Nobody in their "right mind wanted to live in a slum tenement".[16] He argues that tenement life has to be understood dialectically:

the good and the bad, the progressive and the reactionary, the humour and the tears, the struggle and the defeat, the courage and the cowardice, the slum and the palace, were part and parcel of the same phenomenon. Virtue and evil co-existed in the tenement; they faced each other across a landing.[17]

The patterns of behaviour that many poor families exhibited were often consonant with their values and with rational survival strategies in the hostile city. The pre-industrial family economy was only a generation away for many of the migrant families coming from the Highlands or Ireland, and it was one that depended on the labour of all its members. It was quite different from the bourgeois ideal of prolonged or permanent economic dependence for women and children. What was seen by working-class parents as proper initiative and responsibility – for instance, when a son sold newspapers or a daughter sang outside a bar for pennies – was evidence of neglect, cruelty or immorality as far as the child-savers were concerned. In the case of child rearing, middle-class and working-class subcultures saw quite different meanings in the street. The middle class could see no reason for simply "being in the street". According to one female probation officer in the 1920s, the working class had "extraordinary standards about allowing their children to roam about at all hours". She testified that she had "visited houses at 9 o'clock at night [and found] children on the stairs playing, and the parents do not trouble anything about them".[18]

Although offensive to middle-class sensibilities, the streets offered poor families resources for entertainment, companionship and survival.[19] The street was not necessarily a place of danger and temptation, as the middle class characterized it. For the Scottish working class of all ages, a great deal of leisure time was spent in the street: "When housing was uncomfortable or overcrowded, promenading in the streets became a pleasurable pastime."[20] Clearly, for the working class the street was a place for socializing. It was quite acceptable to allow children to play in the street as, before 1930, there were no private gardens and few neighbourhood playgrounds. Homes were far too small, dark, cramped and unsafe for children to be able to play and amuse themselves indoors. It was not a sign of neglect that your children were in the street; where else would they be? But from the middle-class point of view, for girls to be *in* the street was just a step away from being *on* the street. Amid the undeniable poverty the pleasures of the street were free: a game of football, a gossip on a common stair, music and dancing or cuddling in a close were all pastimes that the middle class tended to pathologize or criminalize. This is not to suggest that certain children were not being neglected, beaten and abused – obviously they were – but to focus entirely on a middle-class definition of the situation is to overlook the fact that the working class had their own strategies for dealing with their own problems.

The working-class family: accommodation and resistance

In order to examine these contradictions more closely we must examine the meaning of the child-saving movement more completely, particularly the parents' role in the process. Michael Ignatieff argues that the poor "were not passive victims and objects of the law: they used it for their purposes if they could".[21] M. A. Crowther's study of English workhouses suggests that while "the poor were suspicious of institutions", they supported them: "New hospital beds were filled as soon as possible; pressure on asylums and charitable homes continued to grow."[22] The historian Bettina Bradbury has argued that in Montreal the poor developed a variety of survival strategies to cope with poverty, unemployment, illness and death. "When the future seemed particularly bleak and impossible" some parents gave up their children, temporarily or permanently, to kin, orphanages and other institutions, some "taking them back again when the crisis passed or when they were old enough to work".[23] Some Scottish families turned to these institutions in times of need, as a former industrial day school girl in 1925 explained: "We lost my mother and my daddy had to work and he was so independent he wouldn't leave us running around for neighbours to look after us . . . He found out about this school . . . on his own."[24]

This is not to suggest that institutionalization did not damage intrafamilial relations, even though the family tie remained. Reflecting upon how the years he spent in a reformatory between 1927 and 1934 affected his relationship with his mother, a former inmate revealed: "Honest to God, I think it did me the world of good . . . I finally got rid of my parents . . . It stopped all the [drunken] carry on."[25] In other cases, where children were already suffering from poverty and hunger, their parents' surrender of them to custodial care actually favoured the survival of the family unit. According to one of three brothers who were placed in an industrial school in 1924:

> It was that or the graveyard . . . we were so poor. We were in for neglect . . . They wanted to keep the three of us [boys] together . . . They took us to court one day. Somebody had reported us . . . They reported that we were eatin' out of the bins . . . [If] one of us got a bun or something we'd eat half and bring the other half home to see if anybody else hadn't got anything because we had to live together . . . but in the end they came along and put us into Mossbank which was the best thing . . . [Mother] knew she couldn't do anything. She couldn't even pay the rent.[26]

In contrast to her contemporaries' suspicions that the poor purposefully neglected their children in order to qualify them for industrial schools, Frances Hepburn of the Society for the Prevention of Cruelty to Children observed that while many parents in dire straits "greatly objected to their children being sent to the industrial schools" they understood that it was best for the child.[27] According to the Secretary of the National Vigilance Association, however:

> The position varies very much. There is a certain amount of affection, even in the worst homes . . . it is really quite surprising. When you look at the way in which many of them treat their children . . . not actually ill-treat them but neglect them, you wonder at the amount of affection there seems to be underneath it, especially on the children's side.[28]

Some parents would be "thankful for the help, and others prefer to look after them themselves".[29] Such observations suggest that a more useful perspective may be to see working-class family life in terms of a "culture of survival",[30] in which the daily struggle to make ends meet might mean resorting to the pawnshop, the parish or, in extreme cases, the children's court.

The child-saving movement was one force among others in a highly contested political arena. Admittedly, there was no evidence of anything like a tenants' or prisoners' rights movement developing but this must not be taken as evidence of working-class passivity or fatalism, let alone acceptance. Vulnerable family members quickly learned how to play the institution's game in order to aid their kin. A polite note to a member of the Home Office or a school board official might ensure that a poor mother could visit her boy. One woman wrote: "I am writing in regards to my boy . . . I don't wish him put too far away from home as I couldn't afford the expenses to go to see him."[31] The otherwise costly emigration process might also be set in motion, as the following letter from a "concerned" uncle reveals:

> In regards to William Bain one of your boys his father was killed in France . . . he has an aunt in Sydney Australia anxious to get him as she has a good home for him . . . I hope you will send him to Mossbank until we see what can be done to get him out to Sydney and if you could do anything to assist him in getting out it would be a great favour as there are so many boys going idle in Glasgow and I have 5 of family of my own.[32]

This analysis does not mean that the residential and day school systems acquired consensual support among the working class. Clearly they did not, as this "valentine" sent to the Scottish Education Department by a "village mother" on the occasion of the closure of the *Empress* training ship in 1923 illustrates.

> I wish to thank you for removing the *Empress* Training Ship . . . It makes the shores dirty and unhealthy. The boys land so seldom it must be very bad for them. The officers do so little work it is bad for the other men in the village . . . Why should the rate payer keep it up . . . Why should boys of 14 not be made to work. The village mothers cannot afford to keep their boys at school until they are 16.[33]

What this does indicate is that the problem of child welfare was a process in which the state, ruling class and dominated classes all participated. The residential and day school systems and child protection agencies worked on two levels: to rescue children from families in trouble, and, in cases where the family was still functioning, to serve as a (symbolic) reminder of bourgeois child-rearing expectations.[34] Agents of the Society for the Prevention of Cruelty to Children like Frances Hepburn observed that they had "a certain amount of weight and good deal of influence with parents"; and she used this power as a means of enforcing her wishes on parents: "Sometimes, if they give trouble, they are simply referred to the [temporary] shelter, and they do not give any further trouble after they have paid one visit there."[35] In fact, she recognized that people feared the Society and the inspectors were consequently very well received into some of the homes of the poor. "Those that really want to do better look upon our inspectors as friends, and especially the women inspectors, and they welcome them to their homes ... Of course, those who do not wish to do well receive us because they are afraid of us."[36] The industrial day school girl previously quoted recalled that it was fear that led her father to enrol his daughters of 9 and 11 years old in an industrial day school after their mother's death in 1925.

> That is why my father put us in the school. "If I don't [he said] they will take my weans off me." ... So he put us in that school ... Oh aye, he was worried, he didn't want his family sent away fa him ... if he had went to his work, and left us running about the street, and no doubt somebody would have reported it, and they'd have ... said well you're workin' and cannae look after them, and take them away ... They would take you quicker then, than they would do now.[37]

The majority of children were admitted to institutions on the basis of recommendation of magistrates and other formal institutions. There is abundant evidence that figures such as "the cruelty people"[38] and the parish inspectors were seen as intrusive and unwelcome visitors. A Glasgow woman who grew up on parish assistance in the early years of this century recollects that her mother would treat the family to sausages on Thursdays, the day she received her money.

> He [the inspector] [would] be up at the house, saying: "You're living high today!" "Well," [mother says] "if I can't give my family a bloody decent meal when I get my money I'm a poor mother." That's the words she used to him ... you see they kept tabs on ya ... It was just the way of livin' then. Oh, they had a lot of power over ya, they could take your children off you ... They could take them, quite simple and [put them] in a home.[39]

Many former inmates of industrial schools and magdalene homes believe that they brought up their own children very strictly, out of fear that if they misbehaved they might be taken from them. Of course, these parenting methods would have been applauded by the child-savers, because they represented the adoption of family-centred values and priorities. For people with children in residential care, compliance with the institution's wishes was often their only guarantee of continued contact with their children. One super-intendent confessed that she assessed parents' suitability by their behaviour on monthly visiting days. "If the parents are good", she remarked, "I always let them know about [the licence], but if they are bad I do not".[40]

The children: subcultures of resistance

The child-savers tended to regard the affection of these children for their parents as pathological. They could not make sense of it within the framework of their own cultural milieu, nor understand why it was so difficult to destroy. Reflecting on the close bonds between Scottish children and their parents, the captain of the *Empress* training ship in 1896 declared: "You will never get a boy to say he does not want to go to them – not in Scotland; never. I have heard it very often in England but I have never had it in Scotland."[41] This impression was shared by the captain of the *Mars* in 1920, who noted that "family affection amongst the working classes in Scotland, is developed, to a degree which cannot be surpassed, and children as a rule still believe in the sacred obligation to assist their parents where help is required".[42] Obviously the children did not perceive the "danger" in the same way their would-be protectors did. The reformatory and industrial school superintendents had observed that many of the children felt "homesick and miserable for the first few days".[43] Most were lonely and "long for home".[44] This point is illustrated in the semi-autobiographical account of the Scottish author Jessie Kesson. On Janie's first night in "The Orphanage" in Aberdeenshire in the 1920s:

> All things seemed unreal to Janie. The dormitory most of all
> . . . She felt her head, still with a small sense of shock, although
> it had been shaved hours ago . . . If I got one wish I'd just ask
> for all my hair back again. No, I wouldn't. I'd just ask to get
> home to my Mam again. Not having any hair wouldn't matter
> if I could just get home again.[45]

The child-saving movement did not deal with families on the families' own terms. Whereas modern social work has developed counselling and group therapy to deal with what are now called "dysfunctional" families, the early residential school system elected to treat children as individuals or cases. Thus, they directed their energy towards creating "healthy" families for the future rather than tackling the "unhealthy" families of the present. The institutions developed their own definitions of target populations and strategies for interpreting a family's needs, and positioned parents and children as clients or subjects of their regime of moral reform.

For the most part, the child-savers realized that the children regarded being sent to residential school "as a punishment".[46] Many children clearly knew nothing about what was happening until "they were suddenly taken to the court",[47] and the circumstances surrounding the warrant and the court appearance were almost always negative. Probation officers in the 1920s observed that most of the children had very little explained to them – "as a rule we find that children have been brought to the courts rather hurriedly" – and knew very little about what was happening to them.

> They have had rather a shock and have been bustled out to us, also apparently rather hurriedly, and have been, as it were torn away from their parents. They are not very happy and rather up against things generally when they arrive, and we have to overcome that little prejudice before we can do anything with them. We have to make them fond of the place.[48]

The lack of information and the associated anxiety and depression it caused are clearly illustrated in this exchange between Janie and Peggy, two girls in a children's home in Kesson's novel:

> "When will I get home? I've asked everybody. The Court Man and the Vigilance Officer and Mrs Thane and just everybody. They all let on they don't hear me. But somebody must know when?"
>
> "When you're sixteen, most likely." . . .
>
> "But that's ages!" Janie's distress increased. "That's just years and years. I'm not nine yet . . ."
>
> "My Mam could die by that time . . ."
>
> "I know what I'll do. I'll mark every day off on the calendar till I'm sixteen. It will pass quicker that way."
>
> "That's what I thought when I first came, Janie. Then I just forgot . . ."
>
> "I won't forget." Janie felt very certain. "I'll never forget . . ."[49]

A former inmate of a magdalene home also recalled being made "confused and angry" by the events surrounding her placement in Lochburn in 1944 at the age of 16. She claimed that she had been employed as a nanny in a respectable house in Aberdeen when somehow her parents learned that she had a boyfriend. A probation officer was contacted and he arranged for her to be committed to Lochburn. "She had to go through the horrible process of being examined by a police surgeon and going to court, before she was given a two year sentence in Lochburn."[50] She recalled the humiliating experience of being escorted by train to Glasgow with the probation officer.

Making children "fond of the place" turned out to be quite a challenge for most superintendents. Ample evidence suggests that very few children ever became enamoured with their circumstances. Interviews with former students and an examination of the punishment books suggest the operation of what Paul Willis calls "countercultural resistance" in reformatories and industrial schools. Acts of resistance ranged from innocuous gestures like swearing at or disobeying teachers to absconding and overt acts of aggression which justified the need for strict discipline and corporal punishment. On 6 June 1876 subscribers to the *Daily Telegraph* read about an "epidemic of discontent and insubordination" on the *Mars* training ship. The editorial stated that "eleven lads made a daring escape from the 'Mars' Training Ship having evaded the watch and rowed ashore. Most of the lads were captured, and they confessed that if they had not succeeded in escaping they intended to set fire to the ship."[51] On 8 October 1876 "in consequence of something which the officer said" the boys on the *Cumberland* training ship "locked the captain in his cabin, broke into the storeroom, and feasted till morning".[52] On 8 April 1878 "a serious riot occurred" at the Glasgow Boys' Reformatory

when the acting governor was severely assaulted and wounded . . . Many windows were broken and much furniture smashed. Having armed themselves with broken pieces of furniture, the rioters kept possession of the building until the police arrived . . . The cause of the break out [was] . . . the punishment of one of the boys.[53]

Another riot at the Boys' Reformatory occurred on 18 January 1882, when "50 out of 130 boys took part in the disturbance, which resulted in a considerable destruction of window glass, crockery, and other property . . . A strong detachment of police was required to guard the Institution."[54] On 18 February 1889 the *Cumberland* training ship was totally destroyed by a fire started by four inmates.[55] In some cases resistance turned to tragedy; three boys from the *Mars* training ship drowned during an escape attempt in 1870. Accounts of sensational riots in juvenile reformatories continued into this century, and they are made all the more significant when it is emphasized that this was a generation of young people who "were not known to protest".[56]

There is a wide body of social scientific literature to support the view that home-based factors such as domestic violence, alcoholism and extreme poverty are associated with behavioural and learning difficulties among children. Another body of literature suggests that certain forms of behaviour may "represent a rational and legitimate response to an oppressive environment".[57] Girls and boys in reformatories and industrial schools adopted a variety of strategies for resisting the institutions' education, training and discipline. These ranged from fighting, vandalism and absconding to passive resistance such as the "non-listening syndrome": the "silence behind which an unprepared, unwilling student can retreat".[58] The teacher becomes a ridiculous, futile figure who responds with condescension towards the student. Passive resistance can be more frustrating for teachers to deal with than more extreme forms of misbehavior because it forces them to examine their own pedagogical skills. As indicated in Chapter 5, teachers commonly responded to resistance by denigrating the intelligence and ability of the pupils. Willis's studies of repressive school cultures document the emergence of a dormitory subculture that enables inmates to keep their personal identities intact while providing a release from the regimented routine of daily living.[59] Interviews with former residential school children support this observation. The school becomes a battleground between class and regional cultures. Whatever form the resistance takes, the teachers attribute it to inmates' family background – immoral attitudes, emotional instability, poor genetic endowment – and not to the school's oppressive regime.[60]

In girls' schools the interaction between middle-class women and female inmates demonstrates another form of resistance. Women child-savers often identified male brutality, desertion and drunkenness as the special problems of the women and children, who had to cope with their consequences. But the majority remained bound by ideologies of gender, class and family, and various beliefs about what constituted appropriate work for women and ideal family relations. Unlike middle-class girls, who enjoyed leisure and the protection of a well-appointed family circle far into their twenties, working-class girls were expected to be wage-earners in their teens.[61] The "conception of passive womanhood" espoused in these institutions was totally alien to lower-class inmates. "It had no relationship to girls accustomed to free, independent childhood."[62] In spite of the growing demand for both skilled and unskilled female labour in the factories and the new light industries, especially after the First World War, domestic service continued to be looked upon as the best means of rescuing girls from their plight. Some female social workers recognized that domestic service was not a realistic option for all girls; many girls were "terribly opposed to the mention of domestic service".[63] The female health inspector at an industrial school in Aberdeen testified that there were inmates who were unfit for service. "They drift to the mills, or become what is known in Aberdeen as fish girls."[64] A former industrial day school girl recalled that when she left school in 1916 she could not go into service because her mother wanted her to earn higher wages, so she took a job in a carpet factory.[65] Other girls simply refused to go into service, preferring to go to "work and have their evenings free".[66] A former inmate of Lochburn magdalene home recalled that the inmates taught themselves to faint in order to get themselves out of the laundry work.[67] Nevertheless, the regime of girls' schools continued to focus on domestic training and housewifery rather than training for the trades that the girls were determined to enter.

By the period following the Second World War it was admitted that while girls and young women continued to be taken out of the community for their own protection "it didn't work that way". The experience of being in a reformatory, possibly for years, affected girls in ways "that did not affect boys". It was the opinion of a former headmaster that the education and training the girls received in the schools did not prevent them from falling into "loose living, early marriage, lots of children . . . I think part of it is due to the fact that they were taken away . . . So for the best will in the world, they [the schools] were trying to be kind, but in actual fact in many ways they were creating the climate."[68]

The social and the policing of sexuality, class and family

The child-saving movement was informed by particular discourses and ideologies of the prison, the school, the family, the market and the street. This created a distinct and novel social domain. It was both a new physical space (the reform school) and a set of new forms of knowledge and techniques of power (the regime) that produced a new body of experts (the child-savers) and new clients (the delinquent "family") for surveillance and control. Child-saving institutions operated with particular views about the causes and treatment of delinquency; and gender, class and sexuality were implicated in, and produced by, the theories and practices.

This book has focused on the juvenile reformatory system as a social control mechanism. The reformatory represented the intersection of a number of discourses relating to sexuality, class, gender and the family. Seen from the vantage-point of criticisms of the social as outlined in Chapter 1 and an analysis of the existing literature on the family, the school and the prison, combined with archival data and interviews with former inmates and staff, a broader definition of the social has been constructed. This conceptualization of the social supports feminist commentators such as Michèle Barrett and Mary McIntosh, who reject Foucault's implicit functionalism and Donzelot's conspiracy theory.[69] The preferred framework is the socialist–feminist perspective where ideologies of welfarism are seen as more than just covert mechanisms of social control. The social is not necessarily invasive: it represents, according to Nancy Fraser, the failure of currently constituted market and family institutions to recognize and meet people's needs; and the failure of a criminal justice system, with its bourgeois and patriarchal notions of property and contract, to deliver social justice.[70] To say this might appear to risk naturalizing notions of "needs", but needs are socially and historically constructed. For example, the discovery by the child-savers of the need for children to be protected from their own families suggests that needs, rights and duties can be irreconcilable. Any alliance such as the one which Donzelot claims to have uncovered between the middle-class mother/wife and the new breed of family experts is better conceived as an instrumental and unstable relationship, subject to conflict and reinterpretation. This is particularly apparent in the case of the child-saving movement, when we consider the extent to which the reform school system and its conceptions of delinquency and reform hinged on gendered and sexualized identities which were apparent within the institution, but also existed beyond its confines.[71] This analysis allows us to see the process whereby various state and voluntary agencies emerged to take control of areas, such as family life, which previously were defined as private.

Fraser has examined the contrast between two types of programs. Rights-based programmes, such as unemployment benefits, are those where the client is considered to have a legitimate claim on certain benefits, based, for example, on the contributions made while in employment. Needs-based programmes are those where the client is treated more as a recipient of state welfare or charity, dependent on conformity with administratively defined criteria of needs. In this research on late-nineteenth- and early-twentieth-century social welfare programmes for families it has been demonstrated that the "needs" of different family members might conflict. The working-class child was a "useful", resourceful child who could earn a few pennies and still get to school on time. When the demands of the school conflicted with parents' expectations and the child was absent or tardy, the truancy man entered the scene, and the result might mean a reform school for the child or probation for the family. There was also a different conception of need among working-class parents from that recognized by the child-savers, which led to tension regarding the disposition of the children. One feature of needs-type programmes, however, are the moralizing and therapeutic elements in their provision. Having a particular need that neither the market nor the household could meet was conceptualized as the result of "moral deficiency" in the individual or family unit.

The social is then both an ideological space and a material space. It is the arena of a rubric of laws, regulations, rules, policies and institutions. In this case, these are the certified residential schools and rescue homes for the education and industrial training, moral regulation, surveillance and sexual control of working-class girls and boys. The regime, administered by women and men with distinct and complementary roles, prefigured the roles that inmates were to take up in adult life. During the late nineteenth century and the early years of this century there emerged an idealized version of the Christian home, which was seen as the root of national strength and virtue. According to the supporters of the parish strategy, total separation from parents via boarding-out in a pastoral setting was all that was required for moral regulation. Supporters of reformatory schools favoured limited contact with parents and institutionalization, arguing that the most beneficial elements of family life could be replicated by surveillance and discipline within the institution. In contrast, supporters of industrial day schools argued for limited incarceration, where children were locked in the school only during the school hours. It was hoped that if the children were given supervision and moral guidance during the day they could continue to live with their parents and by their good manners and model behaviour set an example for the rest of the family to follow. Finally, under the probation system, which appears to circumvent the institution altogether, we find that the home actually became an institution where the probation officer practised his or her disciplinary craft on the entire family. Thus, each institution deployed its own ideology, replicating class and patriarchal relations, which influenced legislation and the formation of new institutions, which in turn developed their own familial ideologies.

The social is also closely linked with the rise of the professional experts whose intention is to administer it. But it is not just a repressive sphere; it is also a productive space, a site of contestation. Nobody has absolute authority over the social. It is the terrain where opposition, rebellion and resistance are produced. Obviously no simple class and gender dichotomies can be drawn in this analysis of child-saving agencies. Dominance and resistance can be observed at all levels. Middle-class child-savers united against working-class parents in an effort to protect working-class children, especially girls, from the dangerous streets and in some cases from their own homes. Middle-class women resisted conservative definitions of themselves and their social role; meanwhile working-class parents and children were active, not passive, participants in the process. The social is also the site of discourses about people's needs, specifically about those needs that have broken out of the domestic and/or economic institutions of male-dominated capitalist societies that earlier contained them as "private matters",[72] such as poor women's need to be protected from domestic violence. One of the ways this can occur is through "the state" taking responsibility for matters previously left to the family. The process politicizes the needs, or de-naturalizes them, which may foster "their further politicization".[73]

Stanley Cohen has argued that the history of the nineteenth-century transformation in social control apparatus has been written. However, few histories employ a gender analysis that uses both femininity and masculinity as analytical concepts to examine the production of a juvenile delinquent or to explore the production and implication of gendered "normal and delinquent" sexualities. Implicit in much of what has been written is a set of discourses about adolescent and adult sexuality, which marked homosexuality as the "deviant" behaviour for boys, and for girls precocious promiscuous heterosexuality. Adoption of the view that identities always rest on the negation or repression of something defined as "other" allows us to focus more productively on conflicts over their meaning and to view the social as one of the key sites where conflict and resistance are enacted.

It is now commonplace in the history of sexualities to conceptualize the "homosexual" as a historically constructed role rather than a natural, formed character. To track a "deviant" sexuality for women is to follow a different course, marked not so much by who did what with whom as by doing it too often or too early. If the homosexual is proper masculinity's other, prefigured by the masturbator, the prostitute is proper femininity's other, prefigured by the wayward girl. Although precocious or excessive heterosexual activity was not condoned for boys, it was never condemned in the way that it was for girls. Over the period of this study the language of gender and sexuality remained an integral part of the child-saving movement. While definitions of the causes of juvenile delinquency shifted from a language of "sin" to the influence of Victorian environmentalism and, later, to "moral deficiency" in the discourses of eugenics and impaired "ideal-ego-formation" in psychology, a recurring theme was the deviant sexuality of the girl. Whether cast as a victim of her environment, her genes or her psychological maladjustment, the "vicious girl" continued to manifest problems for herself and others largely through her promiscuous adventures. She persisted in the contamination of others, if not through her "moral pollution" then by transmitting a "culture of poverty" to her children. The folk devil of conservative propaganda today, the single mother, would be a girl immediately recognizable to the Victorian child-savers. She appears in the British rhetoric as the teenage mum who jumps the public housing queues by deliberately getting pregnant. In the United States, according to former Vice-President Dan Quayle, the single mother is responsible for inner-city violence, especially if she is African-American, by raising a generation of fatherless boys. In sum, where she once played a role in reproducing a *lumpen* proletariat or "residuum", a category of physical, mental and moral degenerates, she is now the reproducer of an underclass. In all cases, though, she is blamed for the delinquency of future generations, unwilling or unable to teach her children right from wrong, since she scarcely knows the meaning of it herself. Like her ancestors, by revealing her needs or having them exposed she risks losing custody of her children.

For a special class of girl on the run from male abuse and violence, the juvenile reformatory provided a refuge and a way out, but institutionalization is no guarantee against physical or sexual abuse. In one respect, the institutional practices revealed in this book may have protected some female inmates. The single-sex environments sheltered girls from harassing taunts, wolf-whistles, insults, assaults and "normal" male behaviour that presented problems for girls, but this entailed not permitting them on the street in the first place. The well-publicized cases of the failure of child-protection agencies today has its roots in the nineteenth-century child welfare ideologies and practices. This study suggests that not only did violence and assault continue in the institutions but that the current disclosure of assault and abuse in children's homes reveals a very old problem. "Unnatural" (that is, homosexual) practices featured more often in the list of vices to which boys might be subjected than they did for girls. But the unchallenged assumption that male sexuality was somehow more "natural", including autoerotic and homoerotic behaviour, may well have contributed to the institutionalization of predatory behaviours that were nonconsensual and coercive, redeemed only by the blind eye sometimes turned to boy–boy love affairs. The coincident construction of nonmarital or nonheterosexual sexual activity as "evil" and "filthy", however, turned any type of sexual activity into a dirty secret, something to be ashamed of whether it was consensual or not.

Clearly, for generations of children no refuge was ever found. Since early in this century the juvenile reformatory has become entrenched as part of the disciplinary continuum, sweeping up ever-increasing categories of subjects in its drive, paradoxically to prevent them from entering the penal system. Today, the legacy of these grim hard institutions continues. Modern parents still jokingly threaten mischievous and misbehaving children with a trip to see "Dr Barnardo". More seriously, real fear on the part of many of the poor that their children might be placed "in care" casts its shadow over parent–child relations as another generation learns to fantasize, fear and fight the archipelago of confinement.

Appendix A

॰୫

Admission statistics

Table A.1   Industrial school (Scotland) admissions, 1894/5.

Statute	Boys		Girls			
	Total	%	Total	%	Total	%
Begging	107	14.61	30	12.14	137	13.99
Found wandering	337	46.03	145	58.70	482	49.23
Destitute/orphan	49	6.69	36	14.57	85	8.68
Frequenting company of thieves	131	17.89	8	3.23	139	14.19
Residing in brothel or with prostitutes	6	0.81	12	4.85	18	1.83
Charged with crime	54	7.37	6	2.42	60	6.12
Uncontrollable (parents)	17	2.32	7	2.83	24	2.45
Refractory paupers	1	0.13	–	–	1	0.10
Education Act (truancy)	2	0.27	–	–	2	0.20
Education Act (wandering)	1	0.13	1	0.40	2	0.20
Misbehaving in day industrial school	27	3.68	2	0.80	29	2.96
Total	32	99.93	247	99.94	979	99.65

Source: calculated from reports of Royal Commission on Reformatories and Industrial Schools 1896–7, Appendix V, Table XLVI, p. 211.

Table A.2   Previous convictions for girls and boys admitted to Scottish reformatories, 1861/2 to 1898/9.

Convictions	1861–4 %	1865–74 %	1875–84 %	1885–94 %	1895–8 %	Total %
None						
boys	53.38	60.89	47.99	26.78	14.76	40.76
girls	80.08	76.63	72.01	67.09	51.96	69.55
One						
boys	32.79	30.03	36.72	40.58	41.61	36.34
girls	15.19	19.24	22.64	25.48	41.17	24.74
Two						
boys	10.03	7.32	11.55	19.58	27.38	15.17
girls	3.28	3.26	4.07	4.83	6.89	4.46
Three						
boys	2.23	1.41	2.62	8.58	10.87	5.14
girls	0.40	0.80	0.76	0.96	–	0.38
Four						
boys	1.14	0.22	0.52	3.00	4.96	1.96
girls	1.02	–	0.25	0.64	–	1.91
Five and over						
boys	0.40	0.09	0.57	1.47	0.13	0.53
girls	–	–	0.25	0.96	–	0.24

Source: calculated from the annual reports of Industrial and Reformatory School Inspectors, 1861–2 to 1898–9.
1861 was the first year these data were published in the annual reports.

Table A.3 Age at admission of girls and boys in Scottish industrial schools, 1868–9 to 1898–9.

Age	1868–74 %	1875–84 %	1885–94 %	1895–8 %	Total %
Under 6					
boys	–	–	0.02	0.15	0.13
girls	–	–	0.35	4.84	1.29
6–8					
boys	9.98	7.88	7.03	5.93	7.70
girls	24.08	22.04	19.92	16.10	20.53
8–10					
boys	20.79	17.30	16.39	16.42	17.72
girls	30.77	27.40	24.24	23.81	26.55
10–12					
boys	29.04	35.37	38.03	39.76	35.55
girls	30.37	31.29	27.81	28.95	29.60
12–14					
boys	40.17	39.43	38.50	37.36	38.86
girls	15.13	19.39	27.65	26.28	22.11

Source: calculated from the annual reports of Industrial and Reformatory School Inspector, 1868–9 to 1898–9.
Not including inmates transferred from "other institutions".

Table A.4 Age at admission of girls and boys in Scottish reformatories, 1861–2 to 1898–9.

Age	1861–4* %	1865–74 %	1875–84 %	1885–94 %	1895–8 %	Total %
Under 10						
boys	4.81	2.28	1.86	2.56	3.89	3.08
girls	3.49	1.54	1.52	0.64	–	1.44
10–12						
boys	19.43	22.57	21.01	19.91	18.38	20.26
girls	16.01	12.88	12.21	6.45	8.82	11.27
12–14						
boys	38.81	41.34	40.54	38.07	41.74	40.10
girls	37.98	43.64	37.91	39.03	47.05	41.22
14–16						
boys	36.92	33.79	36.58	39.44	36.37	36.62
girls	42.50	42.09	48.34	53.87	44.11	46.18

Source: calculated from the annual reports of the Industrial and Reformatory School Inspector, 1861–2 to 1898–9.
*1861 was the first year these data was published in the annual reports.
Not including inmates transferred from "other institutions".

Appendix B

❧

Scottish institutions

Table B.1 Certified reformatory schools for boys.

Name	Town	Year founded	No. of beds	Boys' ages
Kibble RS	Paisley	1859	120	12–16
Parkhead RS	Glasgow	1859	200	12–16
Rossie RS	Forfar	1857	90	12–15
Stranraer RS	Wigtown	1850	90	10–16
Wellington RS	Midlothian	1859	110	11–15

Source: Reformatory and Refuge Union, *The classified list of child-saving institutions*, 1912, p. 80.

Table B.2 Certified industrial schools for boys.

Name	Town	Year founded	No. of beds	Boys' ages
Arbroath IS	Arbroath	1855	60	7–16
Ayr IS	Ayr	1848	100	8–12
Clyde Training Ship	Helensburgh	1869	400	11–14
Dumfries IS	Dumfries	1847	120	6–10
Dundee IS	Dundee	1846	200	8–10
Edinburgh Original Ragged IS	Midlothian	1847	200	6–12
Edinburgh Working Boys' Home (RC)	Edinburgh	1891	60	14
Fechney IS	Perth	1843	150	8–13
Mossbank IS	Glasgow	1847	375	8–14
Glasgow ITS	Glasgow	1905	160	10–14
Greenock IS	Greenock	1849	150	9–12
Leith CIS	Leith	1861	135	6–14
Mars Training Ship	Dundee	1869	400	11–14
Oakbank IS	Aberdeen	1841	250	10–12
Paisley IS	Paisley	1847	150	6–14
St Joseph's CIS	Lothian	1889	200	9–13
St Mary's IS	Glasgow	1833	200	7–15
Slatefield IS	Glasgow	1867	150	10–15

Source: Reformatory and Refuge Union, *The classified list of child-saving institutions*, 1912, pp. 80–81.

Table B.3 Certified reformatory schools for girls.

Name	Town	Year founded	No. of beds	Boys' ages
Dalry House Training School	Midlothian	1858	45	under 15
East Chapelton RS	Glasgow	1840	60	under 16

Source: Reformatory and Refuge Union, *The classified list of child-saving institutions*, 1912, p. 82.

Table B.4 Certified industrial schools for girls.

Name	Town	Year founded	No. of beds	Girls' ages
Aberdeen IS	Aberdeen	1877	150	7–16
Ayr IS	Ayr	1848	60	8–12
Dalbeth IS	Glasgow	1858	150	6–10
Dundee, Balgay IS	Dundee	1846	120	6–16
Edinburgh Original IS	Edinburgh	1847	75	6–10
Girls' School of Industry	Perth	1842	60	7–10
Greenock IS	Greenock	1897	40	8–12
House of Refuge for Destitute Girls	Perth	1843	60	6–12
IS for Girls	Stirling	1849	30	8–16
Maryhill IS	Glasgow	1847	200	9–14
Newton Stewart Girls Home	Wigton	1860	50	5–12
Orphanage and IS	Glasgow	1833	200	7–15
St Mary's IS (RC)	Glasgow	1862	190	9–15
Victoria CIS	Leith	1867	60	8–12
Whitehall IS	Aberdeen	1841	80	10–14

Source: Reformatory and Refuge Union, *The classified list of child-saving institutions*, 1912, p. 82.

Table B.5 Day industrial school for girls.

Name	Town	Year founded	No. of beds	Girls' ages
Waverley Park Home	Kirkintilloch	1906	40	under 16

Source: Reformatory and Refuge Union, *The classified list of child-saving institutions*, 1912, p. 82.

Table B.6 Voluntary homes for girls.

Name	Town	Year founded	No. of beds	Girls' ages
Dean Bank Institution	Edinburgh	1832	35	8–13
Greenside Industrial School	Edinburgh	1873	40	5
Home for Working Girls	Edinburgh	1896	20	over 15

Source: Reformatory and Refuge Union, *The classified list of child-saving institutions*, 1912, p. 82.

Table B.7   Certified industrial school for boys and girls.

Name	Town	Year founded	No. of beds	Children's ages
Industrial school	Kirkintilloch	1855	105	8–16

Source: Reformatory and Refuge Union, *The classified list of child-saving institutions*, 1912, p. 84.

Table B.8   Certified day industrial schools for boys and girls.

Name	Town	Year founded	No. of beds	Children's ages
Edinburgh DIS (St John's)	Edinburgh	1898	160	5–14
Glasgow DIS (Green Street)	Glasgow	1879	250	5–14
Glasgow DIS (Hopehill Road)	Glasgow	1910	250	5–14
Glasgow DIS (Rose Street)	Glasgow	1889	250	5–14
Glasgow DIS (Rotten Row)	Glasgow	1882	250	5–14
Glasgow DIS (William Street)	Glasgow	1902	100	5–14
School Board DIS (Hyde Park Street)	Glasgow	1911	180	5–14

Source: Reformatory and Refuge Union, *The classified list of child-saving institutions*, 1912, p. 84.

Table B.9   Voluntary homes for boys and girls.

Name	Town	Year founded	No. of beds	Children's ages
Home for Crippled Children	Edinburgh	1871	24	3–12
Scottish National Society for Prevention of Cruelty to Children	Edinburgh	1877	30	under 16
Scottish National Society for Prevention of Cruelty to Children	Glasgow	1884	25	under 16
Scottish National Society for Prevention of Cruelty to Children	Dumbarton	1902	16	under 16
Scottish National Society for Prevention of Cruelty to Children	Crookston Home, near Cardonald, Glasgow	1903	40	under 16
Scottish National Society for Prevention of Cruelty to Children	Hamilton	1906	12	under 16

Source: Reformatory and Refuge Union, *The classified list of child-saving institutions*, 1912, p. 84.

Table B.10 Magdalene institutions.

Name	Town	Year founded	No. of beds	Girls' ages
Dalbeth (RC) Magdalene Institution	Glasgow	1851	226	15–30
Dundee Home	Dundee	1848	30	18–35
Dundee SA Home	Dundee	1900	53	no limit
Edinburgh IH	Edinburgh	1856	36	no limit
Edinburgh Magdalene Asylum	Edinburgh	1797	115	no limit
Falconer Rescue Home	Edinburgh	1860	30	no limit
Female Refuge	Paisley	1861	30	no limit
Female Rescue Home	Dundee	1876	40	under 20
Glasgow Magdalene Institution	Lochburn, Maryhill	1859	120	under 30
House of Refuge	Greenock	1853	40	over 15
House of the Good Shepherd	Perth	1900	6	14–20
Rescue Shelter	Edinburgh	1895	20	no limit
St Andrew's Home of Mercy	Edinburgh	1858	40	14–20
St Mary's Rescue Home	Glasgow	1900	10	14–25
Salvation Army Home	Glasgow	1889	36	no limit
Springwell House Rescue Home	Edinburgh	1877	12	under 30

Source: Reformatory and Refuge Union, *The classified list of child-saving institutions*, 1912, p. 128.

Appendix C

ᴥ

Industrial trades

Table C.1 Certified reformatory schools for boys.

Name and town	Industrial occupation
Kibble RS (Paisley)	Carpentry, cabinet making, shoe making, tailoring, farming, poultry keeping, turning, dairy work, musicianship, frame making
Parkhead RS (Glasgow)	Carpentry, shoe making, tailoring, farming, poultry keeping, baking, musicianship
Rossie RS (Forfarshire)	Tailoring, farming, poultry keeping
Stranraer RS	Carpentry, shoe making, tailoring, farming, poultry farming, turning, netting, rope making, musicianship, frame making
Wellington RS (Midlothian)	Carpentry, shoe making, tailoring, farming, poultry farming, musicianship

Source: Reformatory and Refuge Union, *The classified list of child-saving institutions*, 1912, pp. 80–81.

Table C.2 Certified industrial schools for boys.

Name and town	Industrial occupation
Arbroath IS	Carpentry, farming, poultry farming, knitting, milling, factory work
Ayr IS	Wood chopping, carpentry, shoemaking, tailoring, farming, poultry farming, paper bag making, knitting, musicianship
Clyde IS Training Ship (Helensburgh)	Carpentry, tailoring, seamanship, sail making, rope making, musicianship
Dumfries IS	Wood chopping, carpentry, shoe making, tailoring, clog and patten making, musicianship
Dundee IS	Carpentry, cabinet making, shoe making, tailoring, farming, poultry farming, musicianship
Edinburgh Original Ragged IS	Carpentry, shoe making, tailoring, farming, poultry farming, musicianship
Fechney IS (Perth)	Wood chopping, shoe making, tailoring, farming, poultry faming, turning
Glasgow ITS (Shettleston)	Shoe making, tailoring, farming, poultry farming
Greenock IS	Carpentry, shoe making, tailoring, brush making, knitting, musicianship
Leith IS	Wood chopping, carpentry, shoe making, tailoring, turning, musicianship
Mars IS (Dundee)	Carpentry, cabinet making, shoe making, tailoring, tinsmithing, farming, poultry farming, mat making, seamanship, blacksmithing, turning, netting, rope making, ship fender making, musicianship, road repairs, carpet making, wood carving
Mossbank IS (Glasgow)	Carpentry, shoe making, tailoring, farming, poultry farming, baking, dairy work, musicianship
Oakbank IS (Aberdeen)	Carpentry, tailoring, farming, poultry farming, musicianship
Paisley IS	Carpentry, cabinet making, shoe making, tailoring, farming, poultry farming, musicianship
St Joseph's CIS (Lothian)	Carpentry, shoe making, tailoring, farming, poultry farming, knitting, musicianship
St Mary's IS (Glasgow)	Wood chopping, shoe making, tailoring, paper bag making, musicianship
Slatefield IS (Glasgow)	Shoe making, tailoring, rope making, musicianship

Source: Reformatory and Refuge Union, *The classified list of child-saving institutions*, 1912, pp. 82–3.

Table C.3 Certified reformatory schools for girls

Name and town	Industrial occupation
Dalry House	Laundry, plain needlework, knitting
East Chapelton RS	Laundry, plain needlework, knitting, dairy work

Source: Reformatory and Refuge Union, *The classified list of child-saving institutions*, 1912, pp. 82–3.

Table C.4 Certified industrial schools for girls.

Name and town	Industrial occupation
Aberdeen IS	Knitting
Ayr IS	Laundry, plain needlework, knitting
Dalbeth IS	Laundry, plain needlework, knitting, dress making and millinery, crochet, netting, fancy needlework, dairy work
Dundee, Balgay IS	Laundry, plain needlework, knitting, lace making, crochet, netting, fancy needlework
Edinburgh Original IS	Laundry, plain needlework, knitting
Glasgow Orphanage and IS	Laundry, plain needlework, knitting, dress making and millinery, crotchet, netting and fancy needlework
Greenock IS	Laundry, plain needlework, knitting, crochet, netting, fancy needlework
Maryhill IS	Laundry, plain needlework, knitting, dairy work
Newton Stewart Girls' Industrial Home	Plain needlework, knitting
Perth Girls' School of Industry	Plain needlework, knitting
Perth Ladies' House of Refuge for Destitute Girls	Laundry, plain needlework, knitting
St Mary's IS (RC)	Laundry, plain needlework, knitting, dress making and millinery, crochet, netting, fancy needlework
Stirling IS for Girls	Plain needlework, knitting, church embroidery
Victoria IS	Plain needlework, knitting
Whitehall IS	Laundry, plain needlework, knitting

Source: Reformatory and Refuge Union, *The classified list of child-saving institutions*, 1912, p. 82–3.

Table C.5   Day industrial school for girls.

Name and town	Industrial occupation
Waverley Park	Knitting, crochet, netting, fancy needlework, carpet making, homemaking

Source: Reformatory and Refuge Union, *The classified list of child-saving institutions*, 1912, pp. 82–3.

Table C.6   Certified industrial school for boys and girls.

Name and town	Industrial occupation
Kilmarnock CIS	Wood chopping, carpentry, tailoring, knitting, turning, running errands/messages, musicianship, fretwork

Source: Reformatory and Refuge Union, *The classified list of child-saving institutions*, pp. 84–5, 1912.

Table C.7   Certified day industrial schools for boys and girls.

Name and town	Industrial occupation
Edinburgh DIS (St John's)	Carpentry
Glasgow DIS (Green Street)	Carpentry, cabinet making, plain needlework, knitting, carpet beating
Glasgow DIS (Hopehill Road)	Carpentry, plain needlework, knitting
Glasgow DIS (Rose Street)	Plain needlework, paper bag making, printing, knitting
Glasgow DIS (Rotten Row)	Plain needlework, brush making, knitting
Glasgow DIS (William Street)	Shoe making, plain needlework, knitting

Source: Reformatory and Refuge Union, *The classified list of child-saving institutions*, 1912, pp. 84–5.

Table C.8   Magdalene institutions.

Name and town	Industrial occupation
Dundee and District Female Rescue Home (Cobden Street)	Laundry, plain needlework
Dundee Home	Laundry, plain needlework
Dundee SA Home	Plain needlework
Edinburgh Falconer Rescue Home	Laundry
Edinburgh IH	Laundry
Edinburgh Magdalene Asylum	Laundry
Edinburgh Rescue Shelters	Laundry, plain needlework
Edinburgh St Andrew's and Home for Mercy	Laundry, plain needlework, knitting, crochet, netting, fancy needlework
Edinburgh Springwell House Rescue Home (Dalry Road)	Plain needlework, knitting
Glasgow Dalbeth (RC) Magdalene Institution	Farming, poultry, baking, laundry, plain needlework, knitting, church embroidery, crochet, netting, fancy needlework
Glasgow Magdalene Institution (Lochburn)	Laundry
Glasgow Magdalene Probationary Home	Laundry
Glasgow SA Home	Plain needlework
Glasgow, St Mary's Rescue Home	Laundry, plain needlework, knitting
Greenock House of Refuge	Laundry, plain needlework, knitting
Paisley Female Refuge	Laundry

Source: Reformatory and Refuge Union, The classified list of child-saving institutions, 1912, pp. 84–5.

Notes

Acknowledgements

1. L. Mahood, "Family ties: lady child-savers and girls of the street, 1850–1925", in *Out of bounds: women in Scottish society, 1800–1945*, E. Breitenbach & E. Gordon (eds) (Edinburgh: Edinburgh University Press, 1992), pp. 42–64.
2. L. Mahood & B. Littlewood, "The 'vicious' girl and the 'street-corner' boy: sexuality and the gendered delinquent in the Scottish child-saving movement, 1850–1940", *Journal of the History of Sexuality* 4, 1994, pp. 549–78.

Chapter 1

1. Interview with former industrial school boy (1923–33), Glasgow, 17 July 1990.
2. Interview with former reformatory school boy (1927–34), Glasgow, 15 August 1989.
3. Interview with former approved school boy (1940–48), Glasgow, 27 June 1990.
4. Interview with former industrial day school boy (1908–10), Perth, 2 July 1990.
5. C. Steedman, C. Urwin, V. Walkerdine (eds), *Language, gender and childhood* (London: Routledge & Kegan Paul, 1985), p. 8.
6. B. Bellingham, "The history of childhood since the 'invention of childhood': some issues in the eighties", *Journal of Family History* 13, 1988, p. 354.
7. P. Corrigan & D. Sayers, *The great arch* (Oxford: Basil Blackwell, 1985).
8. R. P. Dobash, R. E. Dobash, S. Gutteridge, *The imprisonment of women* (Oxford: Basil Blackwell, 1986), p. 35.

NOTES

9. R. Johnson, "Educating the educators: 'experts' and the state, 1833–39", in *Social control in nineteenth century Britain*, A. P. Donajgrodski (ed.) (London: Croom Helm, 1977), p. 91.
10. In this book the concept of "child-savers" follows Anthony Platt's usage. Platt describes the child-savers as a group of middle-class and upper-class social reformers, both men and women. They regarded child welfare as a matter of conscience and morality, seeing themselves as humanitarians dedicated to rescuing and reforming those less fortunate than themselves. Anthony Platt, *The child-savers: the invention of delinquency* (Chicago: University of Chicago Press, 1969).
11. M. Ignatieff, "Total institutions and working classes: a review essay", *History Workshop* 15, 1983, pp. 168–9.
12. "With the passage of the 1968 Social Work (Scotland) Act the procedure for registration was changed and the name 'approved school' was dropped; for want of a more descriptive name, these schools were thereafter referred to by the particular list in which they featured in the records of the Scottish Education Department, List D." N. Boyd, "Historical background", in *The Scottish juvenile justice system*, F. M. Martin & K. Murray (eds) (Edinburgh: Scottish Academic Press, 1982), p. 5.
13. My goal is not to write a comparative history of Scottish and English policies and law, as this has been satisfactorily done elsewhere. See: E. A. G. Clark, "The superiority of the 'Scotch system': Scottish ragged schools and their influence", *Scottish Education Studies* 9, 1977, pp. 30–36. For more on Scottish philanthropy see: O. Checkland, *Philanthropy in Victorian Scotland: social welfare and the voluntary principle* (Edinburgh: John Donald, 1980); K. M. Boyd, *Scottish church attitudes to sex, marriage and the family, 1850–1914* (Edinburgh: John Donald, 1980).
14. Thoughts suggested by the Chief Inspector's report of reformatory and industrial schools, *Seeking and saving*, January 1917, p. 394.
15. *Ibid.*, August 1913, p. 395.
16. S. Cohen, *Visions of social control: crime, punishment, and classification* (Cambridge: Polity, 1985), p. 25.
17. M. Foucault, *The history of sexuality: volume 1: an introduction*, trans. R. Hurley (New York: Random House, 1980), p. 25; B. Smart, *Michel Foucault* (London: Tavistock, 1985), p. 24.
18. Foucault, *The history of sexuality*, p. 118.
19. J. Donzelot, *The policing of families*, trans. R. Hurley (London: Hutchinson, 1979), p. 16.
20. *Ibid.*, p. 18.
21. *Ibid.*, p. 10.
22. *Ibid.*, p. 16.
23. M. Ignatieff, "The ideological origins of the penitentiary", in *Crime and society: readings in history and theory*, M. Fitzgerald, G. McLennan, J. Pawson (eds) (London: Routledge & Kegan Paul, 1986), pp. 37–59.
24. Donzelot, *The policing of families*, pp. 55–6.

25. P. Adams, "Family affairs", *M/F* 7, 1982, p. 10.
26. Corrigan & Sayers, *The great arch*, p. 4.
27. Foucault, *The history of sexuality*, pp. 140–41.
28. Adams, "Family affairs", p. 10.
29. F. Paterson, "Schooling the family", *Sociology* 22, 1988, p. 69.
30. Cohen, *Visions of social control*, p. 135.
31. C. Lasch, *Haven in a heartless world: the family besieged* (New York: Basic Books, 1977).
32. P. Squires, *Anti-social policy: welfare, ideology and the disciplinary state* (Hemel Hempstead: Harvester, 1990), p. 9.
33. M. Barrett & M. McIntosh, *The anti-social family* (London: Verso, 1982), p. 101.
34. Squires, *Anti-social policy*, p. 9.
35. *Ibid.*, p. 20.
36. N. Fraser, *Unruly practices: power, discourse and gender in contemporary social theory* (Cambridge: Polity, 1989), p. 156.
37. *Ibid.*
38. *Ibid.*, p. 157.
39. A. Davin, "Imperialism and motherhood", *History Workshop* 5, 1978, pp. 9–65.
40. S. Damer, *Glasgow: going for a song* (London: Lawrence & Wishart, 1990), p. 103.
41. J. Humphries, "Class struggle and the persistence of the working class family", *Cambridge Journal of Economics* 3, 1977, pp. 241–58.
42. L. Gordon, *Heroes of their own lives: the politics and history of family violence* (London: Virago, 1989), p. 294.
43. *Ibid.*
44. P. Hirst, "The genesis of the social", *Politics and Power* 3, 1981, pp. 65–89.
45. P. Corrigan, B. Curtis, R. Lanning, "The political space of schooling", in *The political economy of Canadian schooling*, T. Wotherspoon (ed.) (London: Methuen, 1987).
46. Technologies-of-power is a concept developed by Foucault to describe agencies and institutions such as jurisprudence, legal medicine, and agencies of social control for the surveillance of dangerous or endangered populations. In the case of this research it refers to child-saving institutions, policies and charities whose goals were the moral regulation of working-class girls and boys, whom they perceived as being at risk of becoming juvenile delinquents.
47. See: S. Cohen, *The evolution of women's asylums since 1500: from refuges for ex-prostitutes to shelters for battered women* (Oxford: Oxford University Press, 1992); N. Rafter, *Partial justice: women in state prisons* (Boston: Northeastern University Press, 1985); Dobash, Dobash, Gutteridge, *Imprisonment of women*.
48. Cohen, *Visions of social control*, p. 31.

49. L. Mahood, *The magdalenes: prostitution in the nineteenth century* (London: Routledge, 1990).

50. N. Williamson, "'Hymns, songs and blackguard verses': life in the industrial and reformatory school for girls in New South Wales: part I, 1867–1887", *Journal of the Royal Australian Historical Society* 67, 1982, p. 379. See also: N. Williamson, "Laundry maids or ladies? Life in the industrial and reformatory school for girls in New South Wales: part II, 1887–1910", *Journal of the Royal Australian Historical Society* 68, 1983, pp. 312–432; N. Williamson, "Factory to reformatory: the founding and the failure of industrial and reform schools for girls in the nineteenth century in New South Wales", *Australia and New Zealand History of Education Society* 9, 1980, pp. 32–41.

51. K. Wimshurst, "Control and resistance: reformatory school for girls in late nineteenth century South Australia", *Journal of Social History* 18, 1984, pp. 278–9. See also: S. Willis, "Made to be moral – at Parramatta Girls' School, 1893–1923", in *Twentieth century Sydney: studies in urban and social history*, J. Roe (ed.) (Sydney: Hale & Iremonger, 1980), pp. 178–92; B. Brenzel, "Domestication as reform: a study of the socialization of wayward girls, 1856–1905", *Harvard Educational Review* 50, 1980, pp. 196–213.

52. Wimshurst, "Control and resistance", p. 273.

53. E. A. Rotundo, "Romantic friendship: male intimacy and middle-class youth in the northern United States, 1800–1900", *Journal of Social History* 23, 1989, pp. 1–25.

54. H. Hendrick, *Images of youth: age, class and the male youth problem, 1880–1920* (Oxford: Clarendon Press, 1990).

55. C. Smith-Rosenberg, "The female world of love and ritual: relations between women in nineteenth-century America", *Signs* 1, 1975, pp. 1–29.

56. G. Block, "Women's history and gender history: aspects of an international debate", *Gender and History* 1, 1989, p. 17.

57. T. C. Smout, *A century of the Scottish people, 1830–1950* (London: Collins, 1986), p. 185

58. M. Valverde, *The age of light, soap and water: moral reform in English Canada, 1885–1925* (Toronto: McClelland & Stewart, 1991).

59. C. Haig-Brown, *Resistance and renewal: surviving the Indian residential school* (Vancouver: Tillacum Library, 1989).

60. E. Balibar, "Class racism", in *Race, nation, class: ambiguous identities*, E. Balibar & I. Wallerstein (eds) (London: Verso, 1991).

61. Foucault argues that power is produced from moment to moment in social relations at all levels, not because it embraces everything, but because it comes from everywhere. Power, therefore, can come from below. It is by virtue of this that he argues that where there is power there is resistance, or the operation of a "reverse discourse". This occurs when the evaluations implicit in a discourse are reversed, for example in gay and civil rights slogans, or more recently, feminist anti-rape and sexual harassment

slogans like "zero-tolerance" and "no-means-no". Foucault suggests that just as there exists a multiplicity of force relations that produce power, there also exists a multiplicity of relations that resist it. Points of resistance are present in every power network. Hence, there is no single locus of "great refusal", and likewise there is no single locus of control. See: Foucault, *The history of sexuality*.

62. V. Satzewich, *Racism and the incorporation of foreign labour* (London: Routledge, 1991).
63. Ignatieff, "Total institutions and working classes", p. 169.

Chapter 2

1. My emphasis. J. Rutherford Hill (Edinburgh Band of Hope), "Some helps and hindrances in rescue and preventive work among women and girls", paper presented at National Conference of Reformatory and Refuge Union, Edinburgh, 1911, pp. 55–6.
2. E. A. G. Clark, "The superiority of the 'Scotch system': Scottish ragged schools and their influence", *Scottish Educational Studies* 9, p. 30, 1977; M. Carpenter, *Reformatory schools*, 1869 edn (New York: Augustus Kelly Publishing, 1851).
3. O. Checkland, *Philanthropy in Victorian Scotland: social welfare and the voluntary principle* (Edinburgh: John Donald, 1980), p. 245.
4. *Cumberland* Training Ship, *Annual report*, 1870, p. 8.
5. A. Davin, "When is a child not a child?", in *Politics of everyday life: continuity and change in work and family life*, H. Corr & L. Jamieson (eds) (London: Macmillan, 1990), p. 43.
6. G. Pearson, *Hooligan: a history of respectable fears* (London: Macmillan, 1983), p. 156–7.
7. P. Squires, *Anti-social policy: welfare, ideology and the disciplinary state* (Hemel Hempstead: Harvester, 1990).
8. In the popular and expert discourses the connection between class, gender and sexuality was naturalized, and one term frequently was made to stand for another in the chain of signification.
9. Contained in a book of cuttings entitled "The dark side of Glasgow", in the Glasgow Room, Mitchell Library, ref. G914.1435. These articles appeared in the *Daily Mail* between 1870 and 1871. Many of the articles are not dated and the pages of the book are not numbered.
10. *Ibid.*
11. L. Nead, "The magdalene in modern times: the mythology of the fallen woman in pre-Raphaelite painting", in *Looking at images of femininity in the visual arts and media*, R. Betterton (ed.) (London: Pandora Press, 1987), p. 76.

12. J. R. Motion, *Desertion cases: supplementary memorandum* (Glasgow: Glasgow Parish Council, 1909), p. 5.

13. R. Ramsay (Chairman of Committee on the Employment of Children), "Juvenile street trading", paper presented at National Scottish Conference on the Employment of Children and Kindred Subjects, Glasgow (Scottish Council for Women's Trades), 5–6 November 1909, p. 28.

14. City of Glasgow Police, *Criminal returns*, 1910, p. 4.

15. *Ibid.*

16. M. Speir (Scoutmaster), *Report of the Departmental Committee on Reformatory and Industrial Schools*, Young Offenders (Scotland) Committee, Minutes of Evidence, PP, 1925 [cited hereafter as PP YOC, 1925], p. 3.

17. J. Miller, *Prostitution considered in relation to its causes and cure* (Edinburgh: Sutherland & Knox, 1859), p. 6.

18. "Shebeens" were unlicensed drinking establishments. J. Bertram, *Glimpses of the social evil in Edinburgh and elsewhere* (Edinburgh: Charles Harvey, 1864), p. 13.

19. Parish of Glasgow, *Memorandum on the social evil in Glasgow and the state of the law for dealing with certain forms of immorality* (Parish of Glasgow, 1911), p. 58.

20. *Report of the Select Committee on Reformatory and Industrial Schools in Scotland*, Appendix VIII, 1896, p. 231.

21. Contained in "The dark side of Glasgow".

22. Edinburgh Magdalene Asylum, *House Committee minute book*, 26 September 1886, 13 October 1886.

23. Edinburgh Magdalene Asylum, *Annual report*, 1887, p. 6.

24. Report of the Glasgow Special Committee on Probation of Offenders, *Seeking and saving*, May 1919, p. 138.

25. *Evening Dispatch*, 23 March 1918. See: National Vigilance Association, cuttings book, 1912–28.

26. *Evening Dispatch*, 25 March 1918.

27. D. Maitland (female probation officer), PP YOC, 1925, Q: 4869.

28. *Ibid.*, Q: 4846.

29. *Ibid.*, Q: 4868.

30. 16 February 1930, National Vigilance Association, cuttings book, 1928–35.

31. J. Donzelot, *The policing of families*, trans. R. Hurley (London: Hutchinson, 1979).

32. T. C. Smout, *A century of the Scottish people, 1830–1950* (London: Collins, 1986), p. 186; Checkland, *Philanthropy in Victorian Scotland*, pp. 30–33.

33. *Seeking and saving*, January 1919, p. 104.

34. Davin, "When is a child not a child?", p. 44.

35. *Ibid.*

36. Transactions of the National Association for the Promotion of Social Sciences, *Annual report* (Edinburgh, 1880), p. 395.

37. M. May, "Innocence and experience: the evolution of the concept of juvenile delinquency in the mid-nineteenth century", *Victorian Studies* 17, 1973–4, p. 21.
38. *Seeking and saving*, June 1910, p. 306.
39. R. Johnson, "Educating the educators: 'experts' and the state, 1833–39", in *Social control in nineteenth century Britain*, A. P. Donajgrodski (ed.) (London: Croom Helm, 1977).
40. J. Playfair, Minutes of Evidence taken before the Select Committee on Criminal and Destitute Children, PP, 1852–3 (26 April 1853), [cited hereafter as PP SC, 1853], Q: 4471.
41. A. Campbell, *Report of the Select Committee on Reformatory and Industrial Schools in Scotland*, Minutes of Evidence, PP, 1896–7, xv [cited hereafter as PP SC, 1897], Q: 24,721.
42. T. Guthrie, PP SC, 1853, Q: 579.
43. J. Bertram, *A deeper glimpse of the social evil* (Edinburgh: Charles Harvey, 1866), p. 9.
44. May, "Innocence and experience", p. 18.
45. "The dark side of Glasgow".
46. F. Mort, *Dangerous sexualities: medico-moral politics in England since 1830* (London: Routledge & Kegan Paul, 1987), p. 170.
47. *Ibid.*
48. Dr A. Watson (medical officer, Aberdeen Female School of Industry), *Report of the Departmental Committee on Reformatory and Industrial Schools*, Minutes of Evidence, PP, 1914 [cited hereafter as PP DC, 1914], Q: 6555.
49. Reformatory and Refuge Union, *Scotsman*, May 1924, located in the cuttings book of the Edinburgh and District Juvenile Organizations Committee, 1920–26. Edinburgh Room, qYHV [C73361].
50. M. Maclauchlan (Superintendent, Dr Guthrie's Girls' School) PP YOC, 1925 (11 February 1926), Q: 1164.
51. Robert S. Allen, PP DC, 1915, p. 246; see also J. M. Roxburgh, *The school board of Glasgow, 1872–1919* (London: University of London Press, 1971), p. 190.
52. V. M. C. Robertson (Justice of the Peace, Glasgow), PP YOC, 1925 (14 January 1926), p. 2.
53. Rutherford Hill, "Some helps and hindrances", p. 55.
54. E. Gordon, "Women's sphere", in *People and society in Scotland: volume II, 1830–1914*, W. H. Fraser & R. J. Morris (eds) (Edinburgh: John Donald, 1989), p. 206.
55. L. Davidoff & C. Hall, *Family fortunes: men and women of the English middle class, 1780–1850* (London: Hutchinson, 1987), p. 23.
56. *Ibid.*, p. 25.
57. Smout, *A century of the Scottish people*, p. 185.
58. D. Garland, *Punishment and welfare* (Aldershot, England: Gower, 1985), p. 153.

59. T. C. Smout, *A history of the Scottish people, 1560–1830* (London: Fontana, 1969), pp. 94–6, 417.
60. Smout, *A century of the Scottish people*, p. 22.
61. D. Gorham, "'The maiden tribute to modern Babylon' re-examined: child prostitution and the idea of childhood in late-Victorian England", *Victorian Studies*, Spring 1979, p. 356; B. Bradbury, "The fragmented family: family strategies in the face of death, illness and poverty, Montreal, 1860–1885", in *Childhood and family in Canadian history*, J. Parr (ed.) (Toronto: McClelland & Stewart, 1982), pp. 109–10.
62. May, "Innocence and experience", p. 14.
63. "The inherent disciplinary character of the social undoubtedly derives from the complex societal transformations that were occurring and creating the kind of political and economic order within which capitalist relations of production, reproduction and exchange might thrive." Squires, *Anti-social policy*, p. 48.
64. See the Transactions of the National Association for the Promotion of Social Sciences, *Annual reports*, 1857–1912. The journal was entitled *Meloria*.
65. Pearson, *Hooligan*, p. 159.
66. Smout, *A century of the Scottish people*, p. 40.
67. R. P. Dobash, R. E. Dobash, S. Gutteridge, *The imprisonment of women* (Oxford: Basil Blackwell, 1986), p. 35.
68. R. Johnson, "Educational policy and social control in early Victorian England", *Past and Present* 49, 1970, p. 98.
69. *Ibid.*
70. Pearson, *Hooligan*, p. 179.
71. M. Carpenter, PP SC, 1852–3, p. 817.
72. F. Paterson, "Schooling the family", *Sociology* 22, p. 73, 1988.
73. G. Steadman-Jones, "The threat of outcast London", in *Crime and society: readings in history and theory*, M. Fitzgerald, G. McLennan, J. Pawson (eds) (London: Routledge & Kegan Paul, 1986), p. 174.
74. Gorham, "'The maiden tribute to modern Babylon'", p. 370.
75. Examples are: A. Thomson, *On the licentiousness of Scotland, and the remedial measures which ought to be adopted* (London: J. Nesbit, 1861); A. C. C. List, *The two phases of social evil* (Edinburgh: Ogle & Murray, 1859).
76. Johnson, "Educating the educators".
77. May, "Innocence and experience", p. 16.
78. A leader of the English ragged school movement, Mary Carpenter, saw them both as equally needy classes. The first, the perishing class, consisted of children "who have not yet fallen into actual crime, but . . . are almost certain from their ignorance, destitution and the circumstances in which they are growing up, to do so". The second, the dangerous class, were those who "have already received the prison brand, or . . . are notoriously living by plunder". The point to be made is that the child-savers recog-

nized that these children were not equally criminal, but were equally at risk of becoming criminal. Mary Carpenter is quoted in Clark, "The superiority of the 'Scotch system'", p. 30; M. Carpenter, *Reformatory schools.*

79. Mrs Cameron (Superintendent, Maryhill School since 1881. She was at Green Street Day Industrial School before transferring to Maryhill.) PP SC, 1897, Q: 7803.

80. Pearson, *Hooligan*, p. 182.

81. May, "Innocence and experience", p. 28.

Chapter 3

1. Interview with former industrial school boy, 1908–10, Perth, 2 July 1990.

2. Interview with former industrial day school girl, 1925–8, Glasgow, 7 August 1989.

3. M. Stevenson and A. Gray (Members of the Edinburgh School Board), *Report of the Select Committee on Reformatory and Industrial Schools in Scotland*, Minutes of Evidence, PP, 1896–7, xv [cited hereafter as PP SC, 1897], Q: 25,347.

4. M. O'Donnel (female probation officer), *Report of the Departmental Committee on Reformatory and Industrial Schools in Scotland*, Young Offenders (Scotland) Committee, Minutes of Evidence, PP, 1925 [cited hereafter as PP YOC, 1925], Q: 2535.

5. P. Squires, *Anti-social policy: welfare, ideology and the disciplinary state* (Hemel Hempstead: Harvester, 1990), p. 19.

6. Scottish Education Department, *Provision of approved schools*, 1923, p. 13.

7. W. M. Douglas (Superintendent of Police, West Division, Glasgow), "The juvenile delinquent", paper presented at National Scottish Conference on the Employment of Children and Kindred Subjects, Glasgow (Scottish Council for Women's Trades), 5–6 November 1909, p. 38.

8. S. MacGill, *Discourses and essays on subjects of public interest* (Edinburgh: Glasgow Society for the Encouragement of Penitents, Waugh & Innes, 1819); S. Mechie, *The church and Scottish social development, 1780–1879* (Westport: Greenwood Press, 1975), p. 42.

9. *Glasgow Courier*, 2 March 1805, p. 2.

10. Glasgow Society for the Encouragement of Penitents, *Annual report*, 1815, p. 8.

11. *Ibid.*

12. A. Coyle, *Inside: rethinking Scotland's prisons* (Edinburgh: Scottish Child, 1991), p. 29.

13. W. Brebner, *A letter to the Lord Provost on the expediency of a House of*

Refuge for juvenile offenders (Glasgow, 1829), p. 7.
14. *Ibid.*, p. 6.
15. *Ibid.*
16. *Ibid.*, p. 10.
17. *Ibid.*, pp. 10–12.
18. O. Checkland, *Philanthropy in Victorian Scotland: social welfare and the voluntary principle* (Edinburgh: John Donald, 1980), p. 249.
19. Glasgow Boys' House of Refuge, *Annual report*, 1838, p. 11.
20. *Ibid.*, p. 16.
21. Checkland, *Philanthropy in Victorian Scotland*, p. 249.
22. J. D. Bryce, *The Glasgow magdalene asylum, its past and present: with relative facts and suggestions* (Glasgow: David Bryce, 1859), p. 4.
23. House of Lords, *Report of Select Committee on the Glasgow Houses of Refuge Bill*, 6 March 1877, p. 1.
24. A. Ralston, "The development of reformatory and industrial schools in Scotland, 1832–1872", *Scottish Economic and Historical Society* 8, 1988, p. 40. In 1832 "benevolent ladies" in Edinburgh established Dean Bank Rescue Home. While little is known about this institution, its aim was "to prevent neglected and destitute girls, exposed by their circumstances to temptation and danger, on the borderland of worse things, from drifting hopelessly downward". Its daughter institution, the Western Reformatory, opened in 1862 (Dean Bank, *Annual report*, 1899).
25. M. May, "Innocence and experience: the evolution of the concept of juvenile delinquency in the mid-nineteenth century", *Victorian Studies* 17, 1973–4, p. 11.
26. T. C. Smout, *A history of the Scottish people, 1560–1830* (London: Fontana, 1969), p. 422.
27. *Ibid.*, p. 423.
28. Cited in H. Corr, "An exploration into Scottish education", in *People and society in Scotland, volume 2*, W. H. Fraser & R. J. Morris (eds) (Edinburgh: John Donald, 1989), p. 293; Checkland, *Philanthropy in Victorian Scotland*, p. 104.
29. S. Checkland & O. Checkland, *Industry and ethos, Scotland, 1832–1914* (London: Edward Arnold, 1984), p. 112.
30. *Ibid.* The authors do not account for the remaining 10,000 cases, which suggests they were in satisfactory schools.
31. Smout, *A history of the Scottish people*, p. 424.
32. T. Ferguson, *The dawn of Scottish social welfare* (London: Thomas Nelson, 1948), p. 534.
33. *Ibid.*, p. 554.
34. W. Watson, quoted in J. Scotland, *The history of Scottish education from the beginning to 1872*, vol. 1 (London: University of London Press, 1972), p. 274.
35. Ralston, "The development of reformatory and industrial schools in Scotland", pp. 40–41.

36. *Ibid.*, p. 41.
37. E. A. G. Clark, "The superiority of the 'Scotch system': Scottish ragged schools and their influence", *Scottish Educational Studies* 9, 1977, p. 29.
38. Ralston, "The development of reformatory and industrial schools in Scotland", p. 42.
39. Quoted in Ralston, "The development of reformatory and industrial schools in Scotland".
40. Bryce, *The Glasgow magdalene asylum*, p. 5.
41. Glasgow Girls' Reformatory (Juvenile Department of the Females' House of Refuge), *Annual report*, 1860, p. 6.
42. *Ibid.*, p. 8. Of the total inmate population of 127 that year 110 had been in prison.
43. Ralston, "The development of reformatory and industrial schools in Scotland", p. 48.
44. Clark, "The superiority of the 'Scotch system'", p. 34.
45. Admissions: 1865: 378; 1866: 605; 1867: 993; 1868:1003. Calculated from the Inspector for Reformatory and Industrial Schools, *Annual reports*, 1854–98.
46. May, "Innocence and experience", p. 27.
47. A. Campbell (Clerk, Edinburgh Burgh Court), PP SC, 1897, Q: 22,185.
48. W. Henderson (Chief Constable, Edinburgh), PP SC, 1897, Q: 21,686.
49. J. Wallace (Sheriff, Argyleshire), *Report of the Select Committee on Reformatory and Industrial Schools in Scotland*, Minutes of Evidence, PP, 1897, Q: 26,162.
50. House of Lords, *Report of Select Committee on the Glasgow Houses of Refuge Bill*, pp. 2–4.
51. F. Stevenson and A. Gray (members of Edinburgh School Board), PP SC, 1897, Q: 25,398.
52. *Cumberland* Training Ship, *Annual report*, 1892, p. 23.
53. Ralston, "The development of reformatory and industrial schools in Scotland", p. 54.
54. Checkland, *Philanthropy in Victorian Scotland*, p. 254.
55. *Cumberland* Training Ship, *Annual report*, 1871, p. 31.
56. Ralston, "The development of reformatory and industrial schools in Scotland", p. 52.
57. *Cumberland* Training Ship, *Annual report*, 1872–73, pp. 27, 28.
58. PP SC, 1897, p. 91.
59. *Ibid.*
60. Scottish Education Department, *Approved schools: methods for dealing with difficult girls and boys: special status for Glasgow Magdalene Institution*. Extract from Mr Pleck's minutes to HMI Mr Forbes, 17 February 1932 (ED 15/136).
61. *Ibid.*, Department minute, 1 March 1934. Letter to Mr Brewer (Glasgow Magdalene Institution).
62. PP SC, 1897, p. 224.

63. *Ibid.*

64. "It seems to be generally agreed among people with experience of [sic] the management of delinquent girls is often a much more difficult problem than in the case of boys. The reasons are obscure: it may be because the offences for which girls tend to be put under custody or supervision are of a special nature; it may be because girls respond less well to supervision or institutional custody. Another possibility is that a high percentage of girls committed to institutions are in need of psychological or psychiatric treatment . . . In post-war years we have had public trouble at Lochburn Home for Girls (now closed as a result) and in the last few weeks our child care and probation inspectorate [sic] have expressed a little anxiety about Cobden Street Home for girls in Dundee." Margaret Geddes, *Some notes on remand homes and approved schools* (Paper no. 6, Scottish Advisory Council on the Treatment and Rehabilitation of Offenders, November 1964). In the 1950s these girls were described in Home Office schools inspectors' reports as "in need of psychiatric treatment", "unstable", "potential suicides", "depressives", "neurotic-schizoid". According to one psychiatrist: "One would expect some unstable girls to express instability in promiscuous sex behaviour." Scottish Education Department, "Proposed working party on management of approved schools for girls: methods for dealing with difficult girls", 3 March 1952 (ED 15/274).

65. A study of Scottish magdalene institutions is found in L. Mahood, *The magdalenes: prostitution in the nineteenth century* (London: Routledge, 1990).

66. "[After] reading the rules of the Scottish Education Department for the Management of Approved Schools these rules seem quite inappropriate for a home such as Lochburn, and on further consideration . . . it would be unwise for the committee to give up their present freedom of control in order to become an approved school. At the same time [we are] entirely in favour of doing everything that could be done by a home that was not approved." Glasgow Magdalene Institution, *Homes Committee minute book*, 1920–35, 10 April 1934.

67. For example: "The Secretary for Scotland had consented to the girls Robina Stewart being licenced to the care of Miss Paterson, matron, for three years." *ibid.*, 10 March 1914. " . . . a girl of fifteen was sent on licence to Miss Paterson, by the Juvenile Delinquency Board . . . she will not be admitted as an inmate until she is 16." *ibid.*, 14 November 1916.

68. M. Carpenter, quoted in Ralston, "The development of reformatory and industrial schools in Scotland", p. 52.

69. J. M. Roxburgh, *The school board of Glasgow, 1873–1919* (London: University of London Press, 1971), p. 192.

70. Interview with former industrial day school girl, 1920–24, Glasgow, 16 August 1989.

71. Glasgow Reformatory and Industrial Schools, *Annual report*, 1886, p. 6.

72. This occurred in the case of the industrial school boy of 1908 quoted at

the beginning of this chapter. The court could sentence children to three months in an industrial school for a breach of an attendance order. These cases were dealt with by the sheriff court.

73. M. Delman, "Child among the bluebells", unpublished manuscript (Drumchapel Writers Group, Glasgow, 1993), p. 10.
74. Ralston, "The development of reformatory and industrial schools in Scotland", p. 52.
75. P. Thane, "Childhood in history", in *Childhood, welfare and justice: a critical examination of children in the legal and childcare systems*, M. King (ed.) (London: Batsford Academic, 1981), p. 19.
76. Smout, *A history of the Scottish people*, p. 96.
77. J. H. Treble, "Juvenile labour and the structure of Glasgow's adult male casual labour market, 1890–1914", unpublished manuscript (Strathclyde University, 1985), ch. 2.
78. R. P. Lamond, *Memorandum on the Children Act, 1908* (Glasgow: Glasgow Parish Council, 1909), p. 11.
79. G. Gillie, *Employment of Children Act, 1903* (Glasgow: Glasgow Parish Council, 1909), p. 7.
80. D. Gorham, "'The maiden tribute to modern Babylon' re-examined: child prostitution and the idea of childhood in late-Victorian England", *Victorian Studies*, Spring 1979, p. 357.
81. *Ibid.*, p. 62.
82. May, "Innocence and experience", p. 8.
83. Emphasis mine, Parish of Glasgow, *Sexual immorality and prostitution in Glasgow* (Glasgow: Glasgow Parish Council, 1911), p. 21.
84. City of Glasgow Police, *Criminal returns*, 1910, p. 4.
85. M. Hill, "A few words on probation", *Report of the Glasgow conference* (Glasgow: Reformatory and Refuge Union, 1924), pp. 86, 87.
86. J. D. Strathen (Procurator Fiscal for Lower Ward of Lanarkshire at Glasgow), PP YOC, 1925, p. 2.
87. J. Christie (Chief Constable, Greenock), PP YOC, 1925 (10 February 1926), p. 3.
88. J. T. Wilson, "The treatment of juvenile delinquency: an appraisal of the Scottish approved school system", unpublished B. Litt. thesis (Glasgow University, 1962), p. 17.
89. O'Donnel, PP YOC, 1925, Q: 2455.
90. Wilson, "The treatment of juvenile delinquency", p. 117.
91. *Glasgow Herald*, 13 February 1932, p. 4. Located in Edinburgh and District Juvenile Organizations Committee, press cuttings, 1931–8. Edinburgh Room, qYHV 756 [C73369].
92. D. Maitland (female probation officer), PP YOC, 1925 (15 December 1925), Q: 4951.
93. *Glasgow Herald,* 13 February 1932, p. 4.
94. O'Donnel, PP YOC, 1925, Q: 2641.
95. City of Glasgow Police, *Criminal returns*, 1910, p. 4. 30 proceedings

dropped; 36 acquitted; 36 sentencing delayed; 114 fined; 7 whipped; 192 admonished.

96. O'Donnel, PP YOC, 1925 (19 November 1925), Q: 2625. She revealed that she tried to get them to go into rescue homes, "but we cannot compel them to go". Q: 2631; "[A girl had to go] of her own free will." Q: 2637.

97. This insight was provided by correspondence with Mr J. Richmond (retired), former deputy head of social work at Balrossie List D School, Kilmalcolm (now retired to Victoria, Australia).

98. Wilson, "The treatment of juvenile delinquency", p. 135.

99. A. Davin, "When is a child not a child?", in *Politics of everyday life: continuity and change in work and family life*, H. Corr & L. Jamieson (eds) (London: Macmillan, 1990), p. 45.

100. Coyle, *Inside*, p. 107.

101. PP SC, 1897, p. 15.

Chapter 4

1. J. Donzelot, *The policing of families*, trans. R. Hurley (London: Hutchinson, 1979), p. 96.

2. J. Lewis describes similar problems in her study of the child and maternal welfare services. See *Politics of motherhood: child and maternal welfare in England, 1900–1939* (London: Croom Helm, 1980), p. 15.

3. E. A. G. Clark, "The superiority of the 'Scotch system': Scottish ragged schools and their influence", *Scottish Educational Studies* 9, p. 30, 1977.

4. G. Greig (former Inspector of the Poor), *Report of the Select Committee on Reformatory and Industrial Schools in Scotland*, Minutes of Evidence, PP, 1896–7, xv [cited hereafter as PP SC, 1897], Q: 22,923–6.

5. *Ibid.*, Q: 22,911.

6. *Ibid.*, Q: 22,931.

7. *Ibid.*, Q: 22,852.

8. *Ibid.*, Q: 22,819. In 1925 the Chief Constable of Greenock indicated that boarding-out was still practised in the 1920s. "It is the practice of the parish councils to board out orphaned children with respectable people in country districts and I understand with success. The children are well cared for and get the advantage of a healthy home atmosphere. They are taught to be industrious." J. Christie, *Report of the Departmental Committee on Reformatory and Industrial Schools in Scotland*, Young Offenders (Scotland) Committee, Minutes of Evidence, PP, 1925 (10 February 1925) [cited hereafter as PP YOC, 1925].

9. W. Dickson (Superintendent, Baldovan Industrial School, Dundee), PP SC, 1897, Q: 23,056.

10. W. Reid, PP SC, 1897, Q: 21,382.

11. *Ibid.*, Q: 23,058–60.
12. Dow, PP YOC, 1925, Q: 1589–93.
13. W. Smith (Superintendent, Oakbank Industrial School, Aberdeen), PP SC, 1897, Q: 23,345; Reid, PP SC, 1897, Q: 21,368.
14. Reid, PP SC, 1897, Q: 21,382.
15. F. Stevenson and A. Gray, PP SC, 1897, Q: 25,520.
16. Reference provided in an unpublished manuscript generously sent to me by Mr J. Richmond (retired), former deputy head of social work at Balrossie List D School, Kilmalcolm.
17. M. Duncan (Superintendent, Green Street Day Industrial School, Glasgow), PP SC, 1897, Q: 24,514.
18. A. Campbell (Superintendent, Dundee Boys' Home), PP SC, 1897, Q: 24,737.
19. A. Pirie (Superintendent, Children's Shelter, Glasgow), PP SC, 1897, Q: 26,039.
20. *Ibid.*, Q: 26,067.
21. *Ibid.*, Q: 26,074.
22. "I do not take boys out of brothels, only girls . . . I have figures of those living in brothels during the whole time that the society has been in existence [11 years], and it amounts to 156 . . . Almost all girls . . . We will take the boys to the shelter. If the parents have been sent to prison we will take them to the shelter for the time being till we get something done for them; but the girls are sent to industrial schools often." *Ibid.*, Q: 26,074–9.
23. F. Hepburn (Edinburgh District Scottish Society for the Prevention of Cruelty to Children), *Report of the Departmental Committee on Reformatories and Industrial Schools in Scotland*, Minutes of Evidence, PP, 1915 [cited hereafter as PP DC, 1915], Q: 7923.
24. *Ibid.*, Q: 7919.
25. Pirie, PP SC, 1897, Q: 26,062.
26. W. Spens (Sheriff for Lanarkshire), PP SC, 1897, Q: 20,912–13.
27. T. C. Macgregor (Deputy Clerk of Peace, Glasgow), PP SC, 1897, Q: 25,316.
28. McDonald, PP SC, 1897, Q: 21,032.
29. Campbell, PP SC, 1897, Q: 24,601.
30. Macgregor, PP SC, 1897, Q: 25,316.
31. Spens, PP SC, 1897, Q: 20,917.
32. *Ibid.*, Q: 20,918.
33. D. Maitland (female probation officer), YOC, 1925, Q: 4890.
34. *Ibid.*, Q: 4892.
35. *Ibid.*, Q: 4893.
36. M. Hill (Church of Scotland Court Sister and probation officer), in *Report of the Glasgow Conference* (Glasgow: Reformatory and Refuge Union, 1924), p. 86.
37. M. Hill, PP YOC (10 December 1925), Q: 4791.
38. M. O'Donnel (probation officer), PP YOC, 1925, Q: 2672.

39. Of the 21 boys committed in 1925 all but two had previously been on probation. Chambers, PP YOC, 4 November 1925, p. 5.
40. "At a preliminary meeting wives of clergyman of the several Christian denominations resolved to make an appeal to such Christian ladies as could devote some time to the care of the fallen. In response to circulars sent by the various clergymen's wives to their congregation, a large and most encouraging public meeting assembled . . . 100 ladies volunteered their services." (Glasgow Magdalene Institution, Annual report, 1861.
41. A. Summers, "A home from home: women's philanthropic work in the nineteenth century", in Fit work for women, S. Burman (ed.) (London: Croom Helm, 1979), p. 45.
42. National Vigilance Association, Annual report, 1911, p. 5.
43. M. Gittell & T. Shtob, "Changing women's roles in political volunteerism and reform of the city", Signs 5, 1980, p. 69.
44. G. Cheape (Dundee Industrial School), paper given at Edinburgh Conference of Reformatory and Refuge Union, 1911, p. 65.
45. Reformatory and Refuge Union of Edinburgh, Annual report, 1878, p. 106.
46. W. Mitchell quoted in J. M. Roxburgh, The school board of Glasgow, 1872–1919 (London: University of London Press, 1971), p. 193.
47. PP SC, 1897, p. 218.
48. L. Gordon, Heroes of their own lives: the politics and history of family violence (London: Virago, 1988), p. 297.
49. The National Vigilance Association was renamed the Guild of Service of Women in the 1940s.
50. B. Scott, A state of iniquity: its rise, extension and overthrow (London: Routledge & Kegan Paul, 1890), p. 117.
51. Ladies' meeting in Glasgow, The Shield, no. 216, 24 October 1874, p. 207.
52. Edinburgh Magdalene Asylum, Ladies' Committee minute book, 22 April 1878.
53. Ibid., 28 April 1898.
54. L. Davidoff & C. Hall, Family fortunes: men and women of the English middle class, 1780–1850 (London: Hutchinson, 1987), p. 50.
55. J. McFarlane and W. Clark, PP SC, 1897, Q: 25,639. (James McFarlane was Convenor of Mossbank Industrial School, Glasgow, and William Clark was Chairman of the Glasgow Juvenile Delinquency Board).
56. Ibid., Q: 25,635.
57. Ibid., Q: 25,634.
58. G. S. Deverell (Captain, Empress Training Ship), PP SC, 1897, Q: 23,909.
59. Ibid., Q: 23,914–19.
60. Ibid., Q: 23,912.
61. Interview with former industrial school headmaster (retired 1980), Paisley, 28 September 1989.
62. M. Reid, A plea for women (1st edn 1843) (Edinburgh: Polygon, 1988), p. 6.

63. Stevenson, PP SC, 1897, Q: 25,532.
64. C. Hunter-Crastor, PP DC, 1915, Q: 3410. Catherine Hunter was matron of Chapelton Girls' Reformatory in Glasgow between 1893 and 1904. She married John Crastor, the superintendent of Wellington Farm Industrial School for Boys, in 1904, and was matron of that institution when she testified before the Departmental Committee in 1915. Because she also testified before the Select Committee in 1897, to avoid confusion she is referred to throughout as Hunter-Crastor.
65. M. Burton (Edinburgh School Board), PP SC, 1897, Q: 23,669.
66. *Ibid.*, Q: 23,673.
67. *Ibid.*, Q: 23,689–94.
68. *Ibid.*, Q: 23,686.
69. Edinburgh Magdalene Asylum, *Ladies' Committee minute book*, 2 May 1876.
70. Dr A. Watson (medical officer, Aberdeen Female School of Industry), PP DC, 1915, Q: 6556–7.
71. McFarlane and Clark, PP SC, 1897, Q: 25,700–701.
72. J. Nicholson (Reformatory Office agent), PP SC, 1897, Q: 21,198.
73. *Ibid.*, Q: 21,205.
74. *Ibid.*, Q: 21,197.
75. *Ibid.*, Q: 21,214.
76. Craik, PP SC, 1897, Q: 28,306.
77. J. T. Wilson, "The treatment of juvenile delinquency: an appraisal of the Scottish approved school system", unpublished B. Litt. thesis (Glasgow University, 1962), p. 111.

Chapter 5

1. Interview with former industrial school boy (1924–33), Glasgow, 17 July 1990.
2. Interview with former industrial school boy (1914–25), Glasgow, 27 May 1993.
3. Interview with former industrial day school girl (1907–16), Glasgow, 2 August 1989.
4. *Empress* Training Ship, *Annual report*, 1900, p. 29.
5. J. Campbell (Clerk to the Burgh Court, Edinburgh), *Report of the Select Committee on Reformatory and Industrial Schools in Scotland*, Minutes of Evidence, PP, 1897 [cited hereafter as PP SC, 1897], Q: 22,205, 22,215–16. According to Campbell, 1896-8 "we do not ask a plea from the child, or grant a warrant to apprehend a child; they are all brought voluntarily". *ibid.*, Q: 22,203.
6. F. Stevenson and A. Gray (members of the Edinburgh School Board), PP

SC, 1897, Q: 25,465.

7. W. C. Spens (Sheriff Substitute for Lanarkshire), PP SC, 1897, Q: 20,857.
8. Interview with former industrial school headmaster (retired 1980), Paisley, 28 September 1989.
9. Calculated from the annual reports of the Industrial and Reformatory School Inspector, 1861–98.
10. PP SC, 1897, p. 211.
11. Twenty-three per cent of reformatory boys (Table A.4) were under 12 and 77 per cent between 12 and 16, while 13 per cent of the girls were under 12 and 87 per cent between 12 and 16.
12. S. Schlossman & S. Wallach, "The crime of precocious sexuality: female juvenile delinquency in the progressive era", *Harvard Educational Review* 48, 1978, p. 66.
13. C. Dow (Superintendent, Maryhill Industrial School for Girls), *Report of the Departmental Committee in Reformatory and Industrial Schools in Scotland*, Young Offenders (Scotland) Committee, Minutes of Evidence, PP, 1925 [cited hereafter as PP YOC, 1925], Q: 1303.
14. Schlossman & Wallach, "The crime of precocious sexuality", p. 66.
15. Interview with former industrial school headmaster (retired 1980), Paisley, 28 September 1989.
16. L. Mahood, *The magdalenes: prostitution in the nineteenth century* (London: Routledge, 1990), pp. 77–8.
17. Glasgow Magdalene Institution, *Annual report*, 1863.
18. S. Humphries, *Hooligans or rebels? An oral history of working class childhood and youth, 1889–1939* (Oxford: Basil Blackwell, 1981), pp. 236–7.
19. J. Brotherhood (Schoolmaster, Parkhead Reformatory, Glasgow), PP SC, 1897 (9 March 1986), Q: 25,206.
20. *Ibid.*, Q: 25,207–8.
21. *Ibid.*, Q: 25,206.
22. J. McFarlane and W. Clark, PP SC, 1897 (10 March 1897); Q: 25,711.
23. F. Hepburn (Secretary, Edinburgh Society for the Prevention of Cruelty to Children), *Report of the Departmental Committee on Reformatory and Industrial Schools in Scotland*, Minutes of Evidence, PP, 1914 (3 November 1914) [cited hereafter as PP DC, 1914], Q: 7938.
24. R. Ross (Chief Constable, Edinburgh), PP YOC, 1925 (15 February 1925).
25. J. Campbell, PP SC, 1897 (4 March 1896), Q: 24,752–3.
26. PP SC, 1887, p. 16.
27. *Cumberland* Training Ship, *Annual report*, 1870, p. 31.
28. W. Quarrier (Founder, Bridge-of-Weir Home for Orphan and Destitute Children), PP SC, 1897, Q: 25,034, 24,886.
29. Mrs Cameron (Superintendent, Maryhill Industrial School), PP SC, 18 December 1895, Q: 7582.
30. PP SC, 1897, p. 30.
31. C. Hunter-Crastor (Superintendent, East Chapelton Girls' Reformatory), PP SC, 1897, Q: 21,910.

32. J. Hutchison (Superintendent, Fechney Industrial School, Perth), PP SC, 1897, Q: 22,309.
33. *Cumberland* Training Ship, *Annual report*, 1873, p. 10.
34. Dr A. Watson (medical officer, Female Industrial School, Aberdeen), PP DC, 1915, p. 240.
35. PP SC, 1897, p. 16.
36. Watson, *ibid.*
37. J. Sliman, "Food, labour and rest for reformatories for girls", *Prison and Reformatory Gazette*, 1 February 1857, p. 37.
38. Interview with former industrial school boy (1928–32), Ayr, 4 September 1990.
39. J. Barman, *Growing up British in British Columbia: boys in private school* (Vancouver: University of British Columbia Press, 1984), p. 84.
40. J. Campbell (Superintendent, Dundee Industrial School), PP SC, 1897, Q: 24,728–30.
41. A. L. Scott (Captain, *Mars* Training Ship), PP SC, Q: 22,594.
42. Dow, PP YOC, 1925, Q: 1452.
43. *Ibid.*, Q: 1354.
44. Stevenson, PP YOC, 1925, Q: 1862–5.
45. Kilmarnock Ragged and Industrial School, *Annual report*, 1896, p. 9.
46. M. May, "Innocence and experience: the evolution of the concept of juvenile delinquency in the mid-nineteenth century", *Victorian Studies* 17, p. 28, 1973–4.
47. J. T. Wilson, "The treatment of juvenile delinquency: an appraisal of the Scottish approved school system", unpublished B. Litt. thesis (Glasgow University, 1962), p. 141.
48. PP SC, 1897, p. 219.
49. *Ibid.*, p. 43.
50. *Ibid.*, p. 221.
51. Scott, PP DC, 1915, Q: 22,642.
52. McGee (Superintendent, St Joseph's Industrial School, Tranent), PP SC, 1897, Q: 23,993.
53. Glasgow Boys' House of Refuge, *Annual report*, 1864, p. 11.
54. Interview with former industrial school headmaster (retired 1980), Paisley, 28 September 1989.
55. Wilson, "The treatment of juvenile delinquency", p. 201.
56. Hunter-Crastor, PP DC, 1915, Q: 3530.
57. R. Deem (ed.), *Women and schooling* (London: Routledge & Kegan Paul, 1978), p. 1.
58. N. Keddie, "Classroom knowledge", in *Knowledge and control*, M. F. D. Young (ed.) (Milton Keynes, England: Open University Press, 1971), p. 141.
59. *Ibid.*
60. F. S. Smith (Manager, Catholic Working Boys' Home, Edinburgh), PP SC, 1897, Q: 23,249.

61. Brotherhood, PP SC, 1897, Q: 25,100.
62. *Ibid.*, Q: 25,146.
63. W. Smith (Superintendent, Oakbank Industrial School for Boys), PP SC, 1897, Q: 23,352.
64. *Ibid.*, Q: 23,362.
65. Scott, PP SC, 1897, Q: 22,725.
66. Hutchison, PP SC, 1897, Q: 22,441.
67. W. M. Dickson (Superintendent, Boys' School, Baldovan and Secretary of Dundee Industrial School for Boys), PP SC, 1897, Q: 23,129, 22,966–70.
68. Stevenson, PP YOC, 1925, Q: 1857. This trend continued into this century, when after the age of 14 girls still received only three hours of education per day.
69. H. E. Harrison (lady Home Office inspector), PP DC, 1915, Q: 1161–3.
70. Hunter-Crastor, PP DC, 1915, Q: 3461–583.
71. Harrison, PP DC, 1915, Q: 1048–51.
72. Interview with former industrial day school girl (1907–16), Glasgow, 2 August 1989.
73. PP SC, 1897, p. 43.
74. Glasgow Boys' House of Refuge, *Annual report*, 1864, p. 12.
75. *Ibid.*, p. 14.
76. *Cumberland* Training Ship, *Annual report*, 1870, p. 13.
77. *Cumberland* Training Ship, *Annual report*, 1896, p. 21.
78. McFarlane and Clark, PP SC, 1897, Q: 25,759.
79. E. Gordon, "The Scottish trade union movement: class and gender, 1850–1914", *The Journal of the Scottish Labour History Society* 32, 1988.
80. Campbell, PP SC, 1897, Q: 24,790–92.
81. Dow, PP YOC, 1925, Q: 1312.
82. A. Summers, "A home from home: women's philanthropic work in the nineteenth century", in *Fit work for women*, S. Burman (ed.) (London: Croom Helm, 1979), p. 59.
83. Harrison, PP DC, 1915, Q: 1068.
84. *Ibid.*, Q: 1218.
85. Hutchison, PP SC, 1897, Q: 22,353.
86. Dow, PP DC, 1915, Q: 4462.
87. *Ibid.*, Q: 4471.
88. W. McMenan (Superintendent, Kilmarnock Industrial School), "Reformatory and industrial schools: disposal and supervision", *Seeking and saving*, June 1909, p. 105.
89. PP SC, 1897, p. 23.
90. Dickson, PP SC, 1897, Q: 23,054.
91. G. Greig (Parish Inspector for the Poor), PP SC, 1897, Q: 22,856.
92. M. Foucault, *Discipline and punish: the birth of the prison*, trans. A. Sheridan (London: Penguin, 1977).
93. Sliman, "Food, labour and rest for reformatories for girls", p. 37.
94. Cameron, PP SC, 1897, Q: 7452.

95. Dow, PP DC, 1915, Q: 4414–29.
96. *Ibid.*, Q: 1611.
97. ". . . they do not get to sleep out of the school." Dickson, PP SC, 1897, Q: 23,001.
98. *Ibid.*, Q: 22,999.
99. Hutchison, PP SC, 1897, Q: 22,330.
100. W. Smith (Superintendent, Oakbank Industrial School), PP SC, 1897, Q: 32,243.
101. *Ibid.*, Q: 22,227–30.
102. R. Chessum, "Teacher ideologies and pupil disaffection", in *Schooling, ideology and the curriculum*, L. Barton, R. Meighan, S. Walker (eds) (Lewes: Falmer Press, 1980), p. 125.
103. Scottish Education Department, *Revision of punishment rules* (1918), 1930.
104. Hutchison, PP SC, 1897, Q: 22,376.
105. *Ibid.*, PP SC, 1897, Q: 22,376–401.
106. *Cumberland* Training Ship, *Annual report*, 1897, p. 25.
107. *Empress* Training Ship, *Annual report*, 1891.
108. *Cumberland* Training Ship, *Annual report*, 1892, p. 10.
109. Mossbank Industrial School, *Register of offences and punishments*, 1893–1924.
110. Hunter-Crastor, PP SC, 1897, Q: 22,075.
111. *Ibid.*, Q: 22,096.
112. *Ibid.*, Q: 21,935.
113. *Ibid.*, Q: 21,931.
114. *Ibid.*, Q: 21,950.
115. Interview with former industrial day school girl (1945–55), Perth, 25 May 1993.
116. Interview with former reformatory school boy (1927–34), Glasgow, 15 August 1989.
117. Interview with former industrial school boy (1924–33), Glasgow, 17 July 1990.
118. Interview with former industrial school headmaster (retired 1980), Paisley, 28 September 1989.
119. Scott, PP SC, 1897, Q: 22,616.
120. Hutchison, PP SC, 1897, Q: 22,402.
121. C. Haig-Brown, *Resistance and renewal: surviving the Indian residential school* (Vancouver: Tillacum Library, 1989), p. 75. My understanding of the residential school system has been significantly broadened by this study of the Indian residential school.
122. Interview with former approved school boy (1940–48), 23 August 1989.
123. *Ibid.*
124. Humphries, *Hooligans or rebels?*, p. 234.
125. Interview with former approved school boy (1940–48), 23 August 1989.
126. K. Clarke, "Public and private children: infant education 1820–1830", in

Language, gender and childhood, C. Steedman, C. Urwin, V. Walkerdine (eds) (London: Routledge & Kegan Paul, 1985); B. Simon, *Education and the labour movement, 1870–1920* (London: Lawrence & Wishart, 1974).
127. Simon, *Education and the labour movement*.
128. PP SC, 1897, p. 66.
129. John Chambers (Minister, Greenlaw Parish, Paisley), PP YOC, 4 November 1925.
130. PP SC, 1897, p. 66.
131. Greig, PP SC, 1897, Q: 22,817.
132. Watson, PP DC, 1915, Q: 6510, 6557.
133. Hutchison, PP SC, 1897, Q: 22,316.
134. Greig, PP SC, 1897, Q: 22,821.
135. Stevenson, PP YOC, 1925, Q: 1739.
136. PP SC, 1897, p. 54.
137. *Ibid.*, p. 227.
138. PP SC, 1897, Appendix XII, "Abstract of replies to circular questions issued to the schools by the committee", pp. 266–70.
139. Because of the selection process (social class and family background), what is known cannot be generalized to the total population of children charged with offences under the various sections of the Industrial Schools Acts. Nevertheless, the records provide information that is of historical and sociological interest and confirms the results of similar studies of residential schools in other regions of Britain and North America, Austria and New Zealand.

Chapter 6

1. *Reformatory and Refuge Union Journal*, January 1881.
2. Interview with former industrial school headmaster (retired 1980), Paisley, 28 September 1989.
3. Chapters 6 and 7 draw heavily on L. Mahood & B. Littlewood, "The 'vicious' girl and the 'street-corner' boy: sexuality and the gendered delinquent in the Scottish child-saving movement, 1850–1940", *Journal of the History of Sexuality* 4, 1994, pp. 549–78. My original interpretation of the subject has been enhanced significantly through my collaboration with Barbara Littlewood.
4. J. Miller, *Prostitution considered in relation to its causes and cures* (Edinburgh: Sutherland & Knox, 1859), p. 14.
5. M. Valverde, *The age of light, soap and water: moral reform in English Canada, 1885–1925* (Toronto: McClelland & Stewart, 1991), p. 28.
6. M. Foucault, *The history of sexuality: volume 1: an introduction*, trans. R. Hurley (New York: Random House, 1980), p. 104.

7. L. Gordon, *Heroes of their own lives: the politics and history of family violence* (London: Virago, 1988), p. 205.
8. F. Hepburn (Secretary, Edinburgh Division, Scottish Association for the Prevention of Cruelty to Children), *Report of the Departmental Committee on Reformatories and Industrial Schools in Scotland*, Minutes of Evidence, PP, 1915 [cited hereafter as PP DC, 1915], Q: 7919.
9. D. Maitland (female probation officer), *Report of the Departmental Committee on Reformatory and Industrial Schools in Scotland*, Young Offenders (Scotland) Committee, Minutes of Evidence, PP, 1925 [cited hereafter as PP YOC, 1925], Q: 1408.
10. Scottish National Society for the Prevention of Cruelty to Children, *Annual report*, 1911, p. 27.
11. Maryhill Industrial School for Girls, *Girls' register*, 3 June 1914.
12. *Ibid.*, 26 March 1920.
13. *Ibid.*, 11 May 1923.
14. *Ibid.*, 19 April 1923.
15. Mrs J. T. Hunter (National Vigilance Association), PP DC, 1914, Q: 3732.
16. F. Rush, *The best kept secret: sexual abuse of children* (New York: McGraw-Hill, 1980).
17. There were "51 cases of 'criminal assault' in Maryhill Industrial School between 1911 and 1926 . . . 12 committed by parents" (Catherine Dow, PP YOC, 19 November 1925, Q: 1400–405). These parents were not allowed to communicate with their girls (*ibid.*, Q: 1408). Between 1922 and 1924, 132 girls had been living in brothels (Q: 1452).
18. V. Bailey & S. Blackburn, "The Punishment of Incest Act 1908: a case study of law creation", *Criminal Law Review*, 1979, p. 714.
19. A. S. Wohl, "Sex and the single room: incest among the Victorian working classes", in *The Victorian family*, A. S. Wohl (ed.) (New York: St Martin's Press, 1978), p. 199.
20. Gordon, *Heroes of their own lives*, pp. 219, 223–6.
21. *Ibid.*, p. 226.
22. Parish of Glasgow, *Immoral houses and venereal diseases* (Glasgow: Glasgow Parish Council, 1911), p. 60.
23. C. Dow (Superintendent, Maryhill Industrial School for Girls), PP YOC, 1925 (19 November 1925), Q: 1452. See also admission books. In 1922 there were 38 girls in Maryhill Industrial School, in 1923, 50 and in 1924, 44.
24. Maitland, PP YOC, 1925 (15 December 1925), Q: 4920.
25. J. Kitzinger, "Who are you kidding? children, power and the struggle against sexual abuse", in *Constructing and reconstructing childhood*, A. James & A. Prout (eds) (London: Falmer Press, 1990), p. 166.
26. Parish of Glasgow, *Immoral houses and venereal diseases: notes for conference*, p. 4.
27. *Ibid.*, p. 19.
28. A. H. Gray, *Exempted shops. Report II: ice-cream shops* (Glasgow: Scottish

Council for Women's Trades, 1911), p. 7.
29. Parish of Glasgow, *Sexual immorality and prostitution in Glasgow*, p. 10.
30. A. Davin, "The precocity of poverty", unpublished paper presented at British Sociological Association Annual Conference, Edinburgh, 1988, p. 5.
31. Maryhill Industrial School for Girls, *Girls' register,* 26 February 1915.
32. *Ibid.,* 27 August 1920.
33. *Ibid.,* 1 January 1932.
34. National Vigilance Association of Scotland, *Minutes of the Ladies' Committee*, 18 May 1919.
35. *Ibid.,* 1 June 1916.
36. Miller, *Prostitution considered in relation to its causes and cures*, p. 15.
37. M. Maclauchlan (Superintendent, Guthrie's Girls' School), PP YOC, 1925 (1 February 1926), p. 2.
38. W. Smith (Superintendent, Oakbank School), *Report of the Select Committee on Reformatory and Industrial Schools in Scotland*, Minutes of Evidence, PP, 1896–7, xv [cited hereafter as PP SC, 1897], Q: 23,220; E. McGee (Superintendent, St Joseph's Industrial School, Tranent), *ibid.*, Q: 23,988.
39. J. Brotherhood, PP SC, 1897, Q: 25,097.
40. Smith, PP SC, 1897, Q: 23,226.
41. Interview with former industrial school headmaster (retired 1980), Paisley, 28 September 1989.
42. M. Smith Wilson, "The danger of venereal diseases in homes and institutions", *Report of the Leeds conference* (Reformatory and Refuge Union, 1930), p. 44. This conference was attended by delegates from Dundee Girls' School, Edinburgh National Vigilance Association, Dr Guthrie's Girls' School, Maryhill Industrial School for Girls, Slatefield Boys' School, Westthron Boys' Industrial School, St Mary's Industrial School for Boys.
43. *Ibid.*
44. Interview with former industrial school headmaster (retired 1980), Paisley, 28 September 1989.
45. Foucault, *History of sexuality*, pp. 27–8.
46. J. McFarlane and W. Clark, PP SC, 1897, Q: 25,730.
47. Letter from George McDonald to Scottish Office, *Mars. Closure, File II*, 28 December 1928, p. 3.
48. *Ibid.*
49. *Ibid.*
50. Interview with former industrial school headmaster (retired 1980), Paisley, 28 September 1989.
51. Mossbank Industrial School, *Register of offences and punishments*, 1893–1924; *Empress* Training Ship, *Punishment returns*, 6 July 1923.
52. Interview with former approved school boy (1940–48), Glasgow, 23 August 1989.
53. *Ibid.*

54. V. Beechey, "Familial ideology", in *Subjectivity and social relations*, V. Beechey & J. Donald (eds) (Milton Keynes, England: Open University Press, 1985), pp. 99, 105.

55. C. Hunter-Crastor (Superintendent, East Chapelton Girls' Reformatory), PP SC, 1897, Q: 22,036.

56. J. Sliman, "Food, labour and rest for reformatories for girls", *Prison and Reformatory Gazette*, 1 February 1857, p. 37.

57. H. E. Harrison (lady Home Office Inspector), PP DC, 1915, Q: 1055.

58. Glasgow Boys' House of Refuge, *Annual report*, 1864, p. 11.

59. *Ibid.*

60. *Ibid.*

61. *Ibid.*

62. J. T. Wilson, "The treatment of juvenile delinquency: an appraisal of the Scottish approved school system", unpublished B. Litt. thesis (Glasgow University, 1962), p. 202.

63. *Empress* Training Ship, *Annual report*, 1895, p. 24.

64. P. Marks, "Femininity in the classroom", in *The rights and wrongs of women*, J. Mitchell & A. Oakley (eds) (London: Penguin, 1976), p. 183.

65. S. Bowles & H. Gintis, *Schooling in capitalist America* (New York: Basic Books, 1977).

66. Davin, "The precocity of poverty", p. 10.

67. R. Ramsay, "Juvenile street trading", paper presented at National Scottish Conference on the Employment of Children and Kindred Subjects, Glasgow (Scottish Council for Women's Trades), 1909, pp. 29–30.

68. *Ibid.*, p. 29.

69. *Ibid.*

70. J. R. Motion, *Desertion cases: supplementary memorandum* (Glasgow: Glasgow Parish Council, 1909), pp. 1–2.

71. G. Gillie, *Employment of Children Act, 1903* (Glasgow: Glasgow Parish Council, 1909), pp. 6–7.

72. W. Dickson (Secretary, Dundee Industrial School), PP SC, 1897, Q: 23,111.

73. *Ibid.*, Q: 23,144.

74. J. Campbell (Superintendent, Dundee Industrial School), PP SC, 1897, Q: 24,649.

75. Smith, PP SC, 1897, Q: 23,255.

76. *Ibid.*, Q: 23,257.

77. W. C. Spens (Sheriff Substitute, Lanarkshire), PP SC, 1897, Q: 20,978.

78. B. Harrison, "Suffer the working day: women in the "dangerous trades", 1880–1914", unpublished paper presented at British Sociological Association Annual Conference, Edinburgh, 1988, p. 18.

79. Letter to W. Asquith, 22 January 1894, Scottish Records Office, *Manufacture of Lucifer matches at Oakbank Industrial School*.

80. *Ibid.*, letter to W. Stapelton from G. Luchington, 12 January 1894.

81. *Ibid*, letter to Inspector Inglis from John P. Cumnie of Directors of

Oakbank Industrial School, 10 August 1894.

82. K. Marx, *Capital*, vol. I (1st edn 1869) (New York: International Press, 1967), pp. 480–501.

83. *Empress* Training Ship, *Annual report*, 1891, p. 25.

84. *Cumberland* Training Ship, *Annual report*, 1872–3, p. 30.

85. G. S. Deverell (Captain, *Empress* Training Ship), PP SC, 1897, Q: 23,789.

86. *Empress* Training Ship, *Annual report*, 1877, p. 18.

87. J. Playfair (Glasgow Juvenile Delinquency Board), Minutes of Evidence taken before the Select Committee on Criminal and Destitute Children, PP, 1852–3 (26 April 1853), Q: 4450 [cited hereafter as PP SC, 1852–3].

88. *Ibid.*, Q: 4451.

89. Quoted in G. Pearson, *Hooligan: a history of respectable fears* (London: Macmillan, 1983), p. 181.

90. *Ibid.*

91. McFarlane and Clark, PP SC, 1897, Q: 25,663.

92. Glasgow Magdalene Institution, *Committee minute books*, 8 April 1919.

93. J. Barman, *Growing up British in British Columbia: boys in private schools* (Vancouver: University of British Columbia Press, 1984), p. 2.

94. C. Haig-Brown, *Resistance and renewal: surviving the Indian residential school* (Vancouver: Tillacum Library, 1989), p. 67.

95. Rev. Professor Cooper, Conference in Glasgow, *Seeking and saving*, August 1913, p. 396.

96. Interview with former industrial school headmaster (retired 1980), Paisley, 28 September 1989.

97. Wilson, "The treatment of juvenile delinquency", pp. 237–8.

98. M. Speir (Scout Master), PP YOC, 1925, 4 November 1925, p. 5.

99. J. Springhall, "Building character in the British boy: the attempt to extend Christian manliness to working-class adolescents, 1880–1914", in *Manliness and morality: middle class masculinity in Britain and America, 1800–1940*, J. A. Mangan & J. Walvin (eds) (Manchester: Manchester University Press, 1987), p. 57.

100. G. S. Smith (Secretary, Boys' Brigade and son of William Smith, founder of the Boys' Brigade), PP YOC, 1925 (2 February 1926), p. 4.

101. Interview with former industrial school boy (1924–33), Glasgow, 17 July 1990.

102. PP SC, 1897, p. 31.

103. Dow, PP DC, 1915, Q: 4549.

104. E. Rosenfeld, "Re-education of delinquent children", *Approved Schools Gazette*, April 1937, p. 189.

105. "Wayward girls", *Approved Schools Gazette*, January 1946, p. 303.

106. Rosenfeld, "Re-education of delinquent children", pp. 189–90.

107. *Ibid.*, p. 192.

108. *Ibid.*

109. "Wayward girls", p. 304.

110. Interview with former industrial school headmaster (retired 1980), Pais-

ley, 28 September 1989.
111. "Wayward girls", p. 304.
112. G. Cheape, "Helps and hindrances in rescue work and preventative work", *Report of Edinburgh conference* (Edinburgh: Reformatory and Refuge Union, 1911), p. 66.
113. Edinburgh Magdalene Asylum, *Annual report*, 1931, p. 5.
114. Mrs Cameron (Superintendent, Maryhill Industrial School for Girls), PP SC, 1897, Q: 7582.
115. Hunter-Crastor, PP DC, 1915, Q: 3480.
116. *Ibid.*, Q: 22,144.
117. Rosenfeld, "Re-education of delinquent children", p. 190.
118. E. Yeo, "Social motherhood and sexual communication", *Women's History Review* 1, 1992, pp. 63–8.
119. Hunter-Crastor, PP SC, 1897, Q: 22,034.
120. E. Gordon, *Women and the labour movement in Scotland, 1850–1914* (Oxford: Oxford University Press, 1991), p. 160.
121. Hunter-Crastor, PP SC, 1897, Q: 22,009. Also M. R. Stevenson admitted that she "never would tell any person what they had done when they came into the school. If I am looking for a situation for a girl, I do not tell what they are in for" (PP YOC, 1925 (19 November 1925), Q: 1870).
122. N. Williamson, "Factory to reformatory: the founding and the failure of industrial and reform schools for girls in the nineteenth century in New South Wales", *Australia and New Zealand History of Education Society* 9, 1980, p. 34; K. Wimshurst, "Control and resistance: reformatory school for girls in late nineteenth century South Australia", *Journal of Social History* 18, 1984, pp. 278–9.
123. A. Summers, "A home from home: women's philanthropic work in the nineteenth century", in *Fit work for women*, S. Burman (ed.) (London: Croom Helm, 1979), p. 54.
124. N. McLeod, *Notes on the industrial training of pauper children* (Glasgow: Andrew Rutherglen, 1853), p. 21.
125. Hepburn, PP DC, 1915, Q: 7984–5.
126. Interview with former industrial school headmaster (retired 1980), Paisley, 28 September 1989.
127. Scottish National Society for the Prevention of Cruelty to Children, Edinburgh District, *Annual report*, 1912, p. 22.
128. Scottish National Society for the Prevention of Cruelty to Children, Glasgow District, *Annual report*, 1912, p. 23.
129. Bella Walker (leader, St Katherine's Club and Division Secretary, Scottish Division, YWCA), PP YOC, 1925 (26 January 1926), Q: 10,502–3.
130. *Ibid.*, Q: 10,308.
131. *Ibid.*, Q: 10,421–6.
132. *Ibid.*, Q: 10,333.
133. *Ibid.*, Q: 10,447.
134. Margaret Irwin, interview with Walker, PP YOC, 1925, Q: 10,499.

135. Scottish National Council of Juvenile Organizations, report on inquiry into juvenile delinquency, *Seeking and saving*, June 1923, p. 133.
136. M. Buchan, "The social organization of fisher girls", in *Uncharted lives: extracts from Scottish women's experiences, 1850–1982*, Glasgow Women's Studies Group (Glasgow: Pressgang, 1983), pp. 35–51.
137. Walker, PP YOC, 1925, Q: 10,457.
138. *Ibid.*
139. *Ibid.*, Q: 10,351.
140. Interview with former industrial school headmaster (retired 1980), Paisley, 28 September 1989.
141. Edinburgh Magdalene Asylum, *Annual report*, 1880, p. 5.
142. *Ibid.*
143. Harrison, PP DC, 1915, Q: 1051–2.
144. Hunter-Crastor, *Seeking and saving*, September 1904, p. 442.
145. *Ibid.*, p. 441.
146. Cameron, PP SC, 1897, Q: 7840.
147. Sliman, "Food, labour and rest for reformatories for girls", p. 39.
148. Hunter-Crastor, PP SC, 1897, Q: 22,025–8.
149. G. Greig (Inspector of the Poor, St Cuthbert's Parish, Edinburgh), PP SC, 1897, Q: 22,922.
150. M. Stevenson, PP YOC, 1925, Q: 1772.
151. P. Walker, "Men and masculinity in the Salvation Army", in *Manful assertions: masculinities in Britain since 1800*, M. Roper & J. Tosh (eds) (London: Routledge, 1991), p. 120; see also J. Springhall, *Youth, empire and society* (London: Croom Helm, 1977), and J. Gillis, *Youth and history: traditions and change in European age relations, 1770–present* (New York: Academic Press, 1979).
152. Interview with industrial school boy (1924–33), Glasgow, 17 July 1990.
153. A. L. Scott, Mars Training Ship, 1925–9. Contained in *Mars* Industrial Training Ship File, Scottish Records Office (ED 15/79).
154. *Cumberland* Training Ship, *Annual report*, 1872–3, pp. 28–9.
155. Interview with former industrial school headmaster (retired 1980), Paisley, 28 September 1989.
156. L. Davidoff & C. Hall, *Family fortunes: men and women of the English middle class, 1780–1850* (London: Hutchinson, 1987), p. 199.
157. *Empress* Training Ship, *Annual report*, 1895, p. 23.
158. *Cumberland* Training Ship, *Annual report*, 1875, p. 26.
159. Miller, *Prostitution considered in relation to its causes and cures*, p. 10.
160. *Ibid.*, pp. 22–3.
161. *Ibid.*, p. 23.
162. M. Pember Reeves, *Round about a pound a week* (1st edn 1905) (London: Virago, 1979), p. 155.
163. Foucault, *The history of sexuality*, p. 24.
164. Letter from George McDonald to Scottish Office, *Mars. Closure, File II*, 28 December 1928, p. 3.

165. R. Forbes (Sub-Inspector of Schools), PP YOC, 1925 (4 November 1925), p. 2.
166. J. Crawford (Scout Headquarters Commissioner), PP YOC, 1925 (15 January 1926), p. 3.
167. F. Mort, *Dangerous sexualities: medico-moral politics in England since 1830* (London: Routledge & Kegan Paul, 1987), p. 194.
168. *Ibid.*, p. 191.
169. Interview with former industrial school headmaster (retired 1980), Paisley, 28 September 1989.

Chapter 7

1. *Cumberland* Training Ship, *Annual report*, 1894, p. 25.
2. G. S. Deverell (Captain, *Empress* Training Ship), *Report of the Select Committee on Reformatory and Industrial Schools in Scotland*, Minutes of Evidence, PP, 1896–7, xv [cited hereafter as PP SC, 1897], Q: 23,798.
3. M. Maclauchlan (Superintendent, Guthrie's Girls' School), *Report of the Departmental Committee on Reformatory and Industrial Schools in Scotland*, Young Offenders (Scotland) Committee, Minutes of Evidence, PP, 1925 [cited hereafter as PP YOC, 1925], Q: 1264.
4. PP SC, 1897, p. 54; *Report of the Departmental Committee on Reformatory and Industrial Schools in Scotland*, Minutes of Evidence, PP, 1915 [cited hereafter as PP DC, 1915], p. 70.
5. M. Ignatieff, "Total institutions and working classes: a review essay", *History Workshop* 15, 1983, pp. 168–9.
6. Quoted in a "leading periodical" reproduced in Kilmarnock Ragged and Industrial School, *Annual report*, 1868.
7. Maclauchlan, Q: 5028.
8. D. Maitland, PP YOC, 1925, Q: 4992.
9. *Ibid.*, Q: 4992.
10. M. Hill (female probation officer), PP YOC, 1925, Q: 4752.
11. F. Hepburn (Secretary, Edinburgh Society for the Prevention of Cruelty to Children), PP DC, 1915, Q: 7985, 8025.
12. L. Gordon, *Heroes of their own lives: the politics and history of family violence* (London: Virago, 1988), p. 295.
13. Scottish National Society for the Prevention of Cruelty to Children, *Annual report*, 1885, p. 6.
14. Edinburgh Magdalene Asylum, *House Committee minute book*, 11 May 1880. Many inmates of magdalene asylums were also taken away from the institution by their parents.
15. Maryhill Industrial School for Girls, *Girls' register*, 19 March 1920.
16. S. Damer, *Glasgow: going for a song* (London: Lawrence & Wishart, 1990), p. 92.

17. *Ibid.*, p. 91.
18. M. O'Donnel (Glasgow probation officer), PP YOC, 1925, Q: 2688.
19. C. Stansell, "Women, children, and the uses of the street: class and gender conflict in New York City, 1850–1860", in *Unequal sisters: a multicultural reader in US women's history*, E. Dubois & V. Ruiz (eds) (London: Routledge, 1990), p. 93.
20. E. King, "Popular culture in Glasgow", in *The working class in Glasgow, 1750–1914*, R. A. Cage (ed.) (London: Croom Helm, 1987), p. 144.
21. Ignatieff, "Total institutions and working classes", p. 170.
22. M. A. Crowther, *The workhouse system, 1834–1929* (London: Batsford Academic, 1981), quoted in *ibid.*, p. 172.
23. B. Bradbury, "The fragmented family: family strategies in the face of death, illness and poverty, Montreal, 1860–1885", in *Childhood and family in Canadian history*, J. Parr (ed.) (Toronto: McClelland & Stewart, 1982), pp. 110, 128.
24. Interview with former industrial day school girl (1925–8), Glasgow, 7 August 1989.
25. Interview with former reformatory school boy (1927–34), Glasgow, 15 August 1989.
26. Interview with former industrial school boy (1924–33), Glasgow, 17 July 1990.
27. Hepburn, PP DC, 1915, Q: 7939.
28. Mrs J. T. Hunter (National Vigilance Association), PP DC, 1915, Q: 5789.
29. *Ibid.*
30. Damer, *Glasgow: going for a song*, p. 88.
31. Letter, *Clyde industrial training ship re: closure*, Scottish Education Department Files, 14 June 1923.
32. *Ibid.*, 13 June 1923.
33. Letter, *Clyde industrial training ship re: closure*, Scottish Education Department Files, 14 February 1923.
34. Gordon, *Heroes of their own lives*, p. 240.
35. Hepburn, PP DC, 1915, Q: 7957.
36. *Ibid.*, Q: 7932.
37. Interview with former industrial day school girl (1925–8), Glasgow, 7 August 1989.
38. D. Maitland, PP YOC, 1925, Q: 4889.
39. Interview with former parish school pupil (1928–35), Glasgow, 7 August 1989.
40. C. Dow (Superintendent, Maryhill Industrial School), PP DC, 1915, Q: 4575.
41. Deverell, PP SC, 1897, Q: 23,789.
42. A. L. Scott, *The evolution of the "Mars" ship* (printed for private circulation only). Scottish Records Office ED 15/79). *Mars* Industrial Training Ship File, 1920–29, p. 19.
43. M. Maclauchlan (Superintendent, Guthrie's Girls' School), PP YOC, 1925

(7 February 1926), Q: 1153.
44. Mrs Cameron (Superintendent, Maryhill Industrial School for Girls), PP SC, 1897, Q: 7762.
45. J. Kesson, *The white bird passes* (Edinburgh: Paul Harris Publications, 1980), p. 110.
46. "I have seldom found girls come willingly to the school". Maclauchlan, PP YOC, 1925 (7 February 1926), Q: 1151.
47. *Ibid.*, Q: 1206.
48. Maclauchlan, *ibid.*, Q: 1106.
49. Kesson, *The white bird passes*, p. 112.
50. BBC Scotland documentary, *Washing away the stain*, research notes, December 1992.
51. "The runaways from the *Mars*", *Daily Telegraph*, 6 June 1876 (Dundee Public Library, 190(27)).
52. *Reformatory and Refuge Union Journal*, November 1876, p. 134.
53. *Ibid.*, July 1878, p. 410.
54. *Ibid.*, January–March 1882, p. 27.
55. "Clyde Industrial Training Ship was totally destroyed by fire yesterday. Fortunately all who were on board escaped without the slightest bodily injury, but so rapidly did the flames make headway that all personal effects and stores had to be sacrificed . . . there were 390 [boys] on board [plus the staff] . . . it is alleged that [some straw] mattresses were deliberately set on fire by some youths, who had by some means or another got possession of the keys to the room . . . From an investigation that was made at the outbreak of the fire there was little reason to doubt that it was deliberately planned." "The burning of the *Cumberland*, alleged incendiarism, four boys arrested", *Glasgow Herald*, 19 February 1889 (Strathclyde Regional Archives, MP 327).
56. Interview Jim Henderson (former *Daily Express* reporter), BBC Scotland documentary, *Washing away the stain*, research notes, 1992.
57. R. Chessum, "Teacher ideologies and pupil disaffection", in *Schooling, ideology and the curriculum*, L. Barton, R. Meighan, S. Walker (eds) (Sussex: Falmer Press, 1980), p. 113.
58. M. L. Wax, R. H. Wax, R. V. Dumont, "Formal education in an American Indian community", *Social Problems* 11, 1964, p. 99.
59. S. Humphries, *Hooligan or rebels? An oral history of working class childhood and youth, 1889–1939* (Oxford: Basil Blackwell, 1981), p. 226.
60. Chessum, "Teacher ideologies and pupil disaffection", p. 119.
61. D. Gorham, "'The maiden tribute to modern Babylon' re-examined: child prostitution and the idea of childhood in late-Victorian England", *Victorian Studies*, Spring 1979, p. 356.
62. N. Williamson, "Factory to reformatory: the founding and the failure of industrial and reform schools for girls in the nineteenth century in New South Wales", *Australia and New Zealand History of Education Society* 9, 1980, p. 39.

63. B. Walker (leader, St Katherine's Club and division secretary, Scottish Division, YWCA), PP YOC, 1925, Q: 10,457.
64. Dr A Watson (medical officer, Aberdeen Girls' Industrial School), PP DC, 1915, Q: 6526.
65. Interview with former industrial day school girl (1907–16), Glasgow, August 1989.
66. Hepburn, PP DC, 1915, Q: 7992.
67. BBC Scotland documentary, *Washing away the stain*, research notes, December 1992.
68. Interview with former industrial school headmaster (retired 1980), Paisley, 28 September 1989.
69. M. Barrett & M. McIntosh, *The anti-social family* (London: Verso, 1982).
70. N. Fraser, *Unruly practices: power, discourse and gender in contemporary social theory* (Cambridge: Polity, 1989).
71. L. Mahood & B. Littlewood, "The 'vicious' girl and the 'street-corner' boy: sexuality and the gendered delinquent in the Scottish child-saving movement, 1850–1940", *Journal of the History of Sexuality* 4, 1994, pp. 549–78.
72. Fraser, *Unruly practices*, p. 157.
73. *Ibid.*

Bibliography

Adams, P. Family affairs. *M/F* 7, 1982, pp. 3–14.

Approved Schools Gazette, April 1937, p. 189; January 1946, p. 303.

Bailey, V. & S. Blackburn. The Punishment of Incest Act 1908: a case study of law creation. *Criminal Law Review*, 1979, pp. 709–18.

Balibar, E. Class racism. In *Race, nation, class: ambiguous identities*, E. Balibar & I. Wallerstein (eds) (London: Verso, 1991).

Barman, J. *Growing up British in British Columbia: boys in private school* (Vancouver: University of British Columbia Press, 1984).

Barrett, M. & M. McIntosh. *The anti-social family* (London: Verso, 1982).

Beechey, V. Familial ideology. In *Subjectivity and social relations*, V. Beechey & J. Donald (eds) (Milton Keynes, England: Open University Press, 1985).

Bellingham, B. The history of childhood since the "invention of childhood": some issues in the eighties. *Journal of Family History* 13, 1988, p. 354.

Bertram, J. *A deeper glimpse of the social evil* (Edinburgh: Charles Harvey, 1866).

Bertram, J. *Glimpses of the social evil in Edinburgh and elsewhere* (Edinburgh: Charles Harvey, 1864).

Block, G. Women's history and gender history: aspects of an international debate. *Gender and History* 1, 1989, pp. 7–30.

Bowles, S. & H. Gintis. *Schooling in capitalist America* (New York: Basic Books, 1977).

Boyd, K. M. *Scottish church attitudes to sex, marriage and the family, 1850–1914* (Edinburgh: John Donald, 1980).

Boyd, N. Historical background. In *The Scottish juvenile justice system*, F. M. Martin & K. Murray (eds) (Edinburgh: Scottish Academic Press, 1982).

Bradbury, B. The fragmented family: family strategies in the face of death, illness and poverty, Montreal, 1860–1885. In *Childhood and family in Canadian history*, J. Parr (ed.) (Toronto: McClelland & Stewart, 1982).

Brebner, W. *A letter to the Lord Provost on the expediency of a House of Refuge for juvenile offenders* (Glasgow, 1829).

Brenzel, B. Domestication as reform: a study of the socialization of wayward girls, 1856–1905. *Harvard Educational Review* 50, 1980, pp. 196–213.

Bristow, E. *Vice and vigilance: purity movements in Britain since 1700* (London: Gill & Macmillan, 1977).

Bruce, N. Historical background. In *The Scottish juvenile justice system*, F. M. Martin & K. Murray (eds) (Edinburgh: Scottish Academic Press, 1982).

Bryce, J. D. *The Glasgow magdalene asylum, its past and present: with relative facts and suggestions* (Glasgow: David Bryce, 1859).

Buchan, M. The social organization of fisher girls. In *Uncharted lives: extracts from Scottish women's experiences, 1850–1982*, Glasgow Women's Studies Group (Glasgow: Pressgang, 1983).

Butt. Housing. In *The working class in Glasgow, 1750–1914*, R. Cage (ed.) (London: Croom Helm, 1987).

Cameron, J. *Prisons and punishment in Scotland: from the Middle Ages to the present* (Edinburgh: Canongate, 1983).

Carpenter, M. *Reformatory schools,* 1869 edn (New York: Augustus Kelly Publishing, 1851).

Cheape, G. Helps and hindrances in rescue work and preventative work. *Report of Edinburgh conference* (Edinburgh: Reformatory and Refuge Union, 1911).

Checkland, O. *Philanthropy in Victorian Scotland: social welfare and the voluntary principle* (Edinburgh: John Donald, 1980).

Checkland, S. & O. Checkland. *Industry and ethos, Scotland, 1832–1914* (London: Edward Arnold, 1984).

Chessum, R. Teacher ideologies and pupil disaffection. In *Schooling, ideology and the curriculum*, L. Barton, R. Meigham, S. Walker (eds) (Sussex: Falmer Press, 1980).

City of Glasgow Police, *Criminal returns,* 1910.

Clark, E. A. G. The superiority of the "Scotch system": Scottish ragged schools and their influence. *Scottish Educational Studies* 9, 1977, pp. 29–39.

Clarke, K. Public and private children: infant education in 1820–1830. In *Language, gender and childhood*, C. Steedman, C. Urwin, V. Walkerdine (eds) (London: Routledge & Kegan Paul, 1985).

Cohen, Sherrill. *The evolution of women's asylums since 1500: from refuges for ex-prostitutes to shelters for battered women* (London: Oxford University Press, 1992).

Cohen, Stanley, *Visions of social control: crime, punishment and classification* (Cambridge: Polity, 1985).

Corr, H. An exploration into Scottish education. In *People and society in Scotland*, vol. 2, W. H. Fraser & R. J. Morris (eds) (Edinburgh: John Donald, 1989).

Corrigan, P., B. Curtis, R. Lanning. The political space of schooling. In *The political economy of Canadian schooling*, T. Wotherspoon (ed.) (London: Methuen, 1987).

Corrigan, P. & D. Sayers. *The great arch* (Oxford: Basil Blackwell, 1985).

Coyle, A. *Inside: rethinking Scotland's prisons* (Edinburgh: Scottish Child, 1991).

Crowther, M. A. *The workhouse system, 1834–1929* (London: Batsford Academic, 1981).

Cumberland Training Ship, *Annual reports*, 1870, 1871, 1872–3, 1873, 1875, 1892, 1894, 1896, 1897.

Cunningham, J. The child under the Poor Law. *Royal Philosophical Society* (Glasgow: Glasgow Parish Council, 1912).

Damer, S. *Glasgow: going for a song* (London: Lawrence & Wishart, 1990).

David, M. *The state, the family and education* (London: Routledge & Kegan Paul, 1980).

Davidoff, L. & C. Hall. *Family fortunes: men and women of the English middle class, 1780–1850* (London: Hutchinson, 1987).

Davin, A. Imperialism and motherhood. *History Workshop* 5, 1978.

Davin, A. The precocity of poverty. Unpublished paper presented at British Sociological Association Annual Conference, Edinburgh, 1988, p. 5.

Davin, A. When is a child not a child? In *Politics of everyday life: continuity and change in work and family life*, H. Corr & L. Jamieson (eds) (London: Macmillan, 1990).

Deem, R. (ed.). *Women and schooling* (London: Routledge & Kegan Paul, 1978).

Delman, M. Child among the bluebells. Unpublished manuscript (Drumchapel Writers Group, Glasgow, 1993).

Departmental Committees on Reformatory and Industrial Schools in Scotland, Reports, 1914, 1915, 1925.

Dickey, B. The establishment of industrial schools and reformatories in New South Wales, 1850–1875. *Journal of Royal Australian Historical Society* 54, 1968, pp. 135–51.

Dobash, R. P., R. E. Dobash, S. Gutteridge. *The imprisonment of women* (Oxford: Basil Blackwell, 1986).

Donzelot, J. *The policing of families*, trans. R. Hurley (London: Hutchinson, 1979).

Douglas, W. M. The juvenile delinquent. Paper presented at National Scottish Conference on the Employment of Children and Kindred Subjects, Glasgow (Scottish Council for Women's Trades), 5–6 November 1909.

Edinburgh Magdalene Asylum, *Annual reports*, 1801–1947.

Edinburgh Magdalene Asylum, *House Committee minute book*, 1876–1934.

Edinburgh Magdalene Asylum, *Ladies' Committee minute book*, 1873–1938.

Empress Training Ship, *Annual reports*, 1877, 1891, 1895, 1900.

Ferguson, T. *The dawn of Scottish social welfare* (London: Thomas Nelson, 1948).

Fitz, J. The child as legal subject. In *Education and the state,* vol. 2, R. Dale et al. (eds) (Sussex: Falmer Press, 1981).

Foucault, M. *Discipline and punish: the birth of the prison*, trans. A. Sheridan (London: Penguin, 1977).

Foucault, M. *The history of sexuality: volume 1: an introduction*, trans. R. Hurley (New York: Random House, 1980).

Fraser, N. *Unruly practices: power, discourse and gender in contemporary social theory* (Cambridge: Polity, 1989).

Garland, D. *Punishment and welfare* (Aldershot, England: Gower, 1985).

Geddes, M. *Some notes on remand homes and approved schools* (Paper no. 6, Scottish Advisory Council on the Treatment and Rehabilitation of Offenders, November 1964).

Gillie, G. *Employment of Children Act, 1903* (Glasgow: Glasgow Parish Council, 1909).

Gillis, J. *Youth and history: traditions and change in European age relations, 1770–present* (New York: Academic Press, 1979).

Gittell, M. & T. Shtob. Changing women's roles in political volunteerism and reform of the city. *Signs* 5, 1980, pp. 67–78.

Glasgow Boys' House of Refuge, *Annual reports*, 1838, 1864.

Glasgow Girls' Reformatory, *Annual report*, 1860.

Glasgow Herald, 13 February 1932, p. 4.

Glasgow Magdalene Institution, *Annual reports*, 1862–1889.

Glasgow Magdalene Institution, *Committee minute books*, 8 April 1919.

Glasgow Magdalene Institution, *Homes Committee minute books*, 1920–35.

Glasgow Special Committee on Probation of Offenders, Report, *Seeking and saving*, May 1919.

Goldman, J. A peculiarity of the English: the social science association and the absence of sociology in nineteenth century Britain. *Past and Present* 114, 1987, pp. 133–71.

Gordon, E. The Scottish trade union movement: class and gender, 1850–1914. *The Journal of the Scottish Labour History Society* 32, 1988.

Gordon, E. *Women and the labour movement in Scotland, 1850–1914* (Oxford: Oxford University Press, 1991).

Gordon, E. Women's sphere. In *People and society in Scotland: volume II, 1830–1914*, W. H. Fraser & R. J. Morris (eds) (Edinburgh: John Donald, 1989).

Gordon, E. & E. Breitenbach (eds). *Out of bounds: women in Scottish society, 1800–1945* (Edinburgh: Edinburgh University Press, 1992).

Gordon, L. What's new in women's history. In *Feminist studies/critical studies*, T. deLaurentis (ed.) (Bloomington, Indiana: Indiana University Press, 1986), pp. 21–40.

Gordon, L. *Heroes of their own lives: the politics and history of family violence* (London: Virago, 1989).

Gorham, D. "The maiden tribute to modern Babylon" re-examined: child prostitution and the idea of childhood in late-Victorian England. *Victorian Studies*, Spring 1979, pp. 353–79.

Gray, A. H. *Exempted shops. Report II: ice-cream shops* (Glasgow: Scottish Council for Women's Trades, 1911).

Guthrie, T. *A plea for ragged schools: prevention better than cure* (Edinburgh: John Elder, 1847).

Haig-Brown, C. *Resistance and renewal: surviving the Indian residential school*

(Vancouver: Tillacum Library, 1989).

Harris, R. & D. Webb. *Welfare, power and juvenile justice: the social control of delinquent youth* (London: Tavistock, 1987).

Harrison, B. "Suffer the working day: women in the "dangerous trades", 1880–1914". Unpublished paper presented at the British Sociological Association Annual Conference, Edinburgh, 1988.

Hendrick, H. *Images of youth: age, class and the male youth problem, 1880–1920* (Oxford: Clarendon Press, 1990).

Hill, M. A few words on probation. *Report of the Glasgow conference* (Glasgow: Reformatory and Refuge Union, 1924).

Hirst, P. The genesis of the social. *Politics and Power* 3, 1981, pp. 65–89.

House of Lords, *Report of Select Committee on the Glasgow Houses of Refuge Bill*, 6 March 1877.

Humphries, J. Class struggle and the persistence of the working class family. *Cambridge Journal of Economics* 3, 1977, pp. 241–58.

Humphries, S. *Hooligans or rebels? An oral history of working class childhood and youth, 1889–1939* (Oxford: Basil Blackwell, 1981).

Hunter, S. L. *The Scottish educational system* (Oxford: Pergamon, 1971).

Ignatieff, M. *A just measure of pain* (London: Macmillan, 1978).

Ignatieff, M. State, civil society and total institutions: a critique of recent social histories of punishment. In *Social control and the state*, S. Cohen & A. Skull (eds) (Oxford: Martin Robertson, 1983), pp. 165–73.

Ignatieff, M. The ideological origins of the penitentiary. In *Crime and society: readings in history and theory*, M. Fitzgerald, G. McLennan, J. Pawson (eds) (London: Routledge & Kegan Paul, 1986), pp. 37–59.

Ignatieff, M. Total institutions and working classes: a review essay. *History Workshop* 15, 1983, pp. 168–9.

Johnson, R. Educating the educators: "experts" and the state, 1833–39. *Social control in nineteenth century Britain*, A. P. Donajgrodski (ed.) (London: Croom Helm, 1977), pp. 77–107.

Johnson, R. Educational policy and social control in early Victorian England. *Past and Present* 49, 1970, pp. 96–119.

Keddie, N. Classroom knowledge. In *Knowledge and control*, M. F. D. Young (ed.) (Milton Keynes, England: Open University Press, 1971).

Kesson, J. *The white bird passes* (Edinburgh: Paul Harris Publications, 1980).

Kilmarnock Ragged and Industrial School, *Annual reports*, 1868, 1896.

King, E. Popular culture in Glasgow. In *The working class in Glasgow, 1750–1914*, R. A. Cage (ed.) (London: Croom Helm, 1987).

Kitzinger, J. Who are you kidding? children, power, and the struggle against sexual abuse. In *Constructing and reconstructing childhood*, A. James & A. Prout (ed.) (London: Falmer Press, 1990).

Lamond, R. P. *Memorandum on the Children Act, 1908* (Glasgow: Glasgow Parish Council, 1909).

Lasch, C. *Haven in a heartless world: the family besieged* (New York: Basic Books, 1977).

Lewis, J. *Politics of motherhood: child and maternal welfare in England, 1900–1939* (London: Croom Helm, 1980).

List, A. C. C. *The two phases of social evil* (Edinburgh: Ogle & Murray, 1859).

Littlewood, B. & L. Mahood. Prostitutes, magdalenes and wayward girls: dangerous sexualities of working class women in Victorian Scotland. *Gender and History* 3, 1991, pp. 160–75.

Logan, W. *The great social evil: its causes, extent, results and remedies* (London: Hodder & Stoughton, 1871).

MacDonald, M. Schooling and the reproduction of class and gender relations. In *Schooling, ideology and the curriculum*, L. Barton, R. Meighan, S. Walker (eds) (Sussex: Falmer Press, 1980), pp. 29–49.

MacDonald, M. Socio-cultural reproduction and women's education. In *Schooling for women's work*, R. Deem (ed.) (London: Routledge & Kegan Paul, 1980), pp. 13–25.

MacDonell, D. *Theories of discourses* (Oxford: Basil Blackwell, 1986).

MacGill, S. *Discourses and essays on subjects of public interest* (Edinburgh: Glasgow Society for the Encouragement of Penitents, Waugh & Innes, 1819).

McLeod, N. *Notes on the industrial training of pauper children* (Glasgow: Andrew Rutherglen, 1853).

Mahood, L. Family ties: lady child-savers and girls of the street, 1850–1925. In *Out of bounds: women in Scottish society, 1800–1945*, E. Breitenbach & E. Gordon (eds) (Edinburgh: Edinburgh University Press, 1992).

Mahood, L. *The magdalenes: prostitution in the nineteenth century* (London: Routledge, 1990).

Mahood, L. & B. Littlewood. The "vicious" girl and the "street-corner" boy: sexuality and the gendered delinquent in the Scottish child-saving movement, 1850–1940. *Journal of the History of Sexuality* 4, 1994, pp. 549–78.

Marks, P. Femininity in the classroom. In *The rights and wrongs of women*, J. Mitchell & A. Oakley (eds) (London: Penguin, 1979).

Marx, K. *Capital*, vol. 1 (1st edn 1869) (New York: International Press, 1967).

Maryhill Industrial School for Girls, *Girls' register*, 1914–40.

May, M. Innocence and experience: the evolution of the concept of juvenile delinquency in the mid-nineteenth century. *Victorian Studies* 17, 1973–4, pp. 7–29.

Mechie, S. *The church and Scottish social development, 1780–1879* (Westport: Greenwood Press, 1975).

Melossi, D. & M. Pavarini. *The prison and the factory: origins of the penitentiary system*, trans. G. Cousins (London: Macmillan, 1981).

Miller, J. *Prostitution considered in relation to its causes and cures* (Edinburgh: Sutherland & Knox, 1859).

Morgan, D. Men made manifest: histories and masculinities. *Gender and History* 1, pp. 87–91.

Mort, F. *Dangerous sexualities: medico-moral politics in England since 1830* (London: Routledge & Kegan Paul, 1987).

Mossbank Industrial School, *Register of offences and punishments*, 1893–1924.

Motion, J. R. *Desertion cases: supplementary memorandum* (Glasgow: Glasgow Parish Council, 1909).

Motion, J. R. *Immoral houses and venereal diseases* (Glasgow: Glasgow Parish Council, 1911).

National Vigilance Association, *Annual report*, 1911–20.

National Vigilance Association of Scotland, *Minutes of the Ladies' Committee*, 1 June 1916, 18 May 1919.

Nead, L. The magdalene in modern times: the mythology of the fallen woman in pre-Raphaelite painting. In *Looking at images of femininity in the visual arts and media*, R. Betterton (ed.) (London: Pandora Press, 1987).

Oakley, C. A. *Second city*, 2nd edn (Glasgow: Blackie, 1967).

Parish Council of Glasgow, *Immoral houses and venereal diseases* (Glasgow: Glasgow Parish Council, 1911).

Parish of Glasgow, *Memorandum on the social evil in Glasgow and the state of the law for dealing with certain forms of immorality* (Parish of Glasgow, 1911).

Paterson, F. Schooling the family. Sociology 22, 1988, p. 65–86.

Pearson, G. *Hooligan: a history of respectable fears* (London: Macmillan, 1983).

Platt, A. *The child-savers: the invention of delinquency* (Chicago: University of Chicago Press, 1969).

Playfair, J. Minutes of Evidence taken before the Select Committee on Criminal and Destitute Children, 26 April 1853, Q: 4471.

Pleck, E. Reviews, *Journal of Social History*, pp. 401–3, 1989.

Rafter, N. Chastising the unchaste: social control functions of a women's reformatory. In *Social control and the state*, S. Cohen & A. Skull (eds) (London: Martin Robertson, 1983), pp. 288–311.

Rafter, N. *Partial justice: women in state prisons* (Boston: Northeastern University Press, 1985).

Ralston, A. The development of reformatory and industrial schools in Scotland, 1832–1872. *Scottish Economic and Historical Society* 8, 1988, pp. 40–55.

Ramsay, R. Juvenile street trading. Paper presented at National Scottish Conference on the Employment of Children and Kindred Subjects, Glasgow (Scottish Council for Women's Trades, 5–6 November 1909).

Reeves, M. Pember. *Round about a pound a week* (1st edn 1905) (London: Virago, 1979).

Reformatory and Refuge Union of Edinburgh, *Annual report*, 1878.

Reformatory and Refuge Union Journal, November 1876, January 1881.

Reid, M. *A plea for women* (1st edn 1843) (Edinburgh: Polygon, 1988).

Report of the Glasgow Special Committee on Probation of Offenders, *Seeking and saving*, May 1919.

Roper, M. Recent books on masculinity. *History Workshop* 29, 1990, pp. 184–90.

Rosenfeld, E. Re-education of delinquent children. *Approved Schools Gazette*, pp. 186–92, April 1937.

Rotundo, E. A. Romantic friendship: male intimacy and middle-class youth in the northern United States, 1800–1900. *Journal of Social History* 23, 1989, pp. 1–25.

535

Roxburgh, J. M. *The school board of Glasgow, 1873–1919* (London: University of London Press, 1971).

Rush, F. *The best kept secret: sexual abuse of children* (New York: McGraw-Hill, 1980).

Rutherford Hill, J. Some helps and hindrances in rescue and preventive work among women and girls. Paper presented at National Conference of Reformatory and Refuge Union, Edinburgh, 1911.

Ryan, M. The power of women's networks. In *Sex and class in women's history*, M. P. Ryan, J. L. Newton, J. Walkowitz (eds) (London: Routledge & Kegan Paul, 1983).

Satzewich, V. *Racism and the incorporation of foreign labour* (London: Routledge, 1991).

Schlossman, S. & S. Wallach. The crime of precocious sexuality: female juvenile delinquency in the progressive era. *Harvard Educational Review* 48, 1978, pp. 65–94.

Scotland, J. *The history of Scottish education from the beginning to 1872*, vol. 1 (London: University of London Press, 1972).

Scott, B. *A state of iniquity: its rise, extension and overthrow* (London: Routledge & Kegan Paul, 1890).

Scottish Education Department, *Approved schools: methods for dealing with difficult girls and boys: special status for Glasgow Magdalene Institution*, 1932.

Scottish Education Department, *Provision of approved schools*, 1923.

Scottish Education Department, *Revision of punishment rules* (1918), 1930.

Scottish National Council of Juvenile Organizations, report on inquiry into juvenile delinquency, *Seeking and saving*, June 1923.

Scottish National Society for the Prevention of Cruelty to Children, *Annual reports*, 1885, 1911.

Scottish National Society for the Prevention of Cruelty to Children, Edinburgh District, *Annual report*, 1912.

Scottish National Society for the Prevention of Cruelty to Children, Glasgow District, *Annual report*, 1912.

Select Committees on Reformatory and Industrial Schools in Scotland, Reports, 1896–7.

Simon, B. *Education and the labour movement, 1870–1920* (London: Lawrence & Wishart, 1974).

Sliman, J. Food, labour and rest for reformatories for girls. *Prison and Reformatory Gazette*, 1 February 1857, pp. 36–8.

Smail, J. New languages for labour and capital: the transformation of discourse in the early years of the industrial revolution. *Social History* 12, 1987, pp. 49–71.

Smart, B. *Michel Foucault* (London: Tavistock, 1985).

Smith-Rosenberg, C. The female world of love and ritual: relations between women in nineteenth-century America. *Signs* 1, 1975, pp. 1–29.

Smout, T. C. *A century of the Scottish people, 1830–1950* (London: Collins, 1986).

Smout, T. C. *A history of the Scottish people, 1560–1830* (London: Fontana, 1969).

Springhall, J. *Youth, empire and society* (London: Croom Helm, 1977)

Springhall, J. Building character in the British boy: the attempt to extend Christian manliness to working-class adolescents, 1880–1914. In *Manliness and morality: middle class masculinity in Britain and America, 1800–1940*, J. A. Mangan & J. Walvin (eds) (Manchester: Manchester University Press, 1987).

Squires, P. *Anti-social policy: welfare, ideology and the disciplinary state* (Hemel Hempstead: Harvester, 1990).

Stansell, C. Women, children and the uses of the street: class and gender conflict in New York City, 1850–1860. In *Unequal sisters: a multicultural reader in US women's history*, E. Dubois & V. Ruiz (eds) (London: Routledge, 1990).

Steadman-Jones, G. The threat of outcast London. In *Crime and society: readings in history and theory*, M. Fitzgerald, G. McLennan, J. Pawson (eds) (London: Routledge & Kegan Paul, 1986).

Steedman, C., C. Urwin, V. Walkerdine (eds). *Language, gender and childhood* (London: Routledge & Kegan Paul, 1985).

Summers, A. A home from home: women's philanthropic work in the nineteenth century. In *Fit work for women*, S. Burman (ed.) (London: Croom Helm, 1979).

Thane, P. Childhood in history. In *Childhood, welfare and justice: a critical examination of children in the legal and childcare systems*, M. King (ed.) (London: Batsford Academic, 1981).

Thomson, A. *On the licentiousness of Scotland, and the remedial measures which ought to be adopted* (London: J. Nisbet, 1861).

Transactions of the National Association for the Promotion of Social Sciences, *Annual report* (Edinburgh, 1880).

Treble, J. H. Juvenile labour market and the structure of Glasgow's adult male casual labour market, 1890–1914. Unpublished manuscript (Strathclyde University, 1985).

Treble, J. H. The characteristics of the female unskilled labour market and the formation of the female casual labour market in Glasgow, 1891–1914. *Scottish Economic and Social History* 6, 1986, pp. 33–46.

Valverde, M. *The age of light, soap and water: moral reform in English Canada, 1885–1925* (Toronto: McClelland & Stewart, 1991).

Walker, P. Men and masculinity in the Salvation Army. In *Manful assertions: masculinities in Britain since 1800*, M. Roper & J. Tosh (eds) (London: Routledge, 1991).

Watson, W. *Ragged and industrial schools* (Edinburgh: Blackwood & Sons, 1872).

Wax, M. L., R. H. Wax, R. V. Dumont. Formal education in an American Indian community. *Social Problems* 11, 1964, p. 99.

Weedon, C. *Feminist practice and post-structuralist theory* (Oxford: Basil Blackwell, 1987).

Weeks, J. *Sex, politics and society: the regulation of sexuality since 1800*

211

(Harlow, England: Longman, 1981).

Williamson, N. Factory to reformatory: the founding and the failure of industrial and reform schools for girls in the nineteenth century in New South Wales. *Australia and New Zealand History of Education Society* 9, 1980, pp. 32–41.

Williamson, N. "Hymns, songs and blackguard verses": life in the industrial and reformatory school for girls in New South Wales: part I, 1867–1887. *Journal of the Royal Australian Historical Society* 67, 1982, p. 379.

Williamson, N. Laundry maids or ladies? life in the industrial and reformatory school for girls in New South Wales: part II, 1887–1910. *Journal of the Royal Australian Historical Society* 68, 1983, pp. 312–432.

Willis, P. *Learning to labour: how working class kids get working class jobs* (New York: Columbia University Press, 1977).

Willis, S. Made to be moral – at Parramatta Girls' School, 1893–1923. In *Twentieth century Sydney: studies in urban and social history*, J. Roe (ed.) (Sydney: Hale & Iremonger, 1980).

Wilson, J. T. The treatment of juvenile delinquency: an appraisal of the Scottish approved school system. Unpublished B. Litt. thesis (Glasgow University, 1962).

Wilson, M. Smith. The danger of venereal diseases in homes and institutions. *Report of the Leeds conference* (Reformatory and Refuge Union, 1930).

Wimshurst, K. Control and resistance: reformatory school for girls in late nineteenth century South Australia. *Journal of Social History* 18, 1984, pp. 278–9.

Wohl, A. S. Sex and the single room: incest among the Victorian working classes. *The Victorian family*, A. S. Wohl (ed.) (New York: St Martin's Press, 1978).

Yeo, E. Social motherhood and sexual communication. *Women's History Review* 1, 1992, pp. 63–8.

Young, J. D. *Women and popular struggles: a history of Scottish and English working-class women, 1500–1984* (Edinburgh: Mainstream, 1985).

Index

213